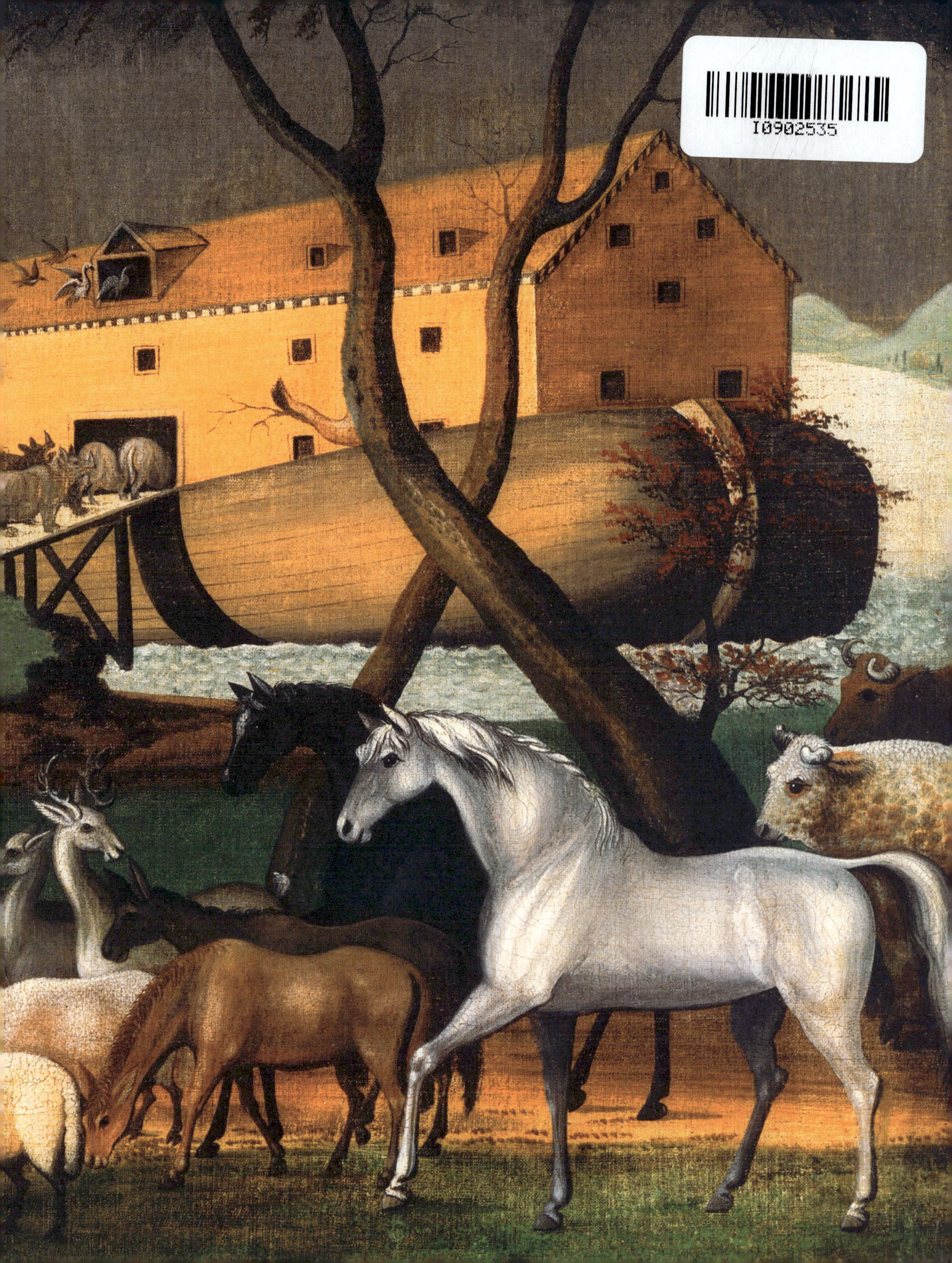

The show's title, **THE ARK,** refers directly to the myth of the **DELUGE:** an event of such **APOCALYPTIC SCALE, FOREWARNED, UNHEEDED,** and **UNSTOPPABLE,** that it appeared it would be the **END OF ALL LIFE** on Earth.

However, through **HUMAN RESOURCEFULNESS, WILL,** and **COMPASSION, THE GREAT FLOOD** marked **A NEW BEGINNING, A DO-OVER, A REBIRTH.**

—Eric Fischl

THE ARK

THE CHURCH

SAG HARBOR, NEW YORK

JUNE 22 - SEPTEMBER 1, 2025

THE ARK

AN EXHIBITION CURATED BY ERIC FISCHL

POINTED LEAF
PRESS

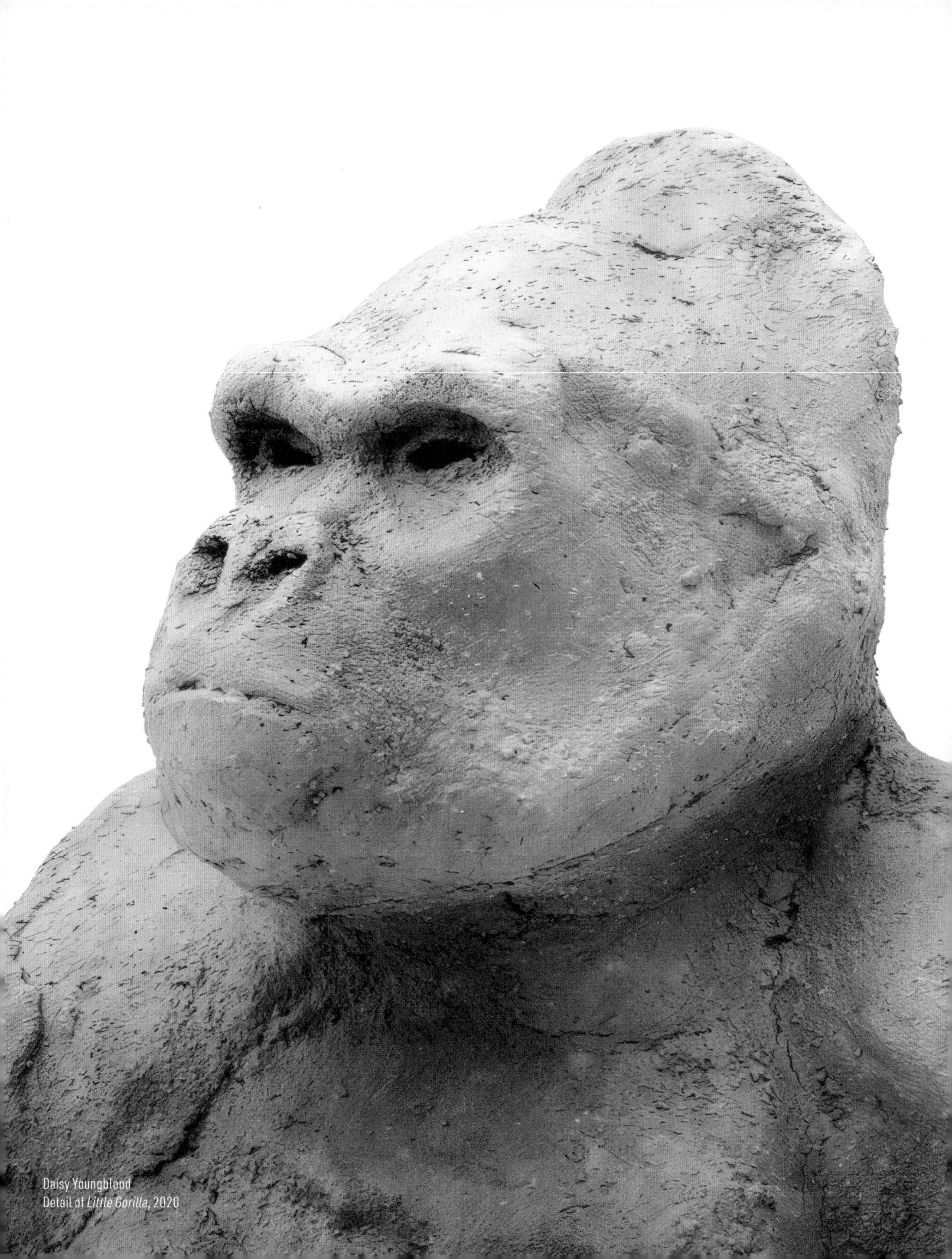

Daisy Youngblood
Detail of *Little Gorilla*, 2020

THE CHURCH, THE ARK Sheri L. Pasquarella 6
THE ANIMALS, THE ART Eric Fischl 8
AND SO IT BEGINS The Artists / The Works 10
ACKNOWLEDGMENTS 133
INDEX 134
CREDITS 135

THE CHURCH, THE ARK

It may seem fitting that a show referencing a biblical narrative is organized by an institution called The Church. Our intention, however, is neither irony nor deification: We are not seeking to espouse or deride tenets of any particular religion. Rather, the themes embedded within this exhibition are sincere inquiries into humanity's relationship to animals, wildlife, and the natural world. As a center for art, creativity, and community that aims to foster creativity on eastern Long Island and celebrate and continue the history of Sag Harbor as a makers' village, the contents of the show go to the heart of our mission. The East End of Long Island has thrived thanks to the fecund opportunities of our flora, fauna, and waterways. This was as true for our Indigenous ancestors as it was for colonial settlers, who set up enterprise in Sag Harbor in the early 1700s as an extension of the global whaling trade. Today, the future of our region demands a careful consideration of humanity's relationship to the natural world, joining with communities the world over in posing timely and essential questions regarding our care for animals and the environment in the postindustrial age.

The Ark marks the fifth summer thematic show here, and our third-ever catalogue. We consider these tremendous achievements for an organization that opened in April 2021. It is our great hope that presenting this gathering of art, as with all of our work, will inspire joy and curiosity in those who experience it, with perhaps some measure of solace or hope.–**Sheri L. Pasquarella**

Sheri L. Pasquarella is the Executive Director of The Church, a multidisciplinary art center and artist residency located in Sag Harbor, New York. Prior to joining The Church in 2022, she was the Owner/ Director of SLP (2005-2022); Director, Gorney Bravin + Lee (2002-2005); Associate Director, Marlborough Gallery (1998-2002); and also conceived and cofounded the New Art Dealers Alliance (NADA) in 2002, of which she is President Emerita. She has served on many boards, has lectured widely, has held teaching posts, and has edited or contributed to numerous books and publications.

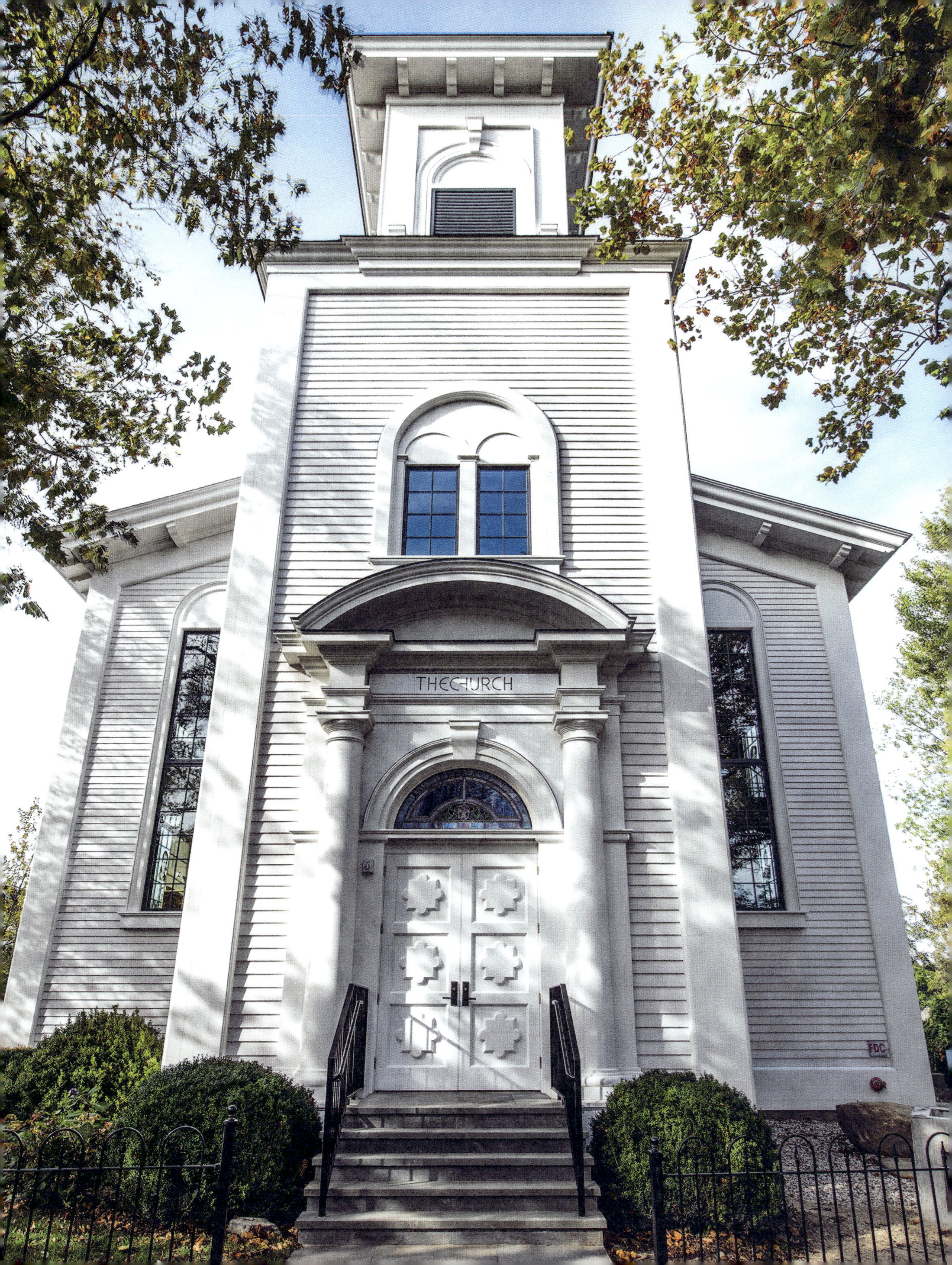
THE CHURCH
FDC

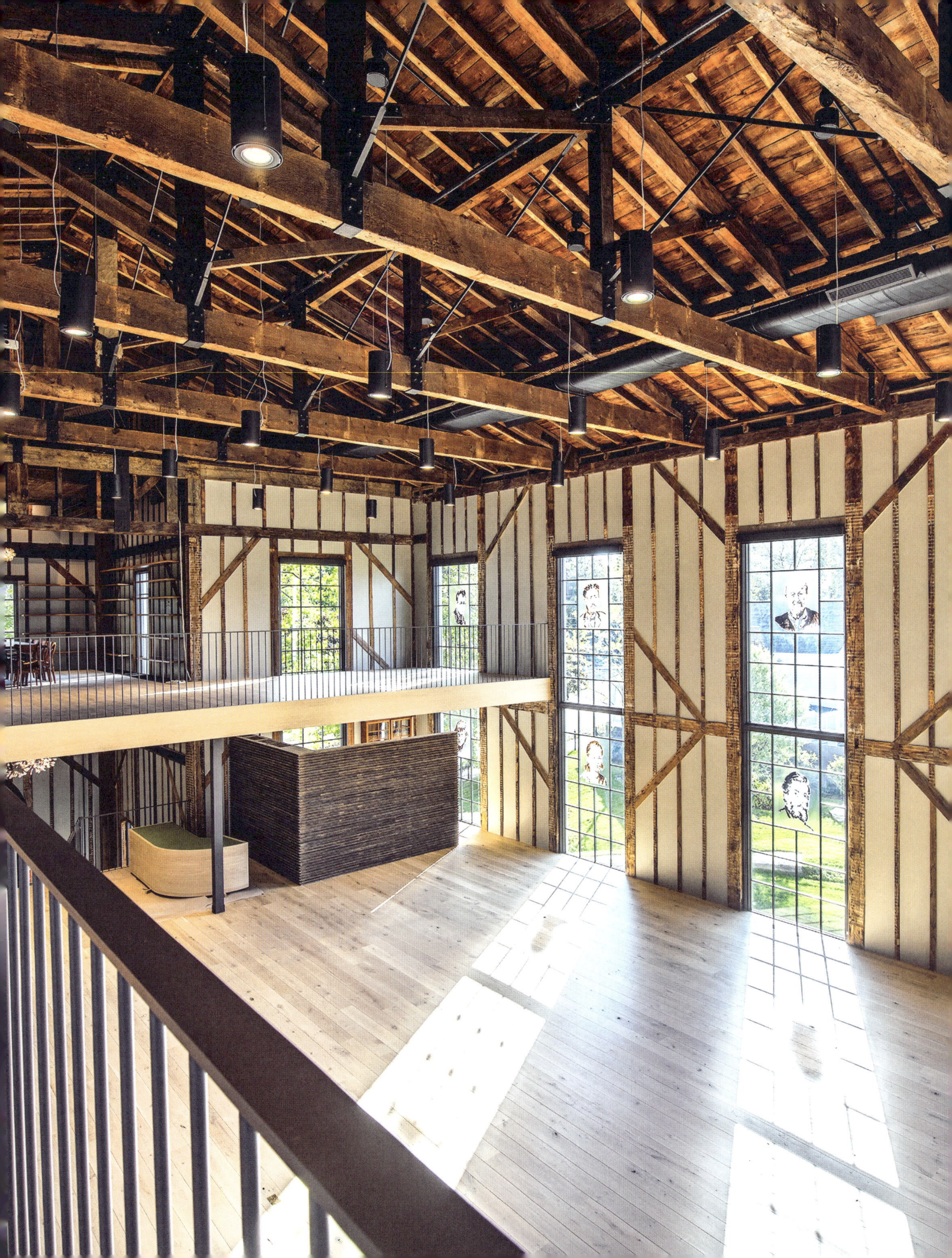

THE ANIMALS, THE ART

Recently I watched a beautifully animated film about a cat, dog, capybara, lemur, and a secretary bird struggling, at first alone and then together, to survive a flood. The movie, *Flow*, has no words, no dialogue–only animals meowing, barking, grunting, and squawking, uncomprehendingly frantic. It is poignantly gripping. A fiction about unlikely bonds formed by creatures who have no ability to understand why or what is happening except that it is happening. On the most basic level, they recognize that they need each other if they are to have any chance of survival.

All the myths of the Deluge are similar: the gods became so angered at the extent of human corruption that they created an event of apocalyptic scale that had been forewarned, but went unheeded, and was thus unstoppable. It appeared in all likelihood that it would be the end of life on Earth. As the lesson of the inundation goes, when the gods left us, they left it up to us to figure out how to come back from the brink of our own self-created destruction. Were it not for our resourcefulness, will, and compassion, the flood would have been the end, but instead marked a renewal and a rebirth.

In a time such as now, when our zeitgeist is fraught with an inescapable sense of apocalyptic doom and chaos, we can turn to art to remind and reassure us that we have dealt with this before.

Art, by its very nature, seeks connection through objects of beauty, feeling, imagination, and craft that pierce our preconceptions of meaning and meaningfulness to make us experience anew our most important affirmations and transitions: Life, Death, Tragedy, Joy, Wonder, Beauty, Birth, Union, Uncertainty, Will, and Hope.

The Ark resonates along similar lines. This exhibition covers the emotional geography of several generations of artists. They have captured some of our deepest pleasures and fears through a wide range of creative invention and self-expression focusing on animals. There are sculptures that capture an animal's inherent beauty, a physical manifestation of instinct and survival. There are also sculptures of animals that personify truths within human life that are best approached indirectly because they are rooted in the sublime: wordless wonder and terror.

These sculptures portray the animal variously as trickster or prophet, fossil or memory, playful or mad, fierce and desperate, guide and protector, trophy or prize, all beauty and perfection. These are not just representations of animals. They are kindred and totemic spirits that embody the mysteries and truths about our struggles with and for attachment against our deepest fears of vulnerability and isolation.

As a metaphor for survival, the legend of Noah's Ark is an embrace of optimism against uncertainty. Through touch, feel, and the making of forms that animate materiality, the work in *The Ark* reasserts this legend as a way to reawaken within us a sensitivity to our own need for harmony, community, and union as well as a renewed awareness of our place and role in the nature of things and the nature of being. For humans to survive, animals must also survive. For humanity to triumph, we must come to understand why compassion for animals brings us closer to our own humanity and, in turn, closer to each other.**–Eric Fischl**

Eric Fischl is an American figurative painter and sculptor of psychologically and emotionally charged scenes of relationships between men and women, mothers and sons/daughters, fathers and daughters/sons, husbands and wives. In his own words, "I paint people. I paint people doing things. Sometimes doing things they shouldn't be doing." His work is collected widely in the United States and Europe by both major museums and important collectors. He published his memoir, *Bad Boy: My Life On and Off the Canvas,* in 2013. In 2020 he, along with his wife, the painter April Gornik, founded The Church, a community art center and artist residency in Sag Harbor, New York, the place they call home.

Rembrandt Bugatti
Girafe en Train de Boire, 1907
Bronze, $5^{3}/_{4}$ x $7^{7}/_{8}$ x $6^{3}/_{4}$ inches

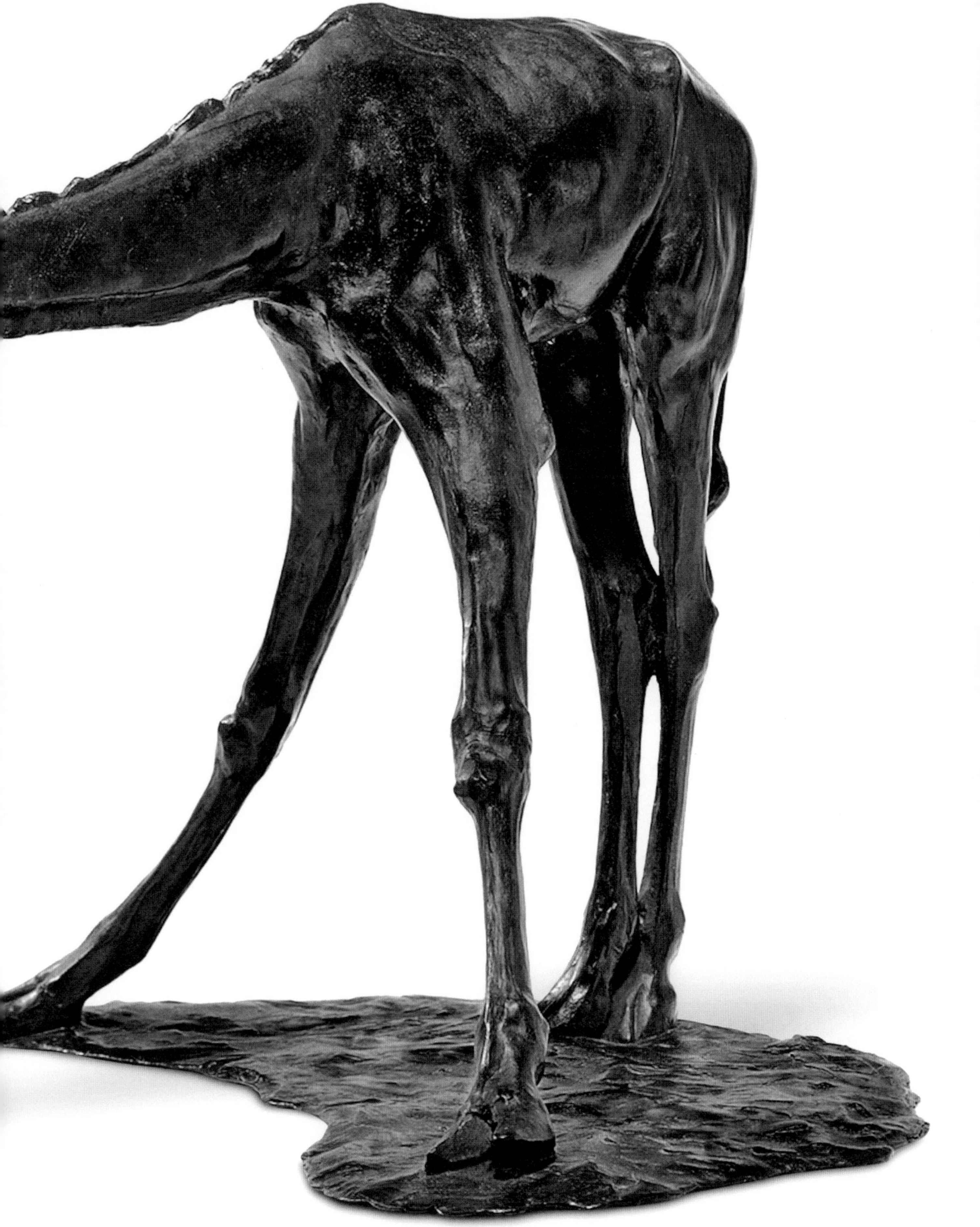

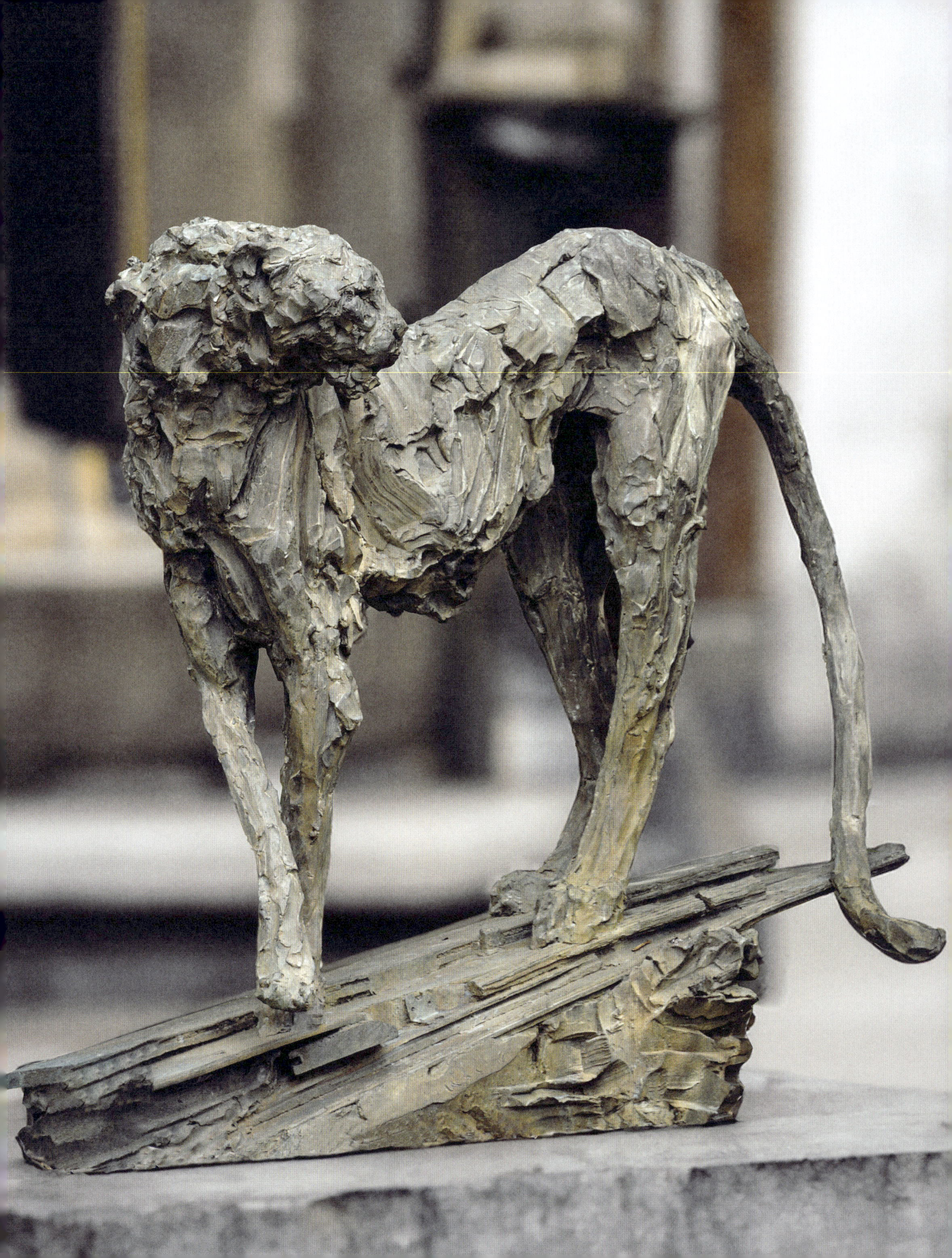

I see my sculptures as a tribute to nature and a silent warning about the fragility of wildlife. I am deeply troubled by the destruction of habitats and the extinction of species and work to capture the strength and dignity of animals while sounding an urgent alarm: Nature is disappearing.–Patrick Villas

Patrick Villas
Cheetah, 2006
Bronze, $38^5/_8$ x $42^1/_2$ x $18^1/_2$ inches

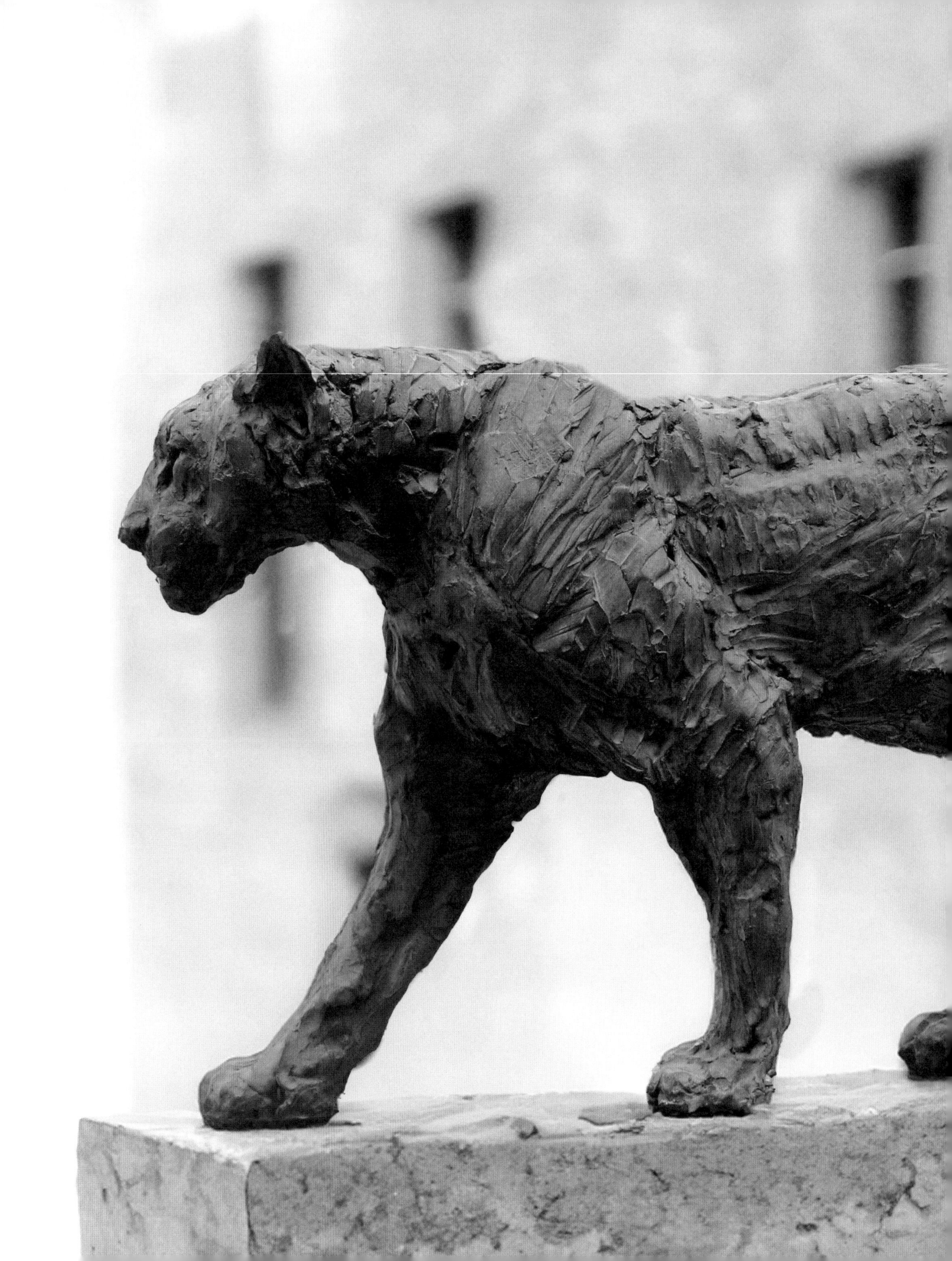

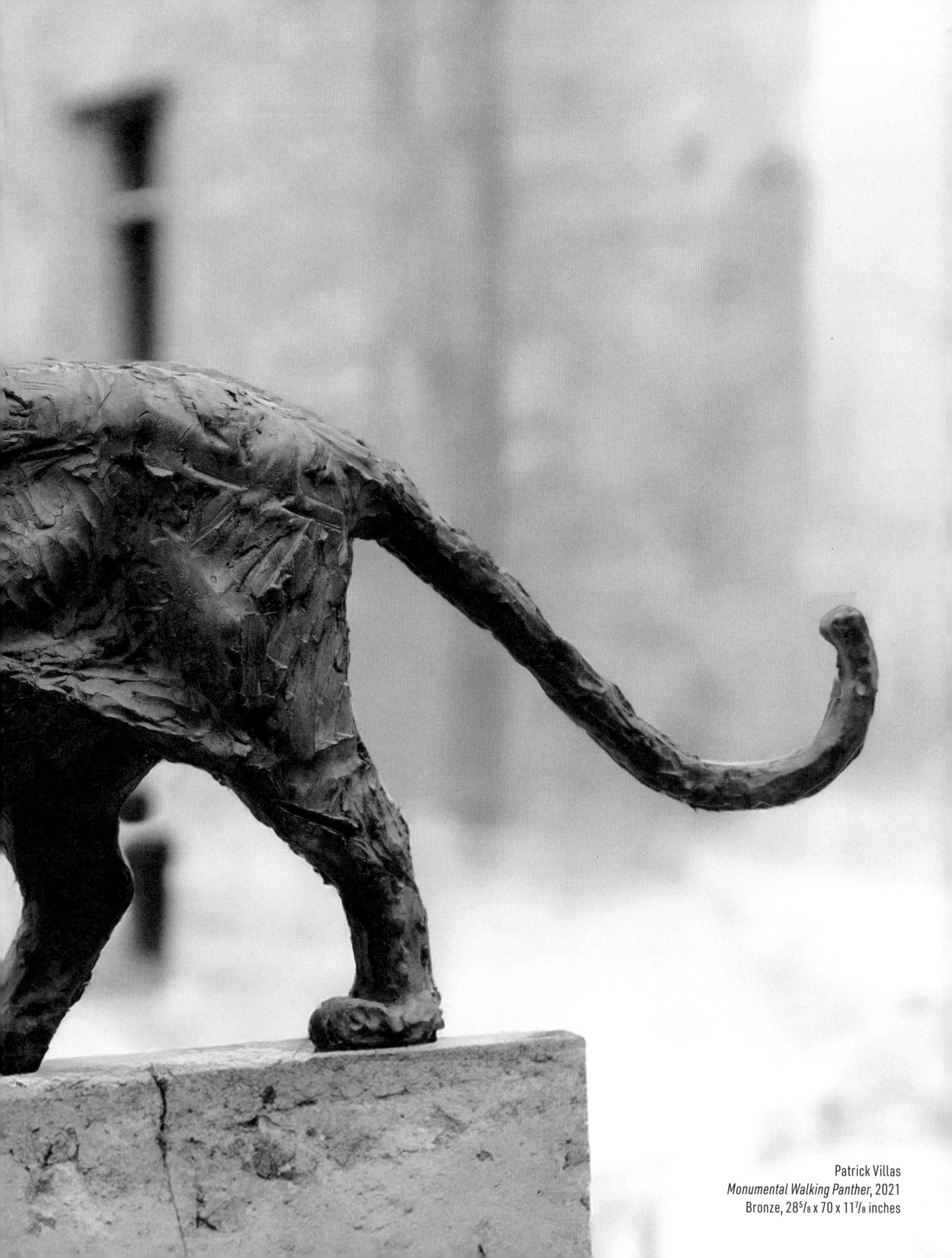

Patrick Villas
Monumental Walking Panther, 2021
Bronze, $28\frac{5}{8}$ x 70 x $11\frac{7}{8}$ inches

Germaine Richier
La Mante, moyenne, 1946
Bronze, 27 1/8 x 14 5/8 x 6 1/4 inches

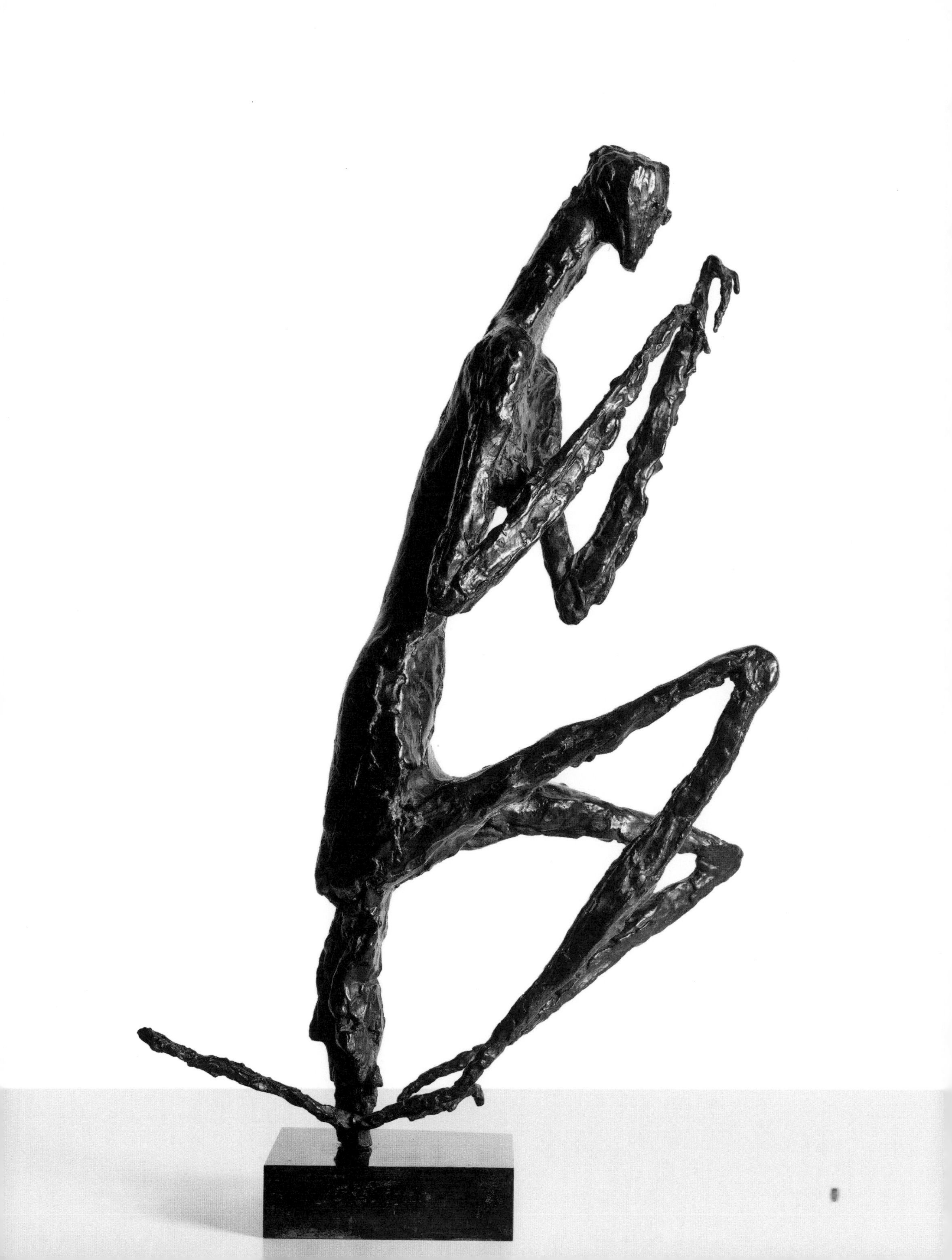

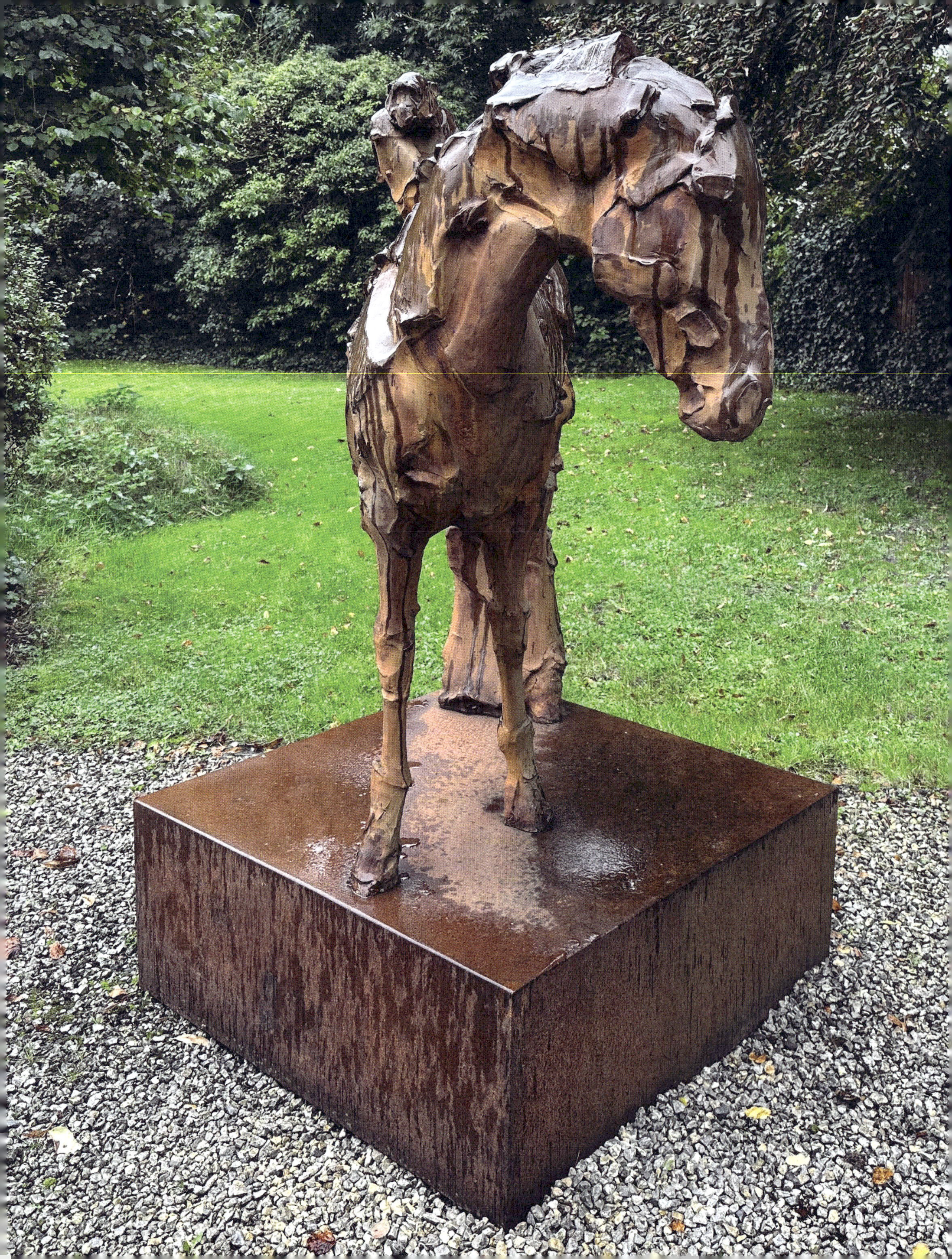

For me, art is an action that allows me to accept reality. I try to respond through gesture to the questions that cross my mind and to search endlessly for the absolute form. One day, standing in front of a Henry Moore sculpture, I understood how shapes could talk to each other and to the air around them. Moved to tears, I felt myself becoming those forms. At that moment, I knew that the path of creation would be long and exciting! Modeling is a natural consequence of this evolution. I also find my painterly touch in the texture of my sculptures. The imprint is touching, it makes me want to plunge my hands into the earth, so spontaneous and joyful does this gesture seem. It's a pleasure and a game with light. I need the texture to hold on to it. I only validate sculptures that move me, the only reference is my own sensation. Specific to *Grand Paradigm* is the notion of superiority that is challenged in this sculpture. Humanity has taken this arrogant place toward other species. The change of paradigm is inevitable. But I especially liked that these two beings listen to each other. They allowed me to emphasize cooperation and understanding through silence.
–Catherine Thiry

Catherine Thiry
Grand Paradigm, 2017
Iron composite, 57 x 59 x 23⅝ inches

My work is about the "Spirit and Essence" of life that I try to express in pure refined minimalist form. I focus on birds partly as their lives contain an extraordinary evolutionary intensity expressed in their form and movement but also because my whole life I have felt connected to them. As a child growing up in the mountains and near lakes, I would often dream as a bird, and now, as an artist, I feel that all living things share feelings and emotions and I try to distill some of these into my work. I am a carver–a whittler–a basic ancient activity of expression unchanged since the dawn of humanity and I feel connected to sculptors working across thousands of years in disparate cultures across the planet. The themes have not changed nor has the subject matter and, although we now live in a highly complex industrial society, it is the shamanistic realm where the human and animal spirits connect with simple, primitive truths in the order of nature and our place in it that are important.
–Anthony Theakston

Anthony Theakston
Spirit Owl, 2025
Bronze, $16^{1}/_{2}$ x $9^{7}/_{8}$ x $2^{3}/_{8}$ inches

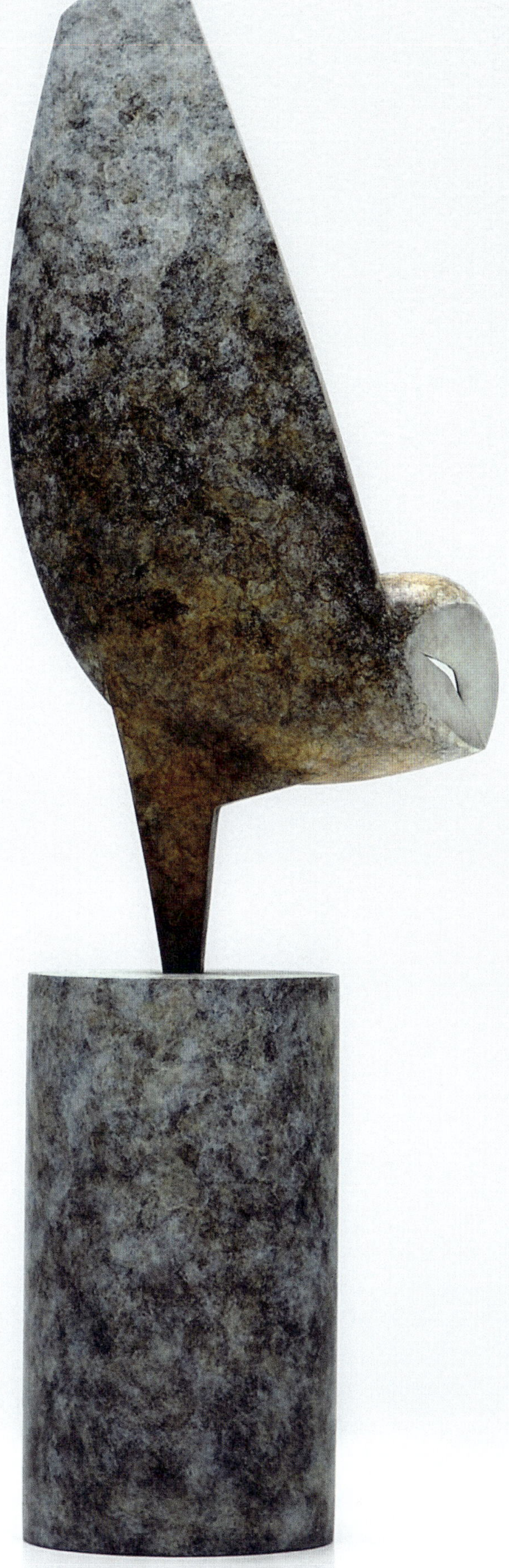

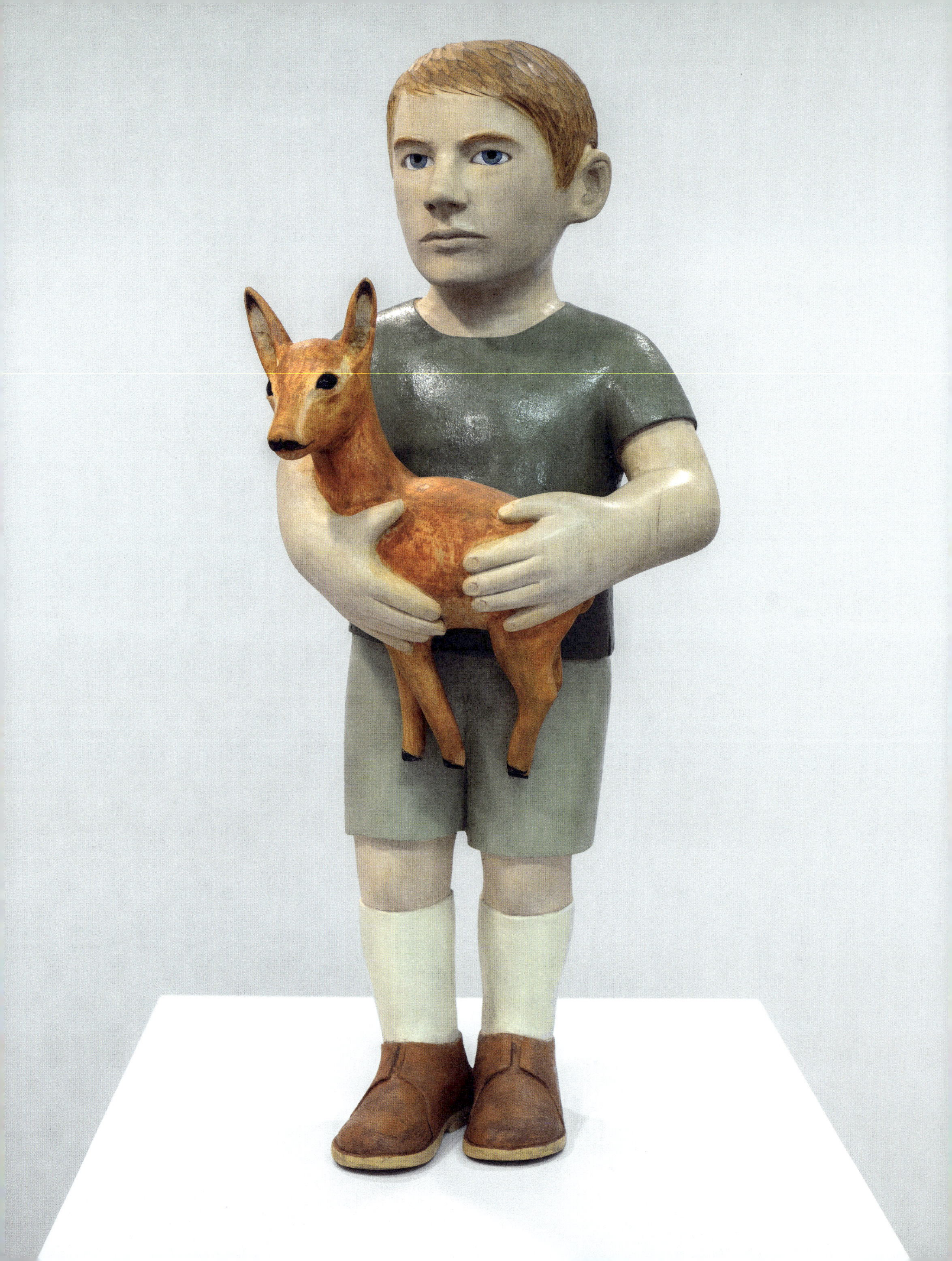

Mr. Right (2019) is a portrait of my father, the second of two wooden sculptures that I have made of him. Both sculptures juxtapose him with animals. The first one sees him riding a leopard, entitled *The Hero* (1995). My father was born and grew up in Holland, shortly after World War II. He was fascinated by animals from a young age and, when he was 16, he was allowed to move to South Africa on his own! There, he completed his schooling and studies and hitchhiked back through Africa to visit Holland at the age of 21. The photograph of him that inspired *Mr. Right* was taken in 1970 in South Africa in Kruger National Park, shortly before he married my mother. These two sculptures are not literal portraits, but allegorical interpretations of my family history.–Claudette Schreuders

Claudette Schreuders
Mr. Right, 2019
Enamel and oil paint on jelutong wood, 23 5/8 x 9 7/8 x 9 7/8 inches

William Kentridge
Pigeon, 2021
Bronze, $11\frac{3}{4}$ x $7\frac{7}{8}$ x $4\frac{1}{8}$ inches

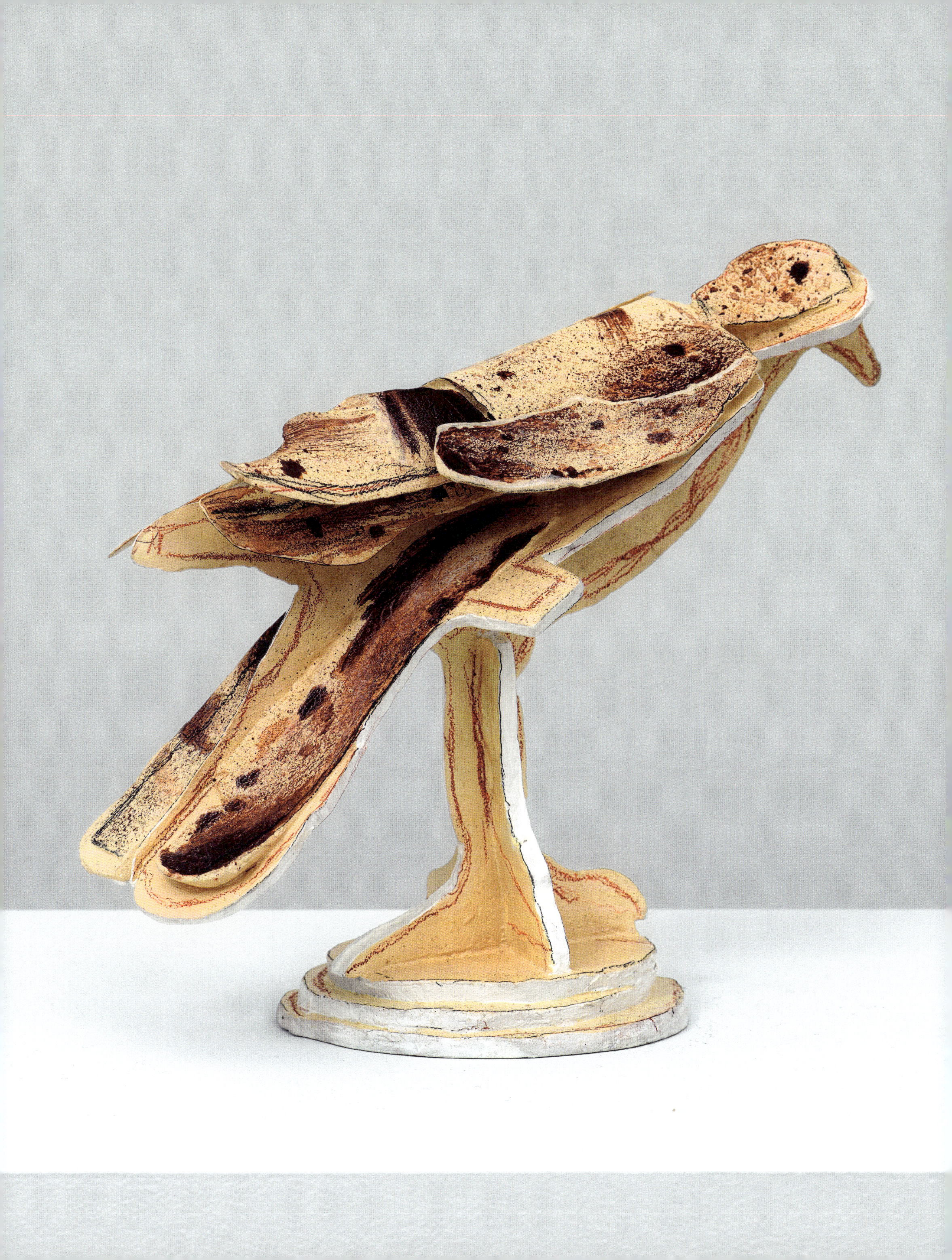

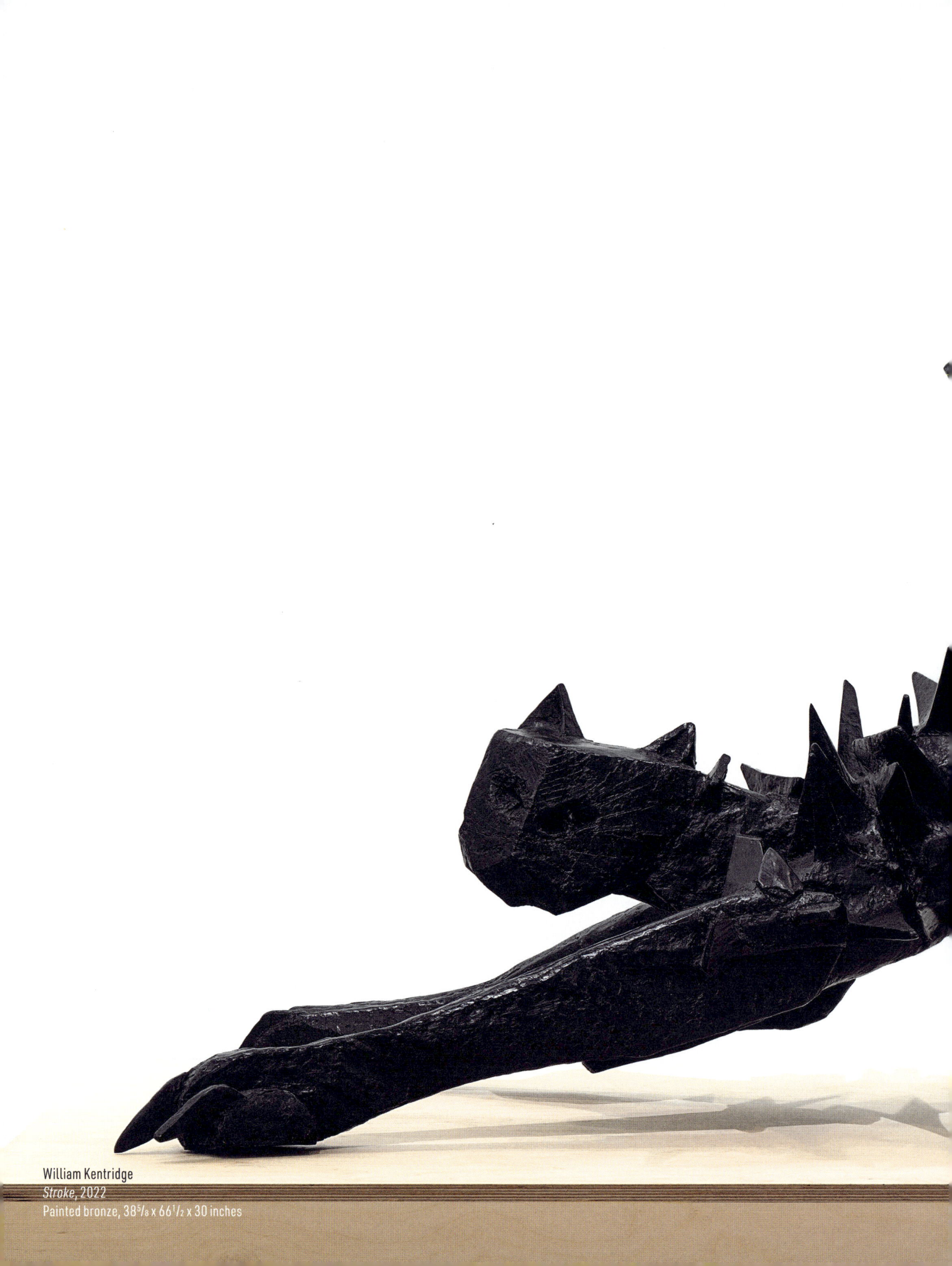

William Kentridge
Stroke, 2022
Painted bronze, 38 5/8 x 66 1/2 x 30 inches

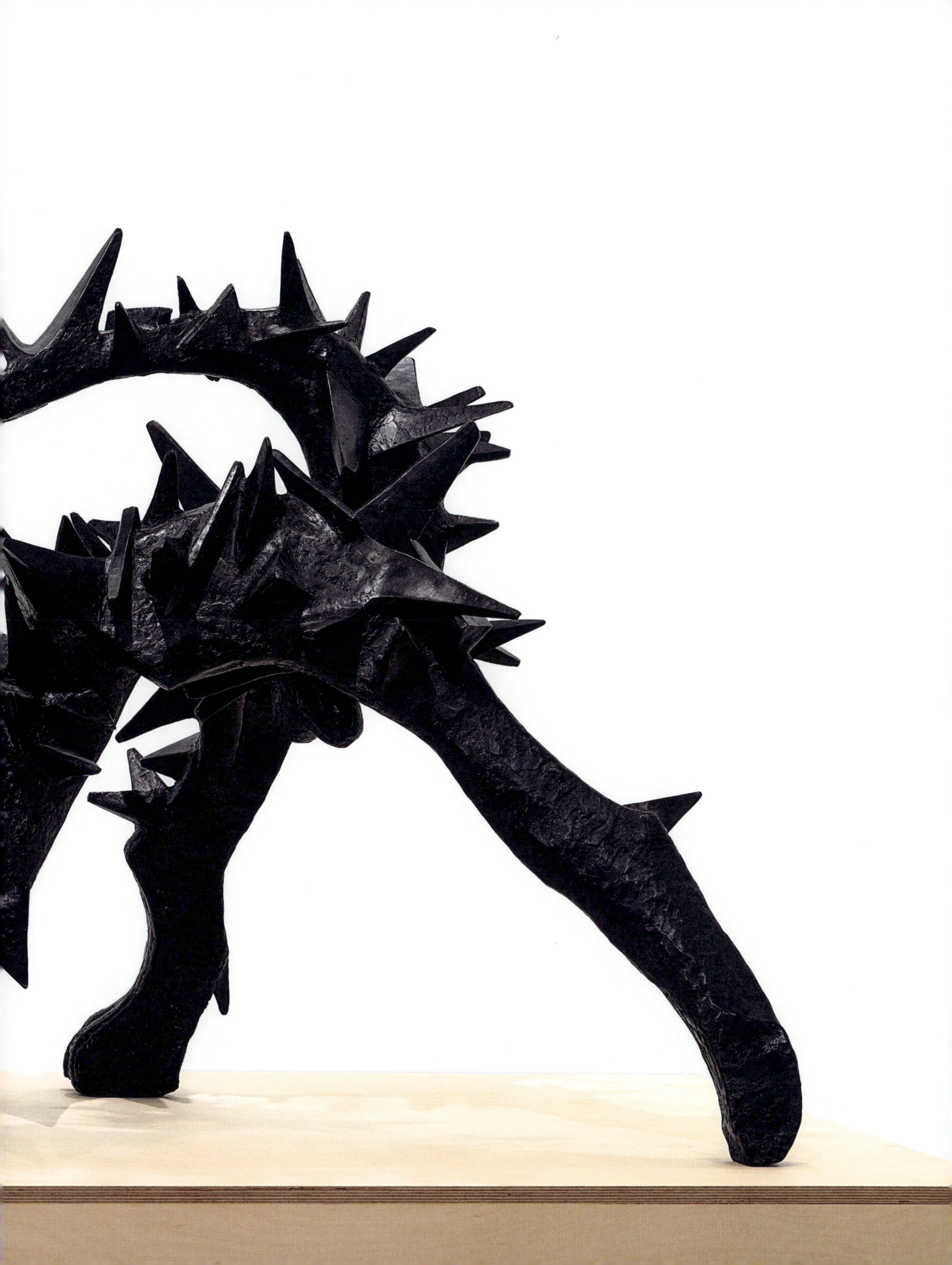

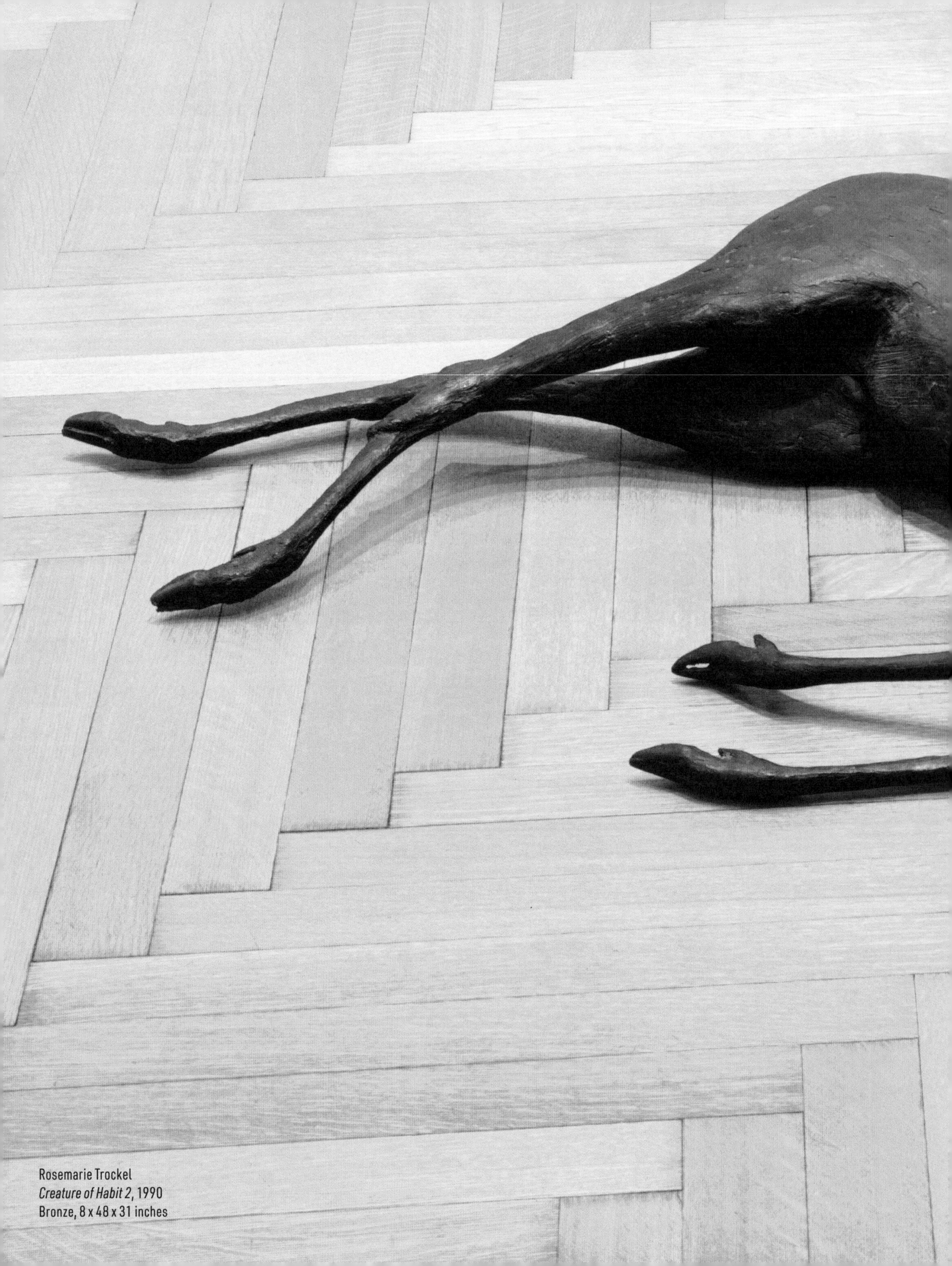

Rosemarie Trockel
Creature of Habit 2, 1990
Bronze, 8 x 48 x 31 inches

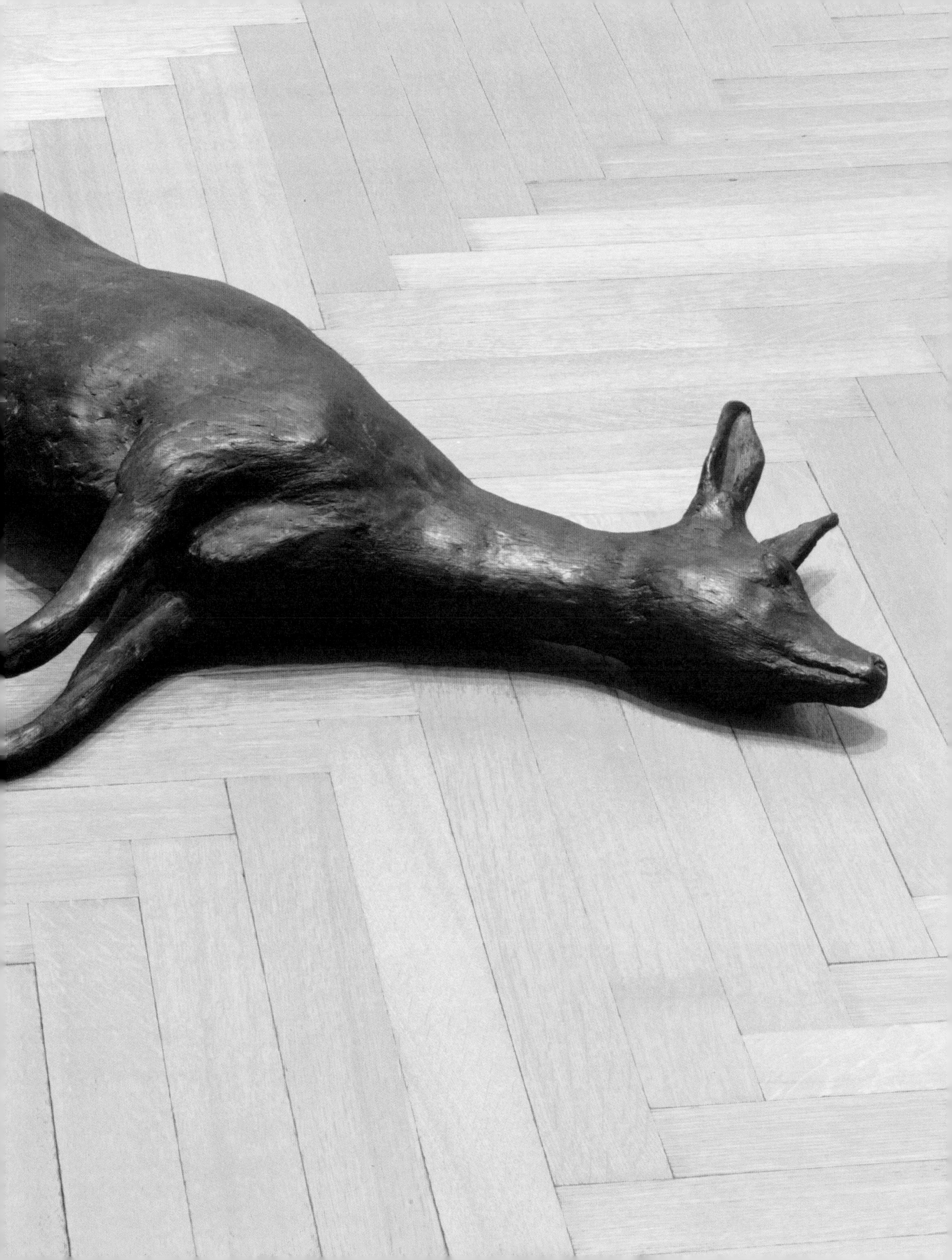

My work around animals allows me to investigate biology, history, psychology, and spirituality. I've been fascinated with prehistoric art's depiction of reverence for animals and have an attraction to the long lineage that connects us with our ancestral past and the human condition. Animals operate on a different frequency. They are attuned to themselves and others and have a sense of vulnerability and innocence that fewer and fewer humans possess. Employing sculpture as a medium allows for physical manipulations and interaction with the material and the animal, in a way, the muscle memory of the hand becoming an integral part of the process. Using porcelain and raw bone powders suspended in resin imbues the forms with a ghost-like translucency, giving them the illusion of life.–John O'Reilly

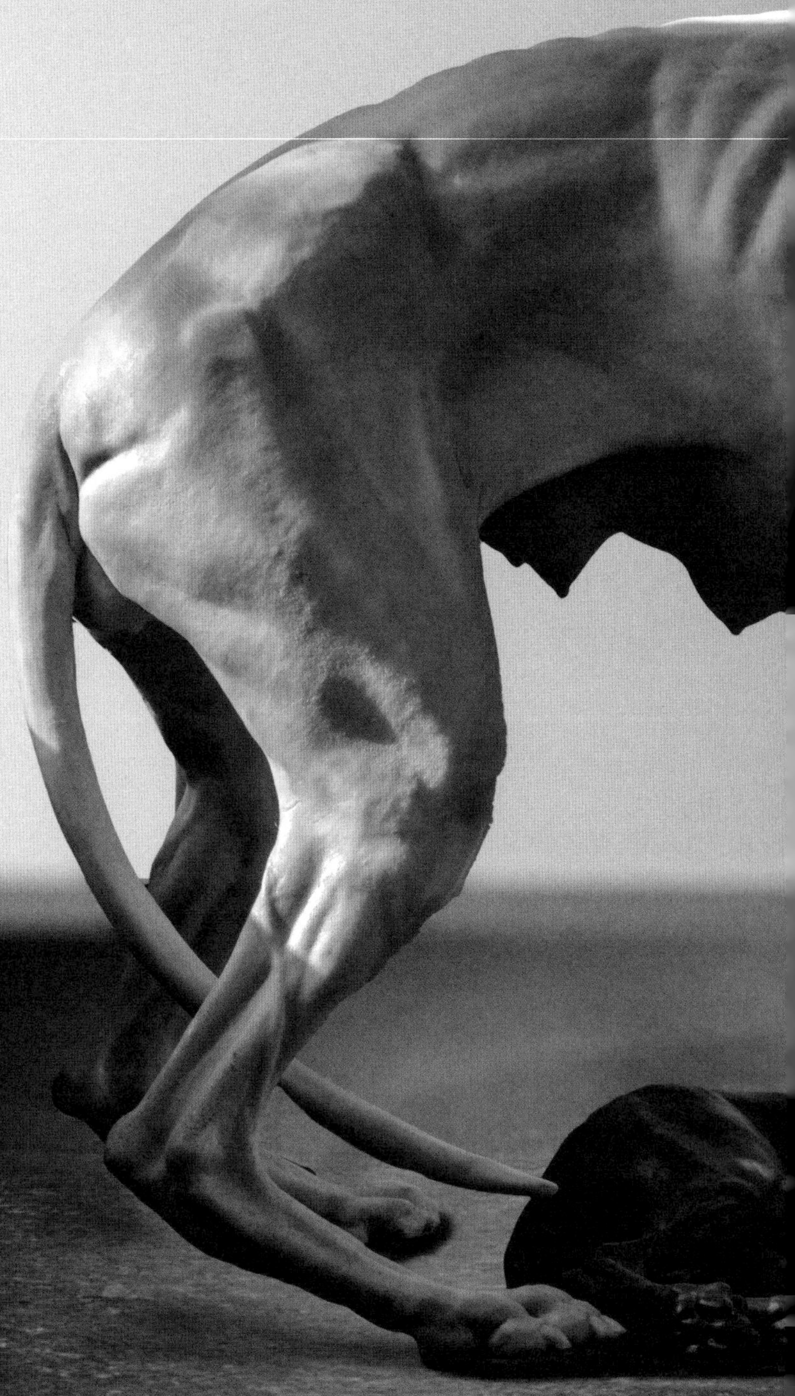

John O'Reilly
Intertwined, 2012
White dog: resin graphite, 23 x 34 x 24 inches
Black dog: resin porcelain and bone powder, 5 x 21 x 17 inches

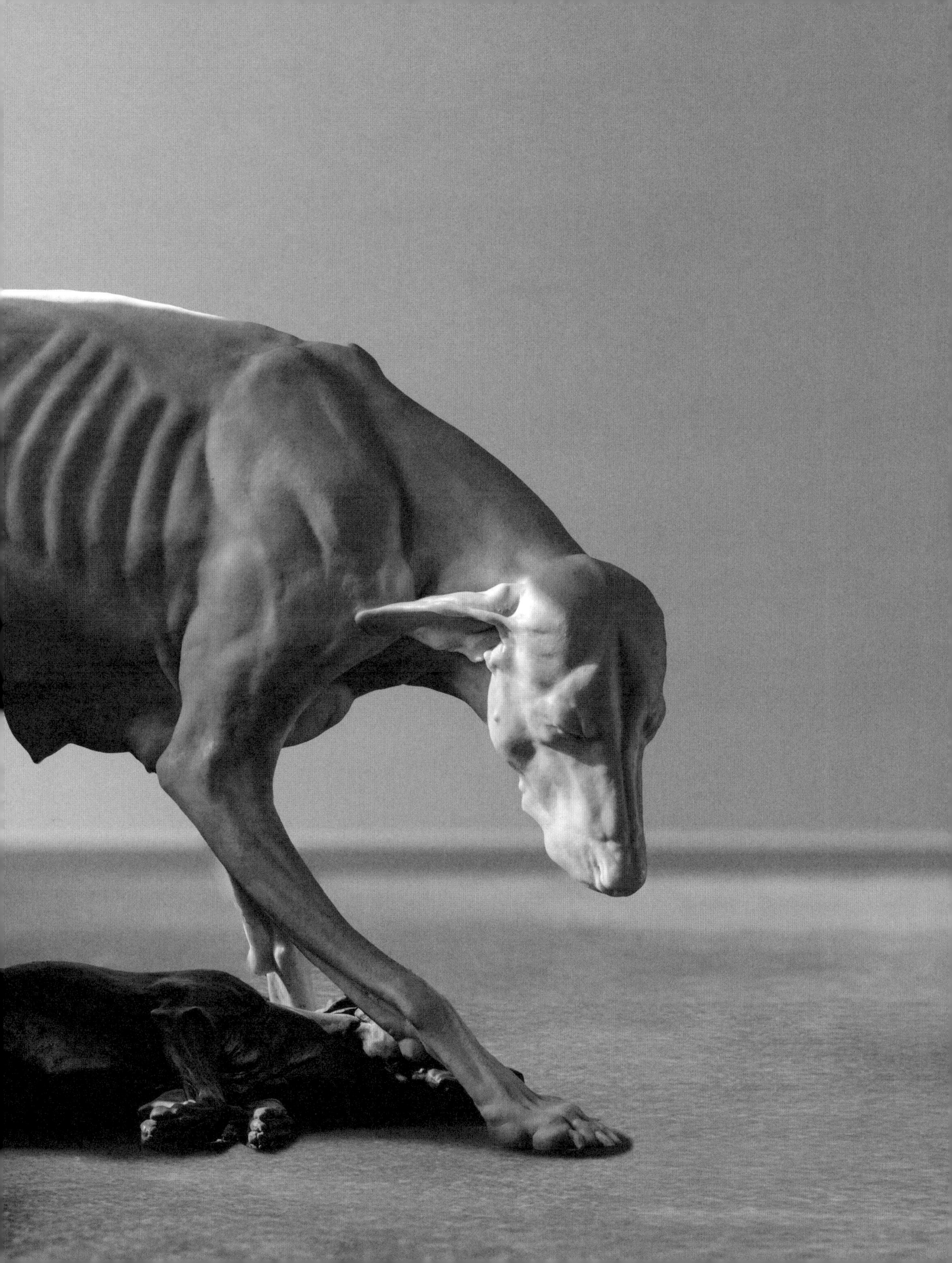

For years I have been making porcelain portraits of the dead winged beings in my collection, but I have focused primarily on birds. To me, birds are everything—they are delicate and vulnerable and resilient and creative. They are mysterious geniuses and practical survivors. They are everything I experience in a day—awe and exuberance and the yearning to pay tribute to the tragic and the quietly heroic. After years of making houseflies and owls and dragonflies and sparrows, I assembled this piece last fall, during the annual butterfly migration, when every year I rediscover the monarchs waggling their way down our beaches en route from Canada to Mexico. I find great optimism in their seemingly random flight pattern that has successfully perpetuated the species for centuries. Although I sculpt the subjects in the position they were found (lying down), I realized I wanted the butterflies to be upright—as though live ones were alighting among the dead birds and insects. I was overcome by a feeling of spirituality and hope—that what's essential in all of us corporeal beings would somehow be carried forward safely, a kind of transcendence.—Monica Banks

Monica Banks
Detail of *Restless Things*, 2024

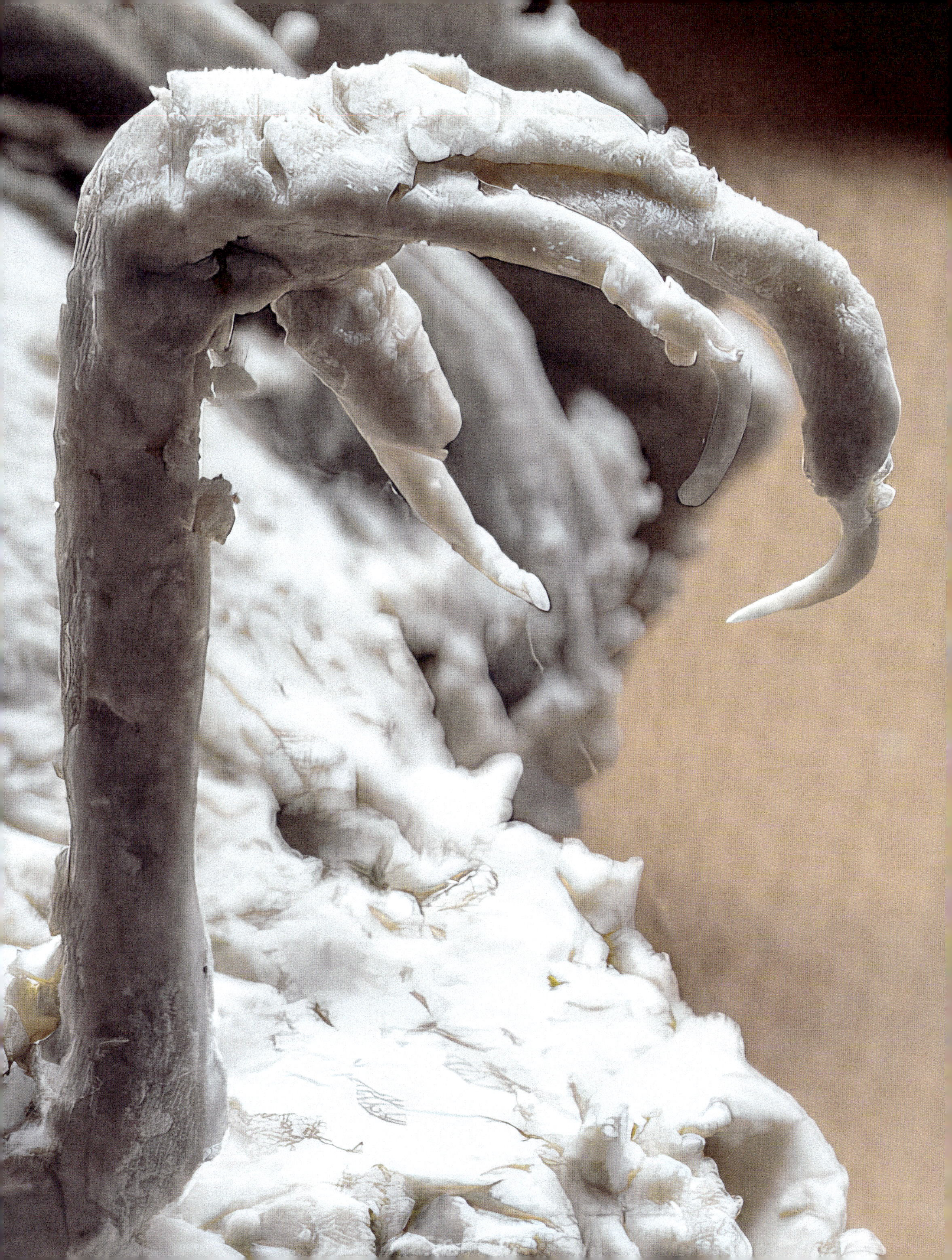

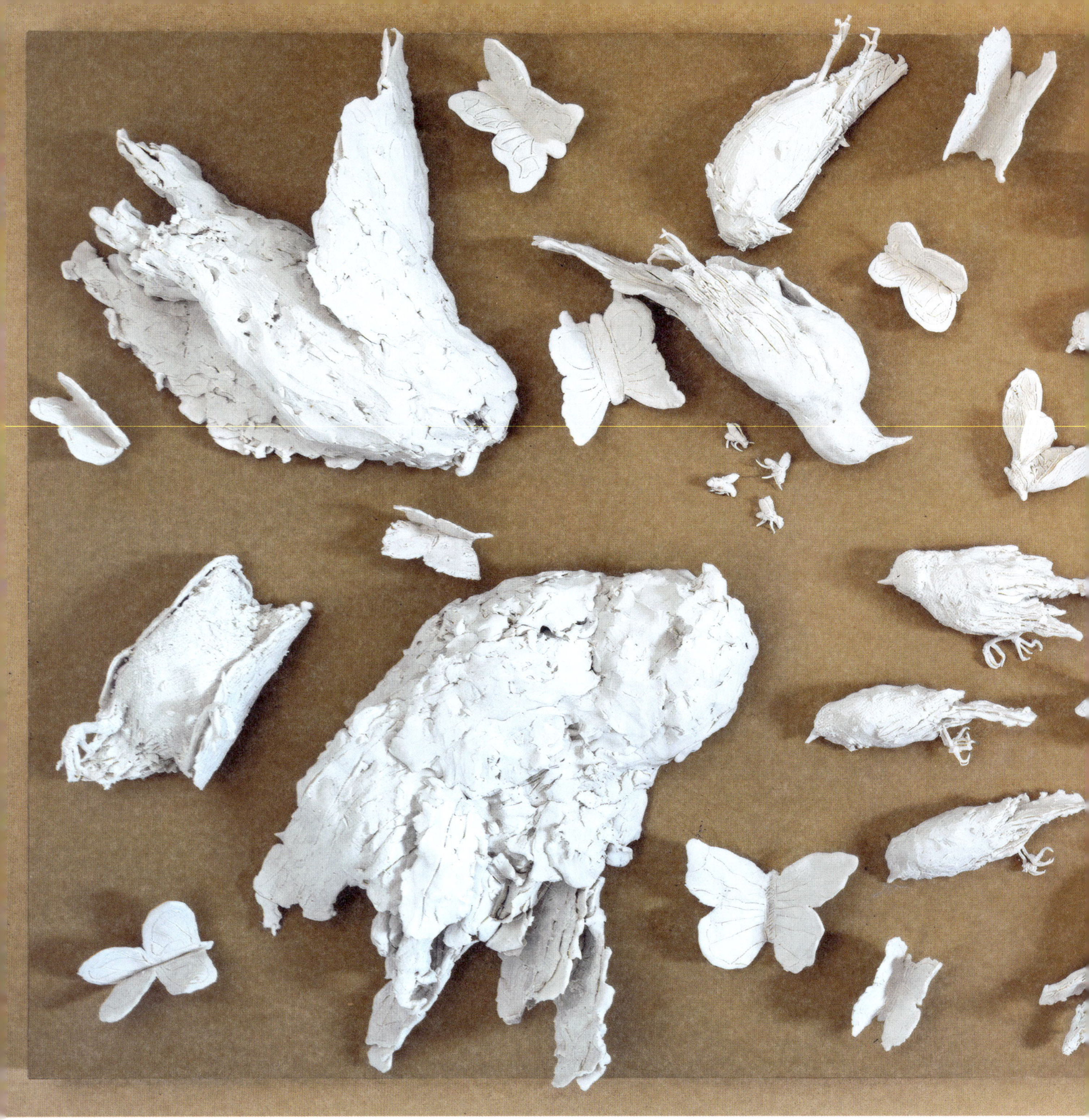

Monica Banks
Restless Things, 2024
Porcelain on painted board, 4 x 37 x 18 inches

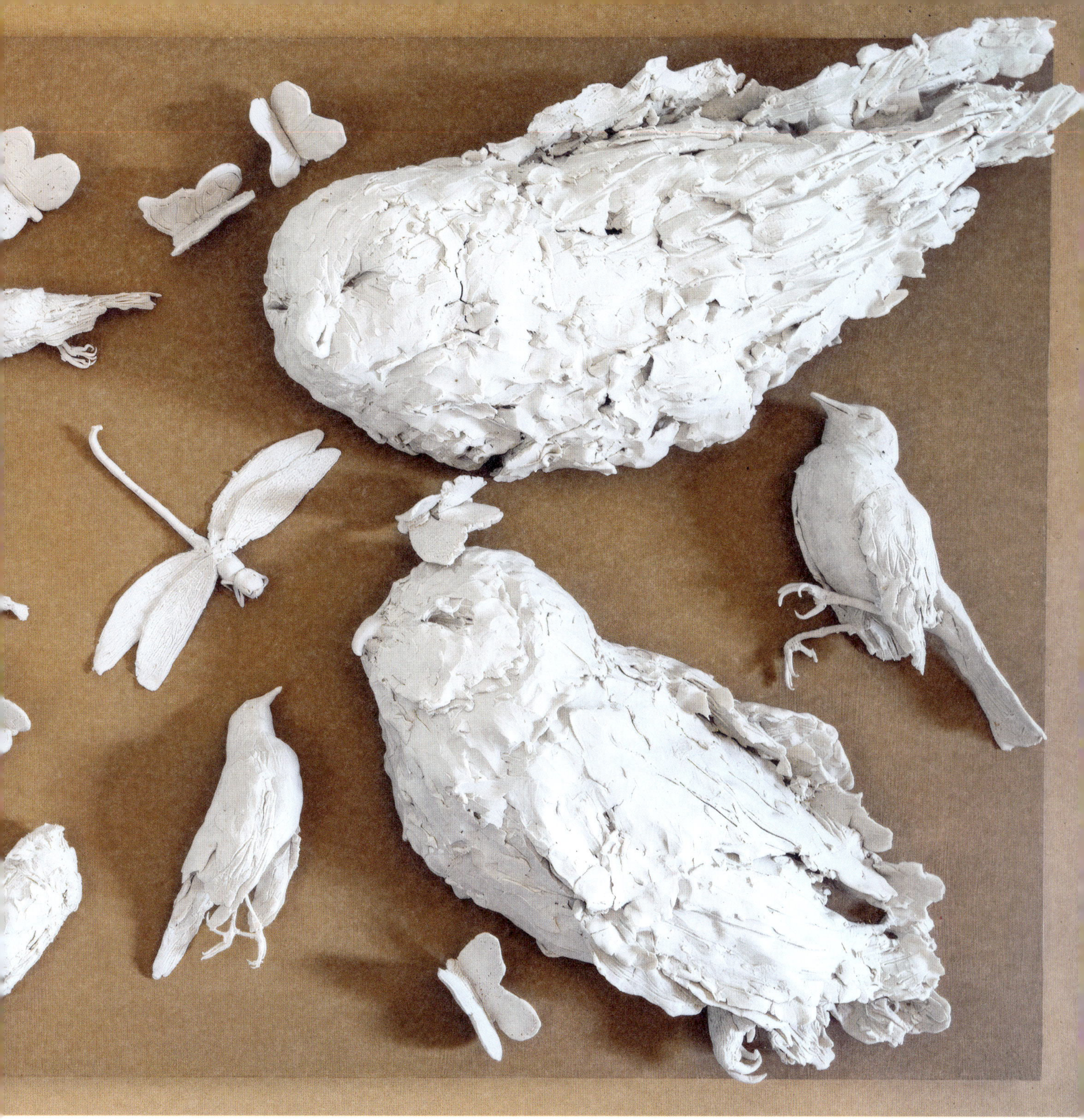

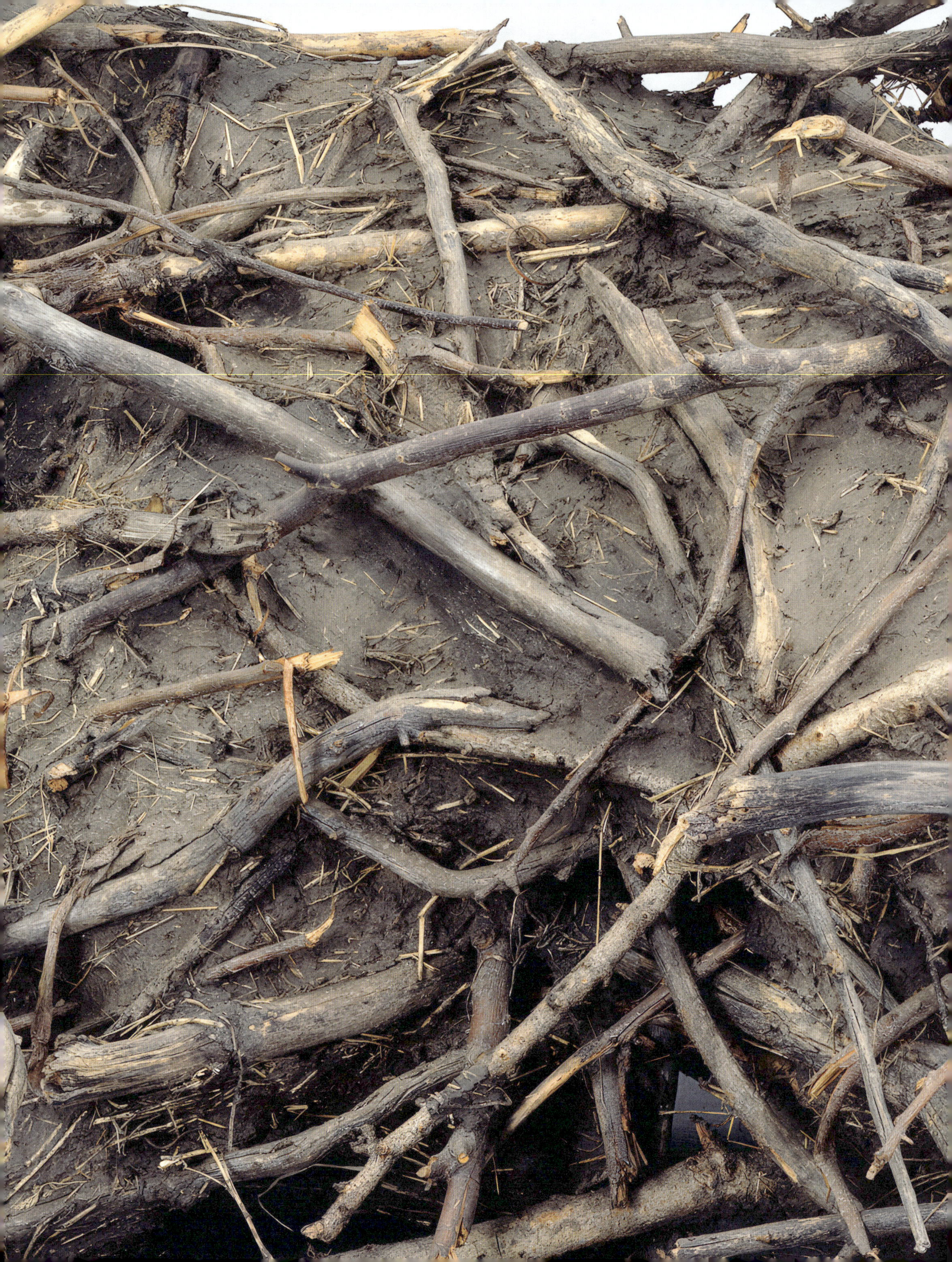

I first used the image as a metaphorical substitute for myself–it was a way of doing a self-portrait one step removed from the specificity of Deborah Butterfield. The first horses were huge plaster mares whose presence was extremely gentle and calm. They were at rest, and in complete opposition to the raging war-horse (stallion) that represents most equine sculpture. The next series of horses were made of mud and sticks and suggested that their forms were left clotted together after a river flooded and subsided. They were dark and almost sinister, reflecting the realization that I was perhaps more like the war-horse than the quiet mares. For me they represented the process of attitudes and feelings taking shape after a "flood" of experiences. The materials and images were also meant to suggest that the horses were both figure and ground, merging the external world with the subject. After moving to Montana in 1976 and having my horse at home, I became so interested in how his form changed when lying down. Still thinking of myself as the horse, I also thought of the female figure in art history–the reclining nudes, the voluptuous female form lounging and being seductive–and envisioned these huge, round, sensual mares lounging around an art gallery on the floor, resting, sleeping. As a prey animal, horses are built to sleep standing up and can flee in an instant, but recline when they feel safe and secure in their environment. For me, then, as a mare, to make oneself vulnerable in the art world, is to show a position of strength.–Deborah Butterfield

Deborah Butterfield
Detail of *Resting Horse*, 1977

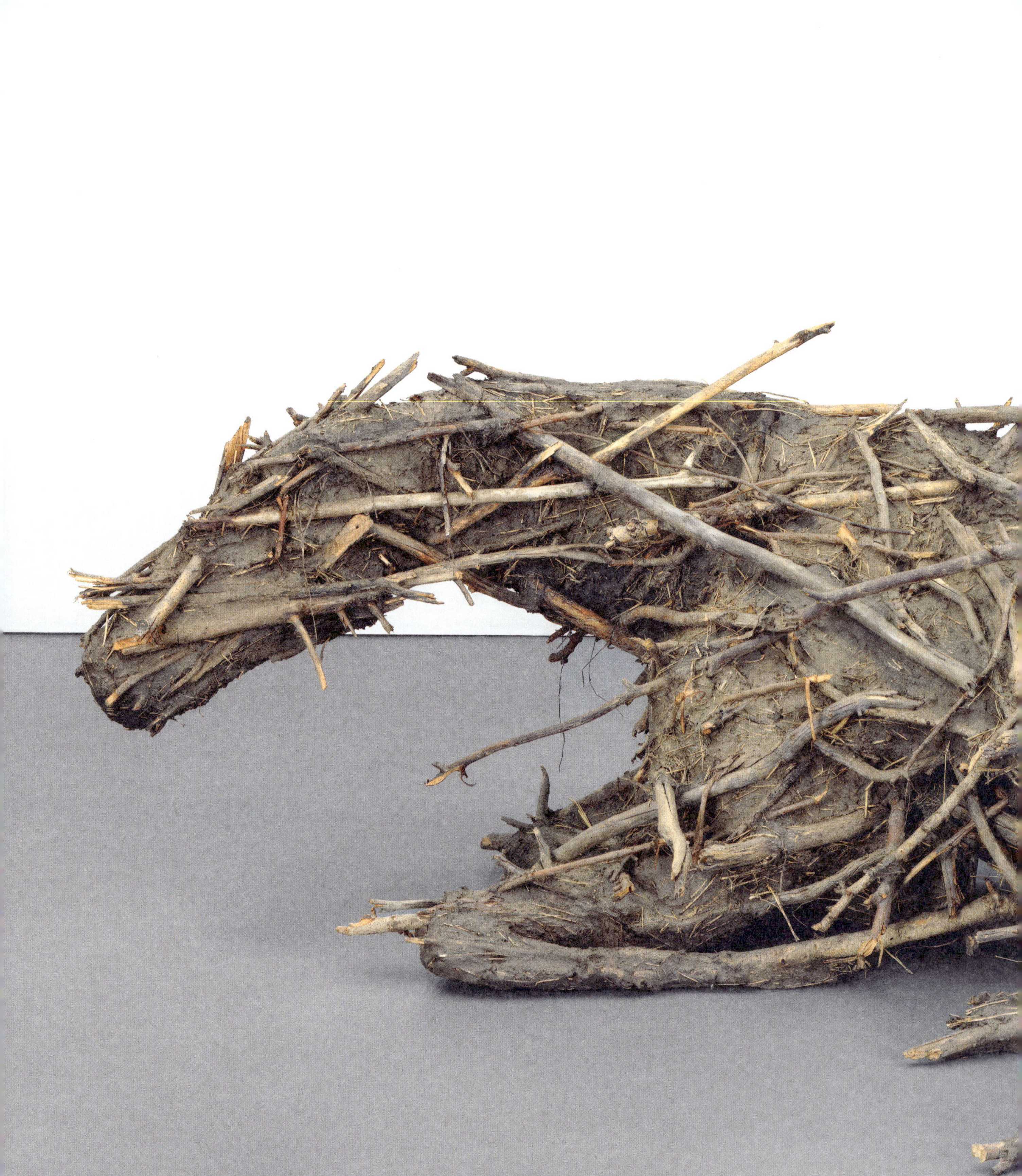

Deborah Butterfield
Resting Horse, 1977
Steel, wire, twigs, clay, paper pulp, dextrine, plaster, and fiberglass, 34 11/16 x 100 7/8 x 54 3/4 inches

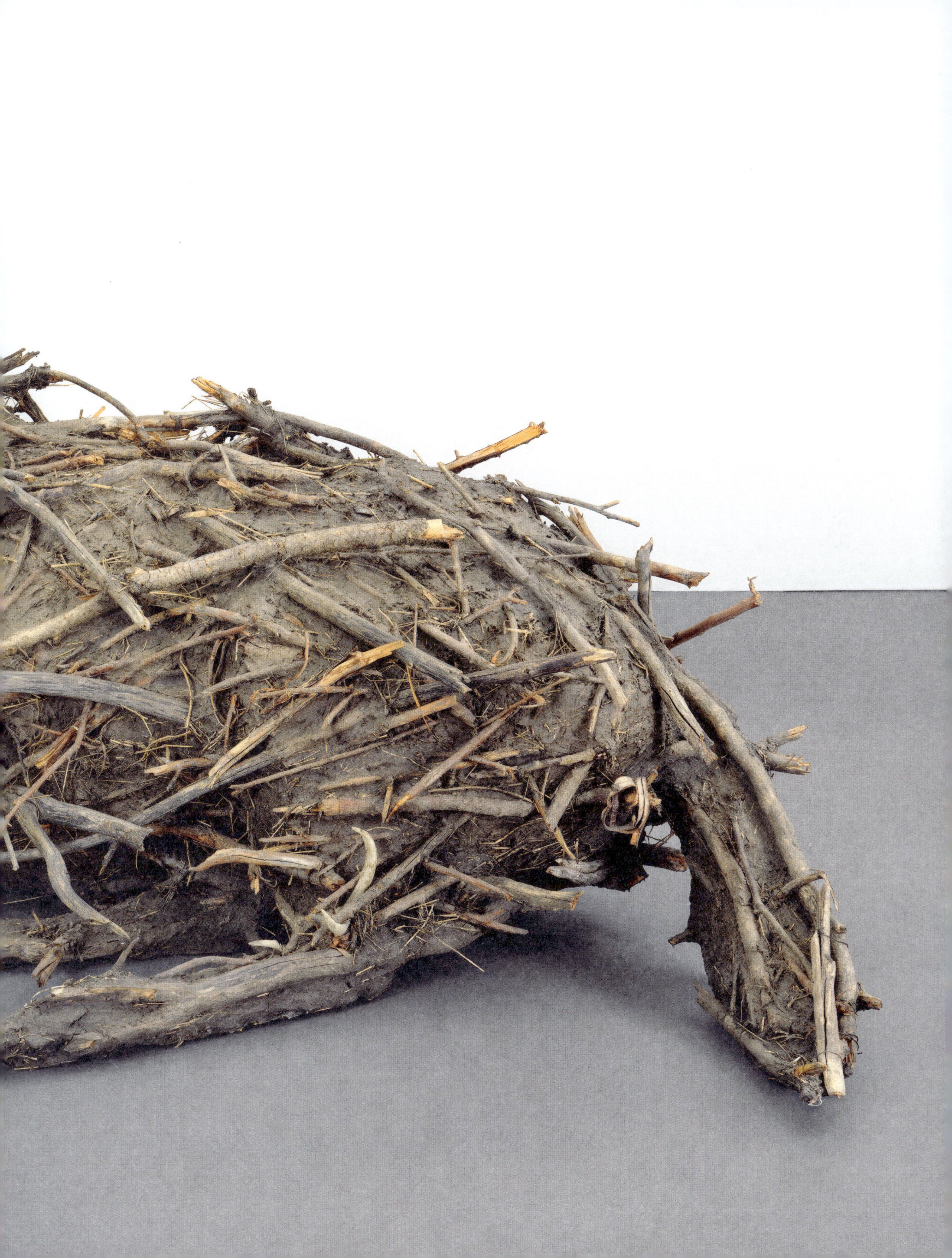

I want to create my own architecture so that the relationships of my forms and objects are fixed. Sometimes I need the large scale so that the person can literally move in relationship to the form. The difference between the real space and the psychological space interests me and I want to explore both. For example, the spiders, which are portraits of my mother, are large because she was a monument to me. I want to walk around and be underneath her and feel her protection.

–Louise Bourgeois, August 2007

Louise Bourgeois
Detail of *Spider Couple*, 2003

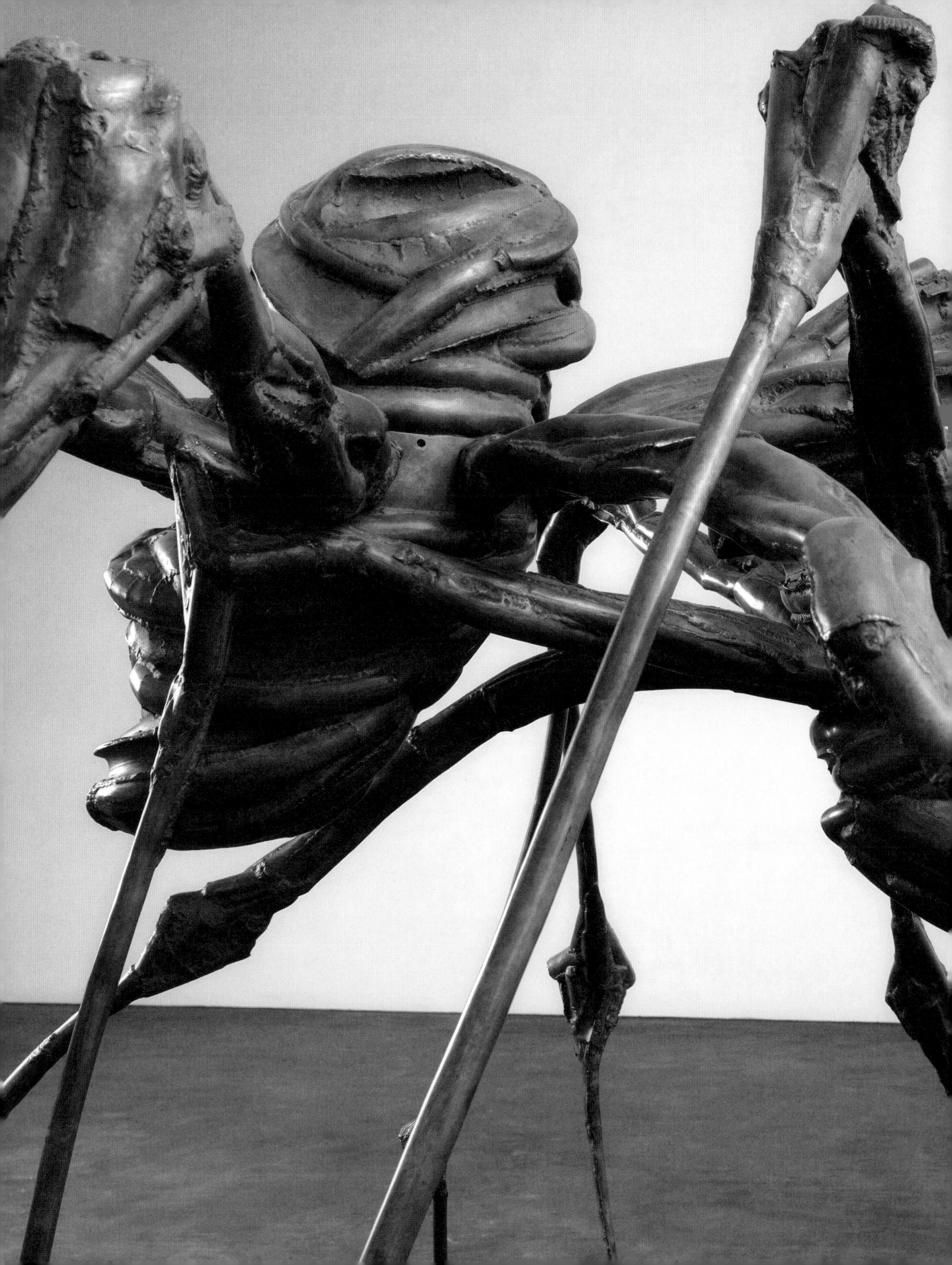

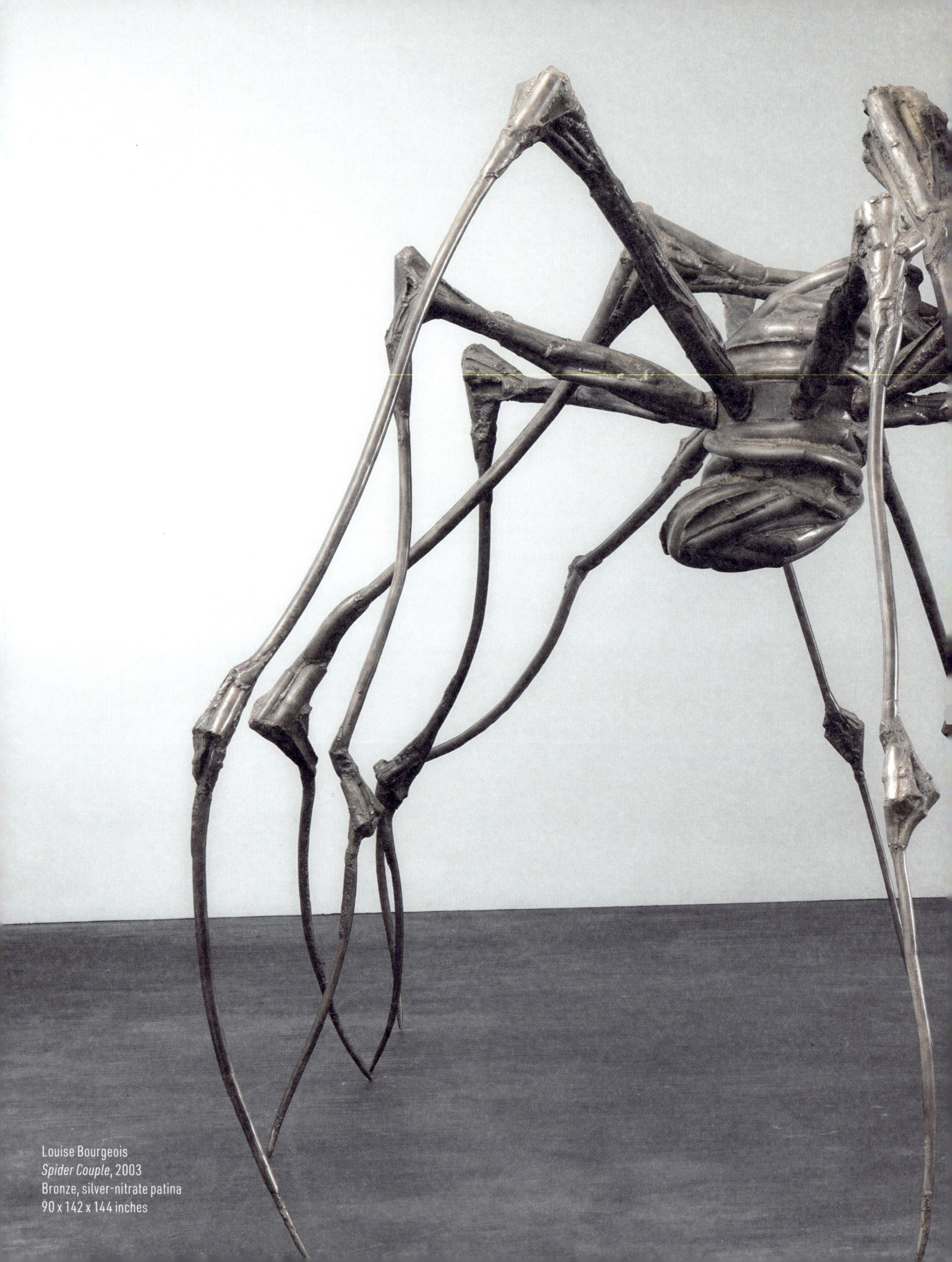

Louise Bourgeois
Spider Couple, 2003
Bronze, silver-nitrate patina
90 x 142 x 144 inches

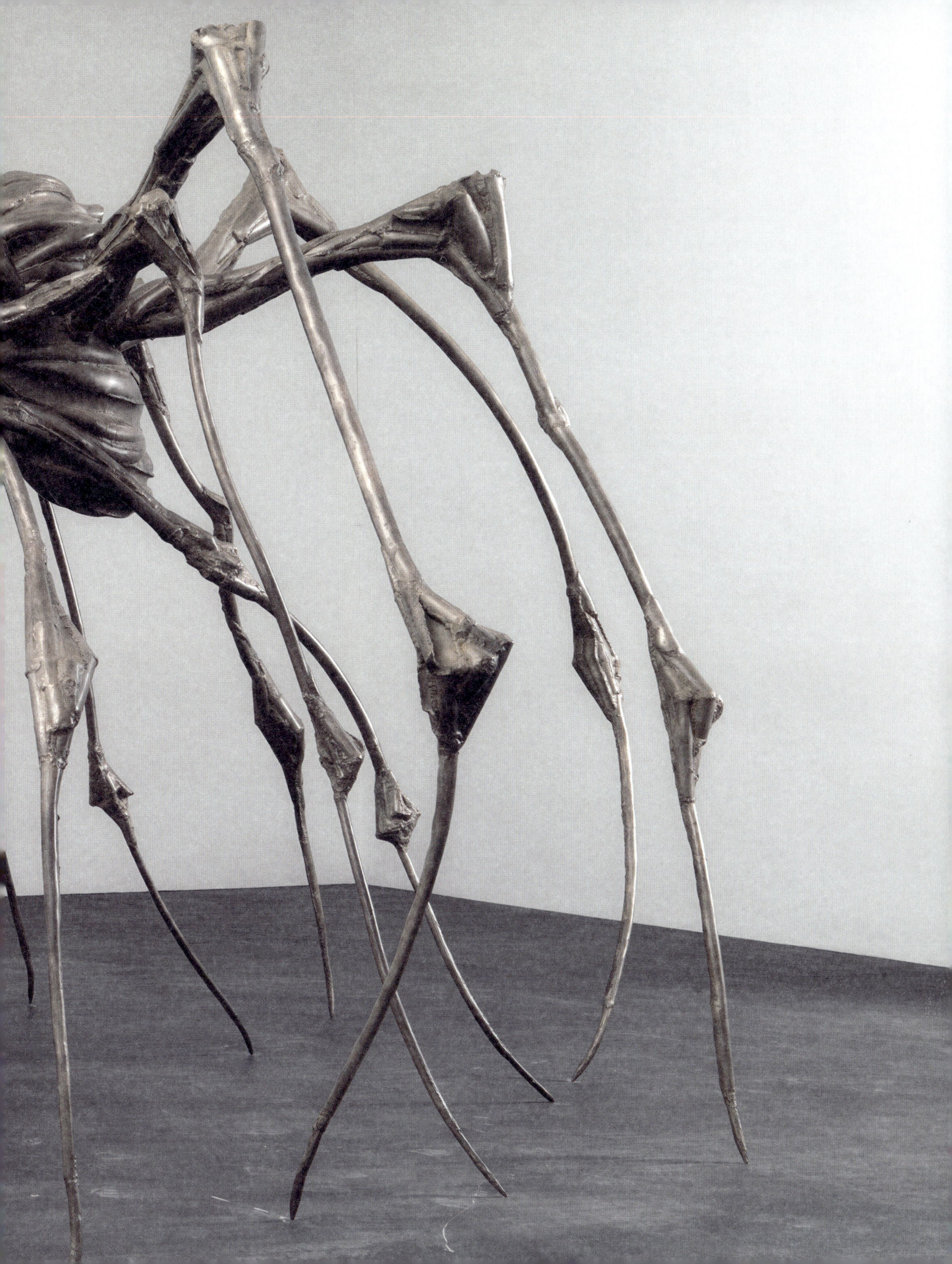

Ravish exudes visceral tension, an undulating mass of iridescent green rooster feathers, coiled and contorted in a moment of ecstasy, or perhaps torment. Seductive yet unsettling, its serpentine form recalls the mythic, the primal, the bodily. A creature neither fully alive nor entirely inert, it hovers in a liminal space, beckoning and forbidding in equal measure. Feathers, symbols of flight and freedom, are reconfigured into something weighty, something constrained. The muscular twists and knots evoke intestines, sinew, or creatures locked in an embrace both intimate and confrontational. The title itself, *Ravish*, speaks to paradox: to captivate and enthrall, yet also to violate and overwhelm. The piece thrums with this tension, oscillating between the tangible and the otherworldly. Encased within a cabinet, *Ravish* seems almost too large for its confines, pressing against the glass as though caught in arrested motion. The vitrine is both frame and barrier—evoking museum cases, cages, and scientific preservation. It isolates and amplifies, emphasizing withheld movement and unresolved energy.—Kate MccGwire

Kate MccGwire
Ravish, 2023
Mixed media with rooster feathers in bespoke cabinet, $28^{5}/_{8}$ x $19^{7}/_{8}$ x $19^{7}/_{8}$ inches

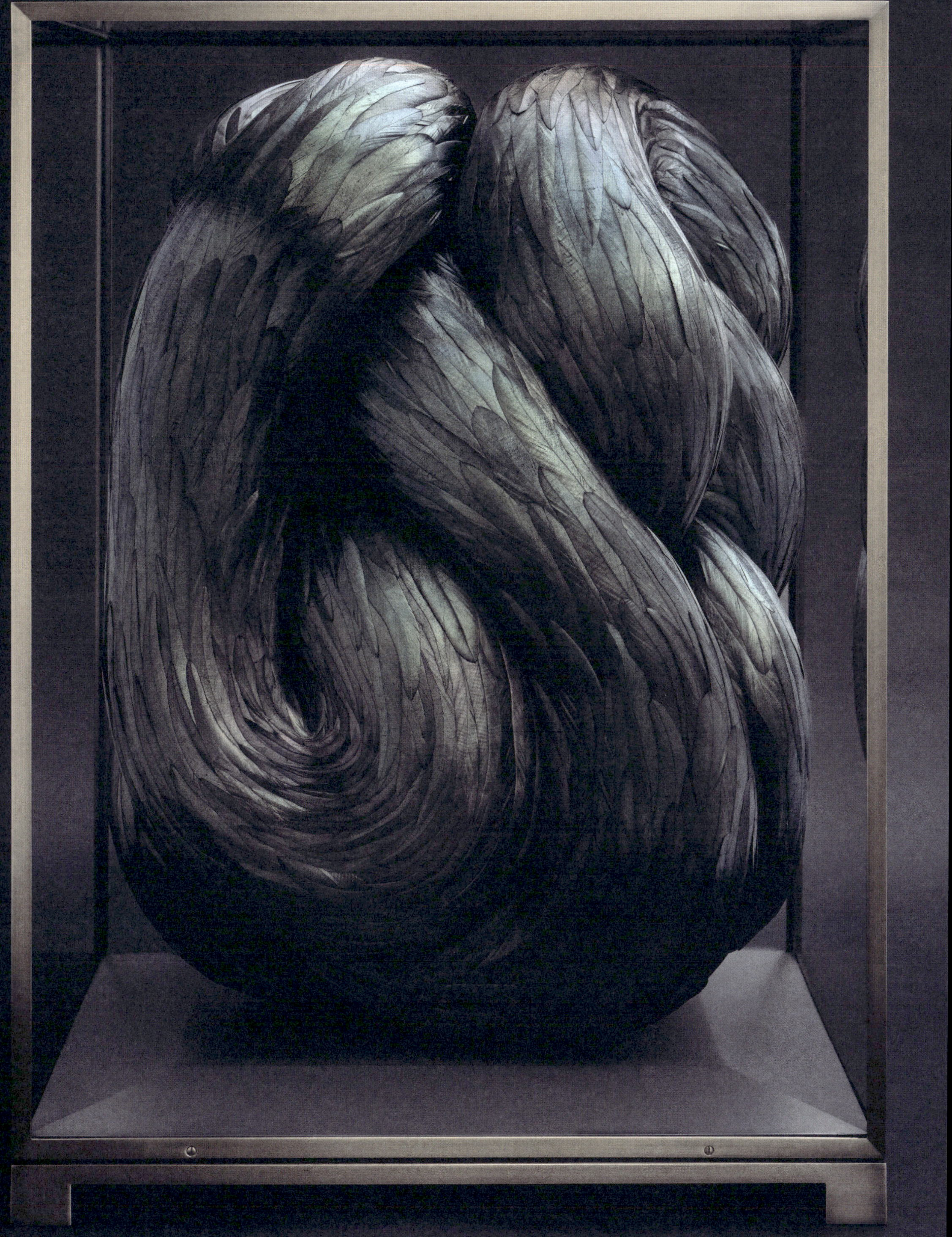

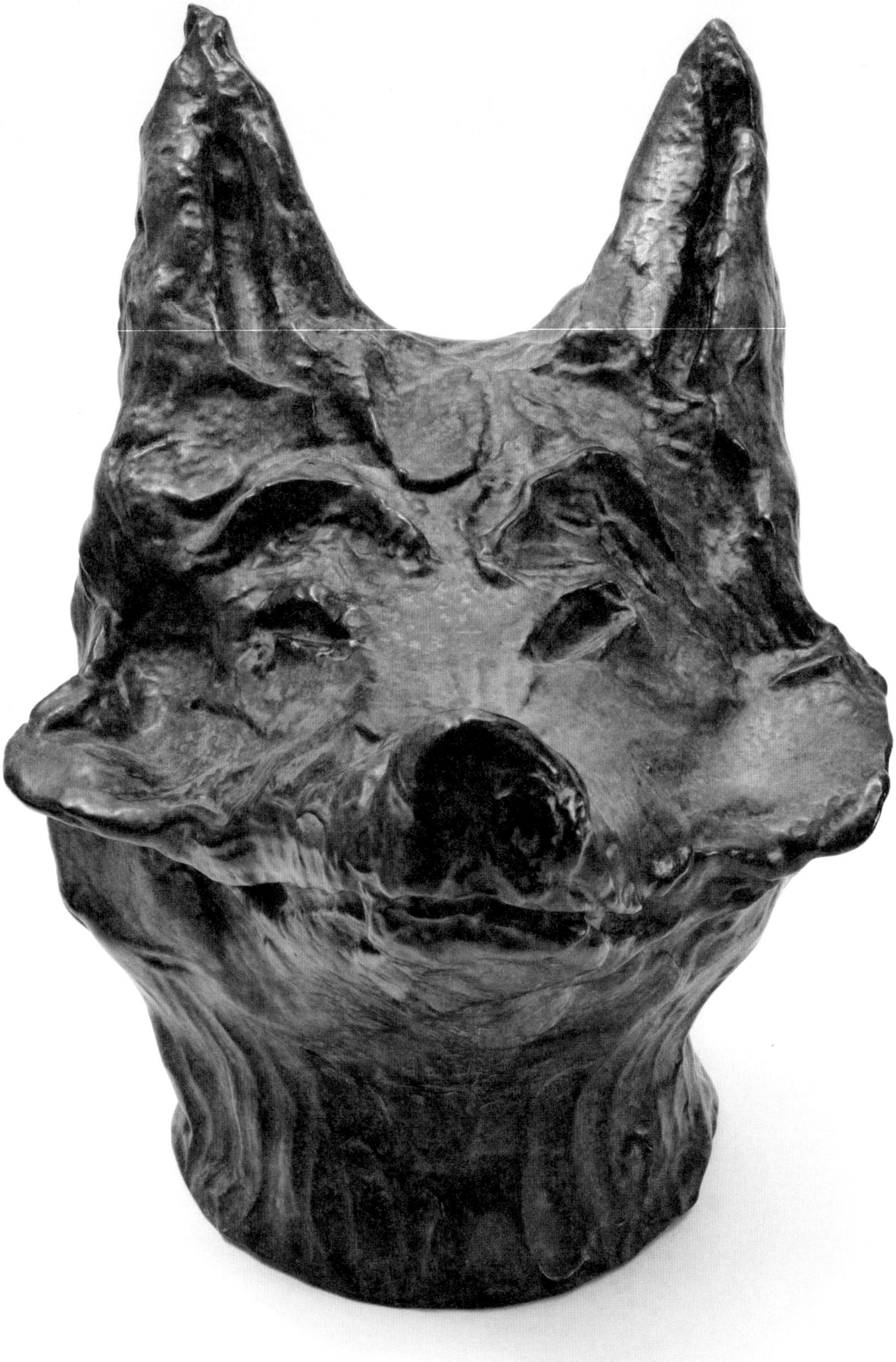

Jaune Quick-to-See Smith
Urban Trickster, 2021
Cast bronze, 28 x 20 1/2 x 24 inches

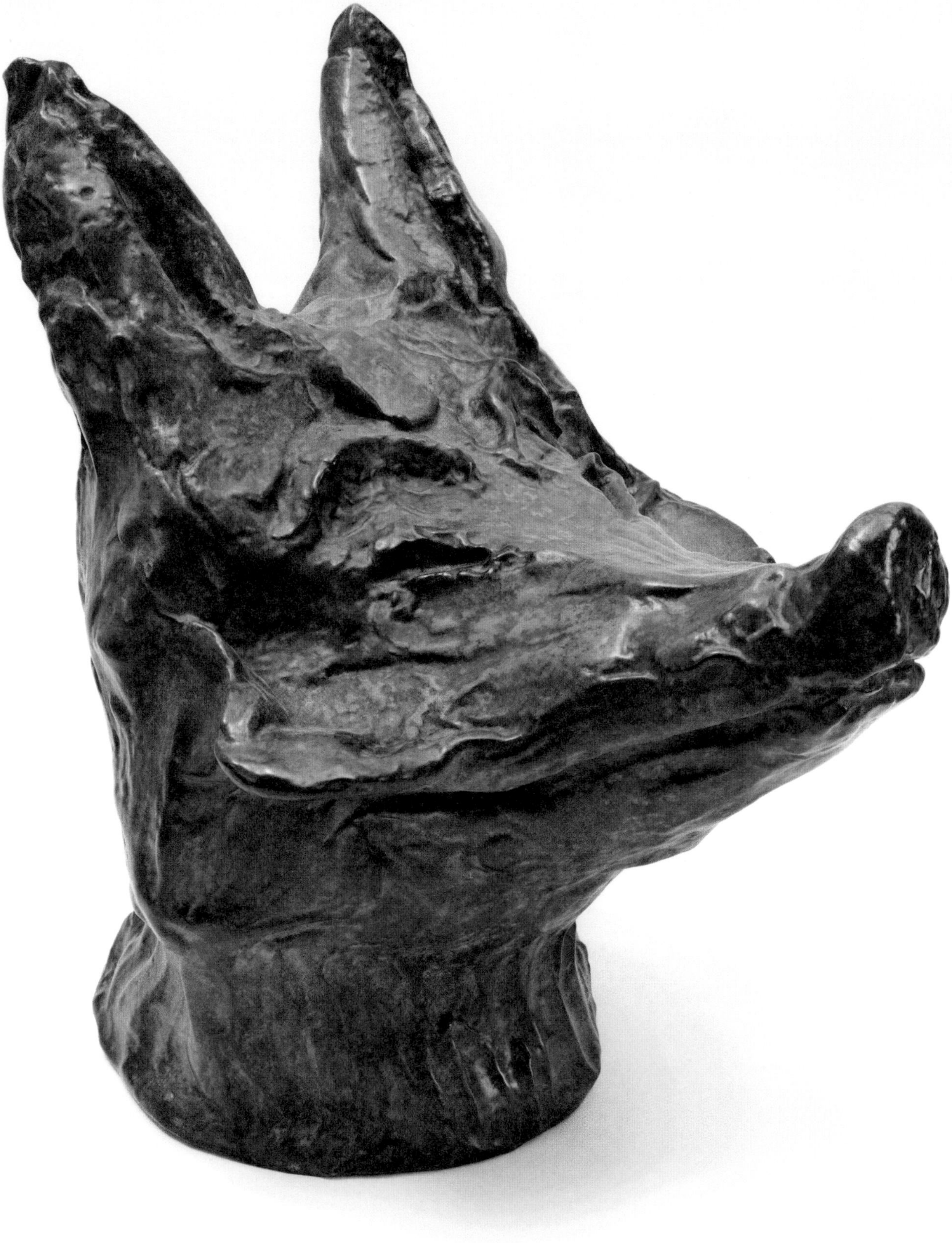

Jörg Immendorff
Malerstamm-Baldung, 2002
Bronze, 35 1/2 x 25 x 13 3/4 inches

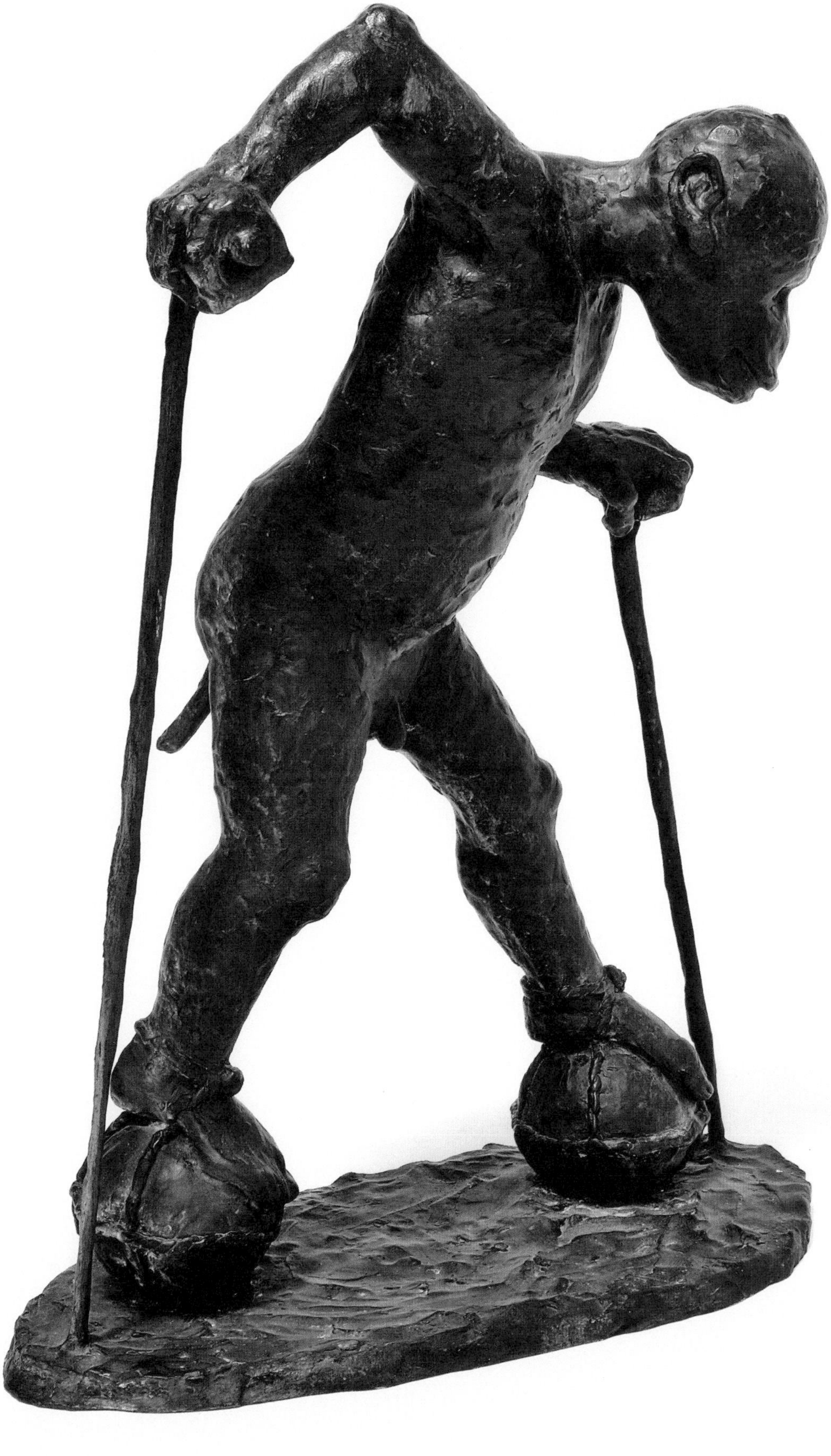

I like cats because, in my experience, I don't understand them and they don't understand me. This could be very irritating but is soothed by the big dose of indifference that is characteristic of cats and that I find corresponds to a big smattering of general indifference that I have on board myself.—Sarah Lucas

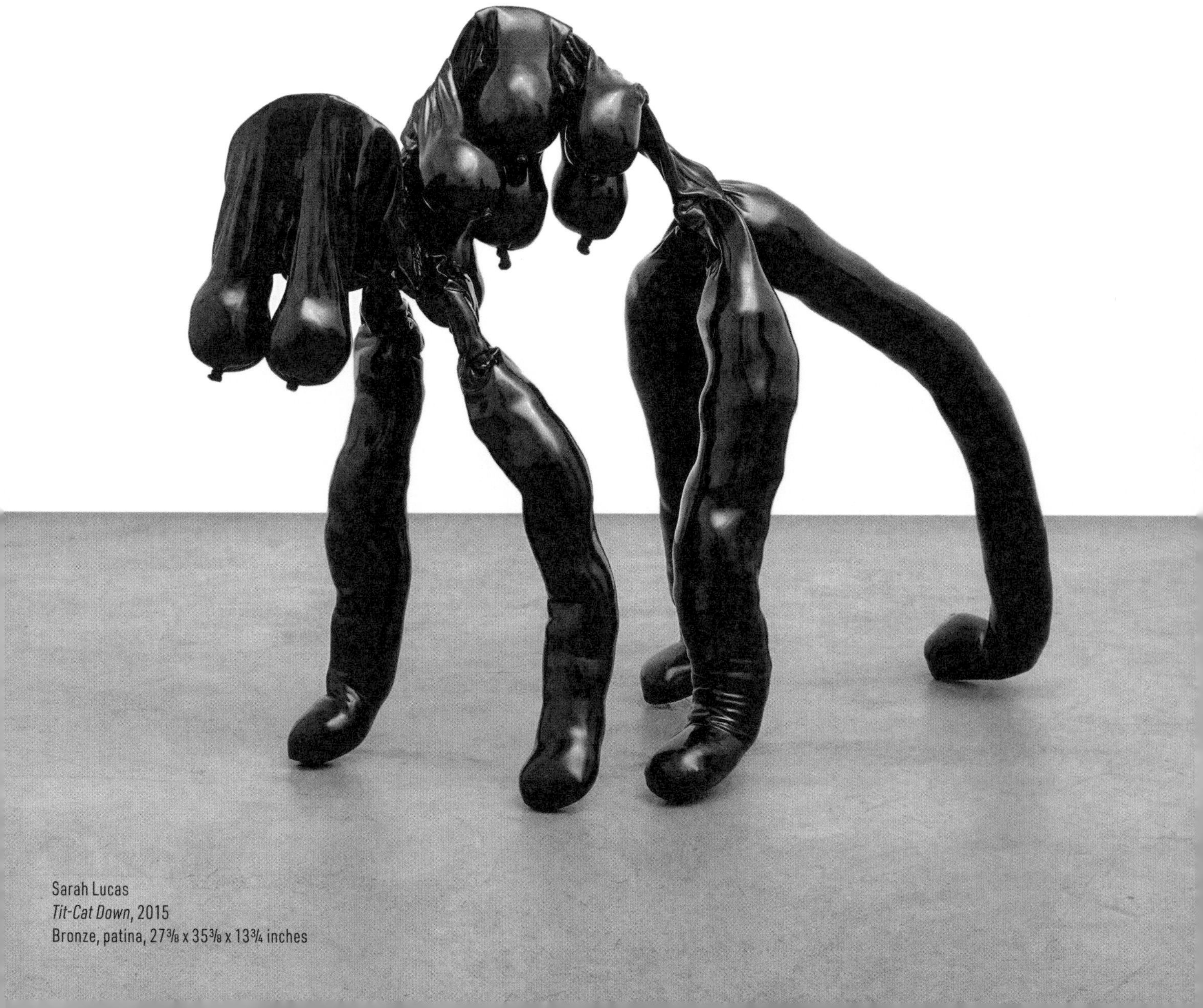

Sarah Lucas
Tit-Cat Down, 2015
Bronze, patina, 27⅜ x 35⅜ x 13¾ inches

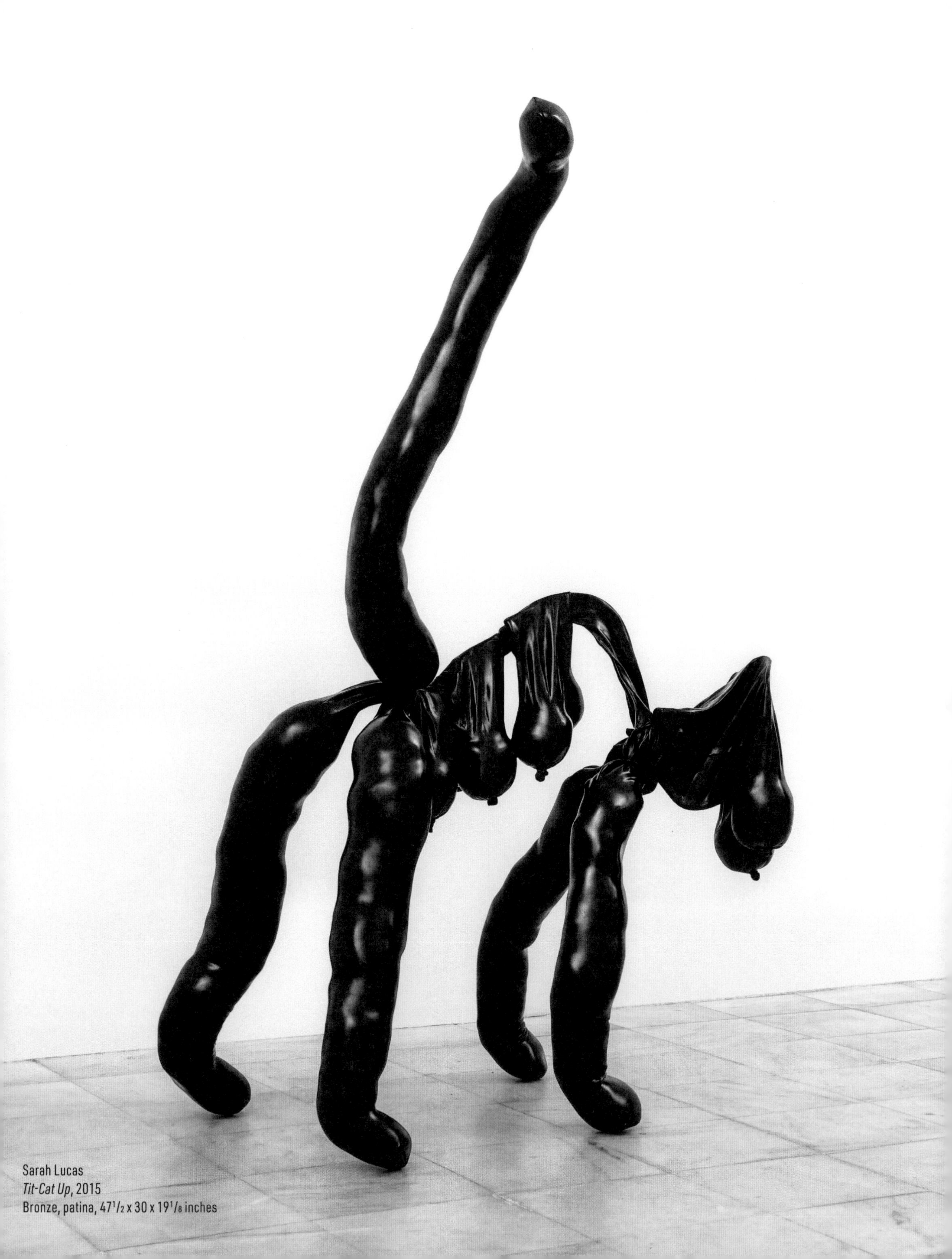

Sarah Lucas
Tit-Cat Up, 2015
Bronze, patina, 47 1/2 x 30 x 19 1/8 inches

Daniel Firman
Wurza, 2008
3D printing PETG, metal, and paint, 216 1/2 x 78 1/4 x 126 1/2 inches
A version of this work entitled *Le Sommeil en Forêt*, 2025, has been created especially for the exhibition

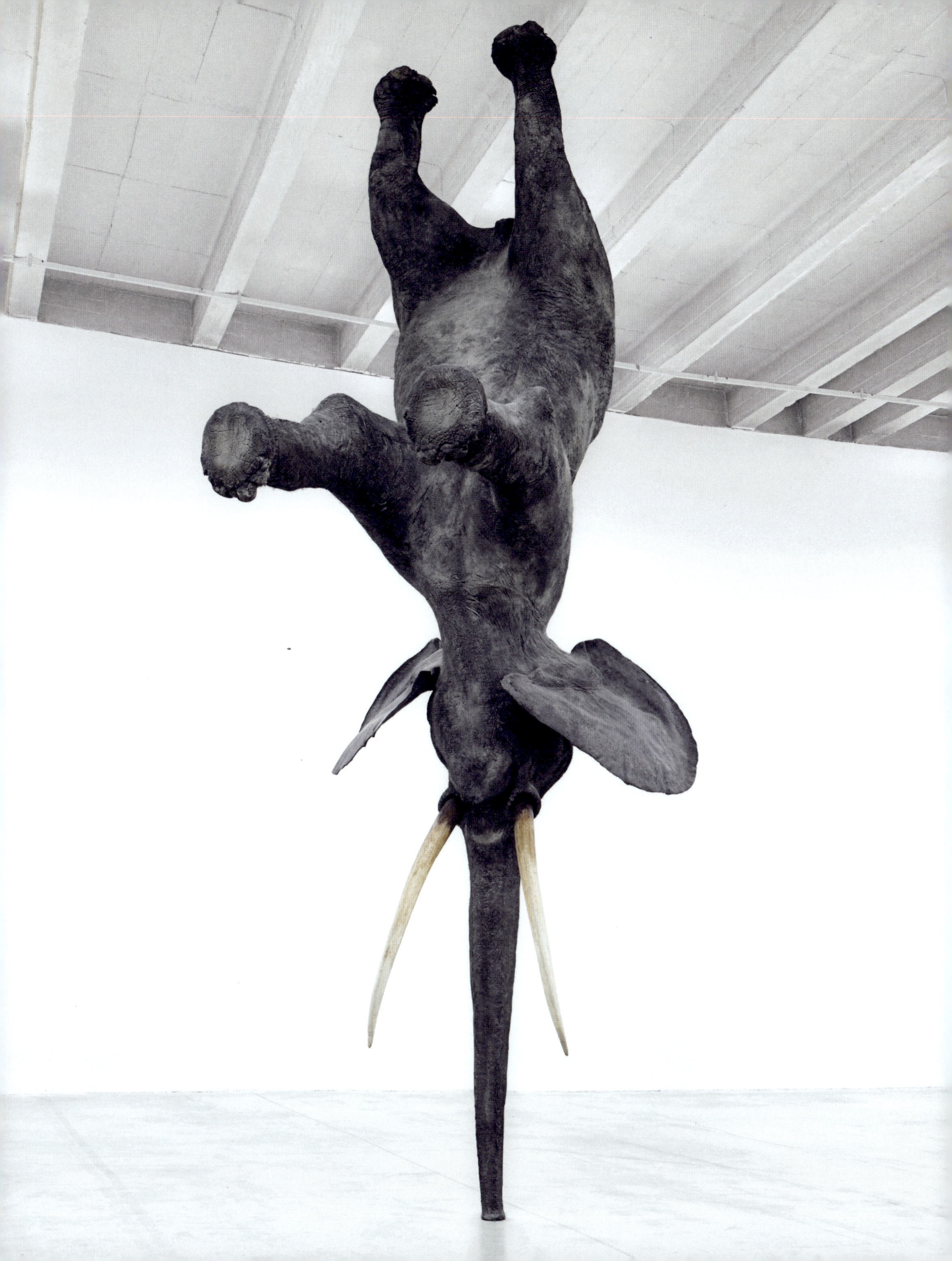

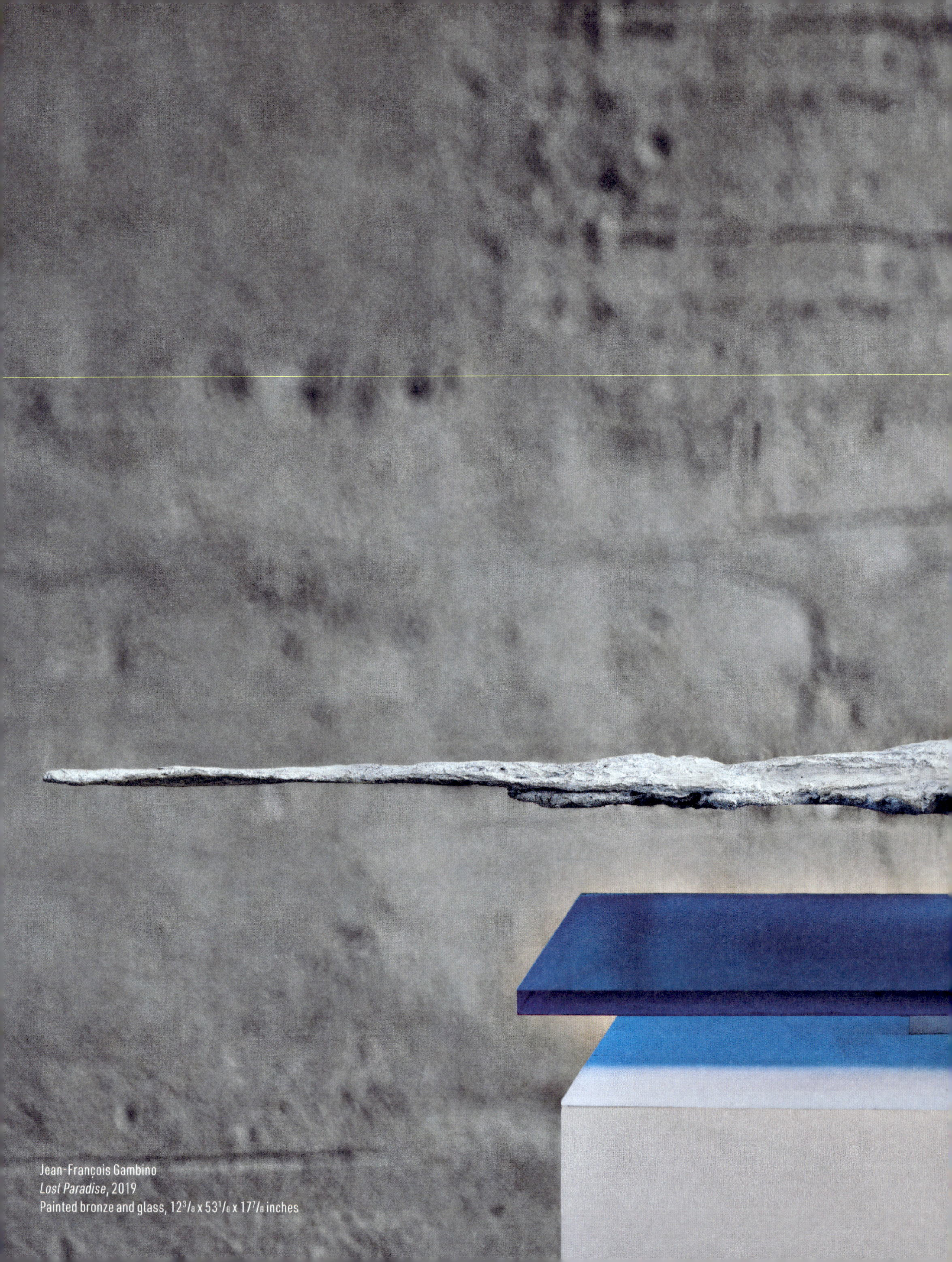

Jean-François Gambino
Lost Paradise, 2019
Painted bronze and glass, $12^{3}/_{8}$ x $53^{1}/_{8}$ x $17^{7}/_{8}$ inches

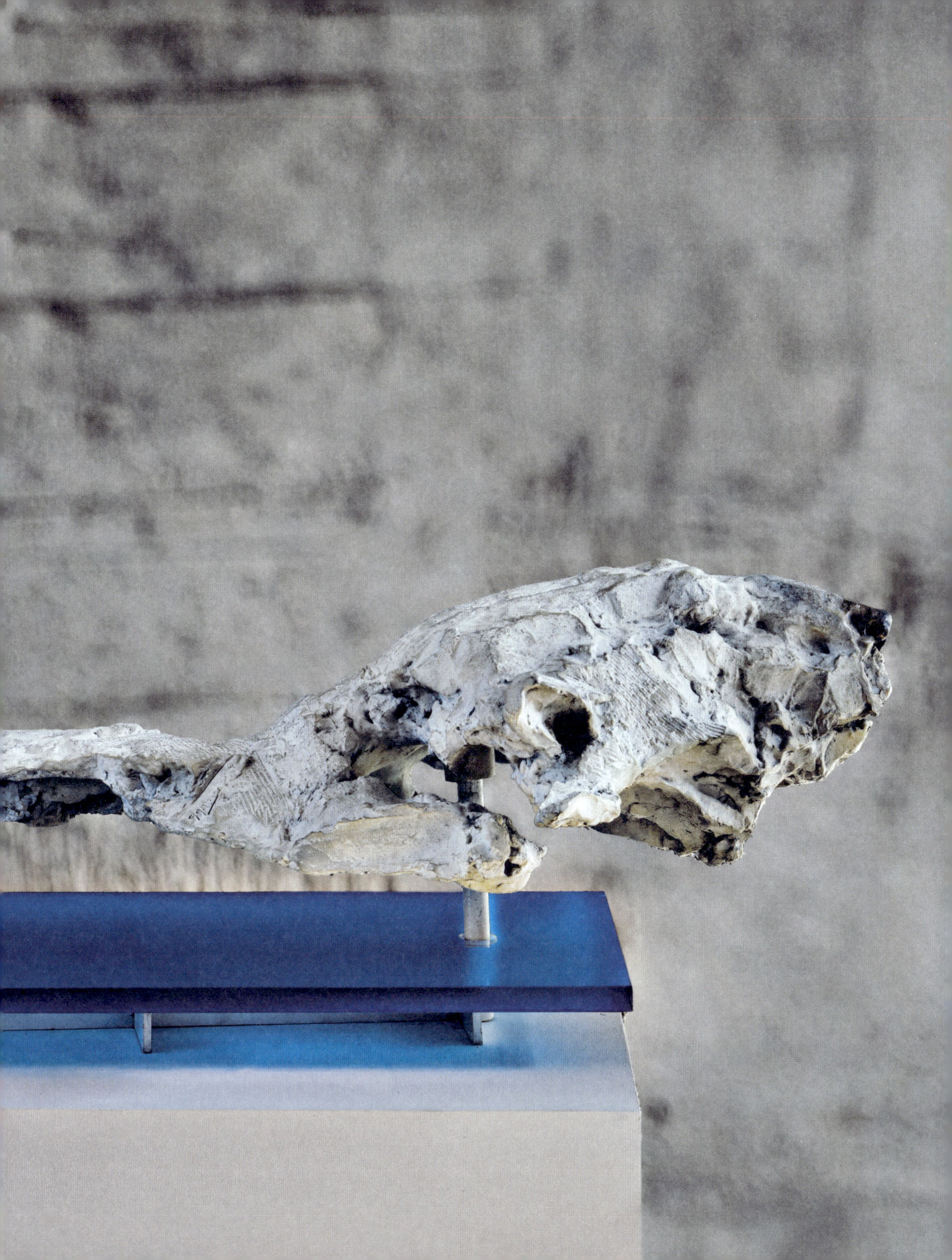

The
pigeons
suggest an
indistinct crowd, the
colonizers of a space that they claim
through the silent power of their presence,
establishing a strong sense of community and belonging.
They "observe" from above the movements of the visitors looking at
them. Impassive and eerily calm onlookers, pigeons are a habitual feature of
the urban landscape and their presence in the exhibition space imparts a feeling of
restlessness. Far from the visitors, the birds seem to loiter in the nooks and most anonymous
places; suggesting a reversal between the inside and outside, they mark the confines of the space and
transform it into an urban environment that abounds with life.–Lucia Aspesi, Fiammetta Griccioli, and Mariagiulia Leuzzi

Maurizio Cattelan
Detail of *Ghosts*, 2021

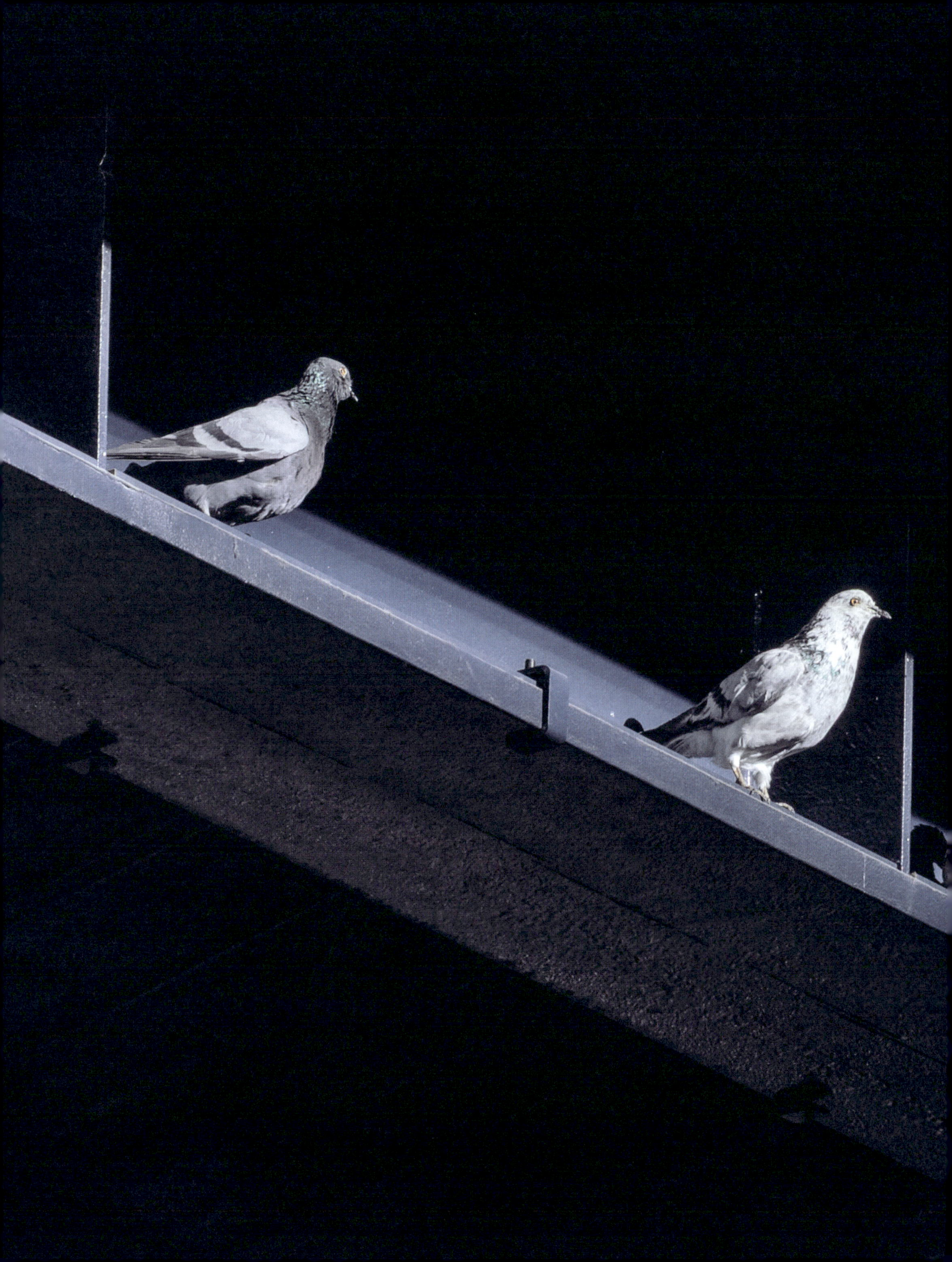

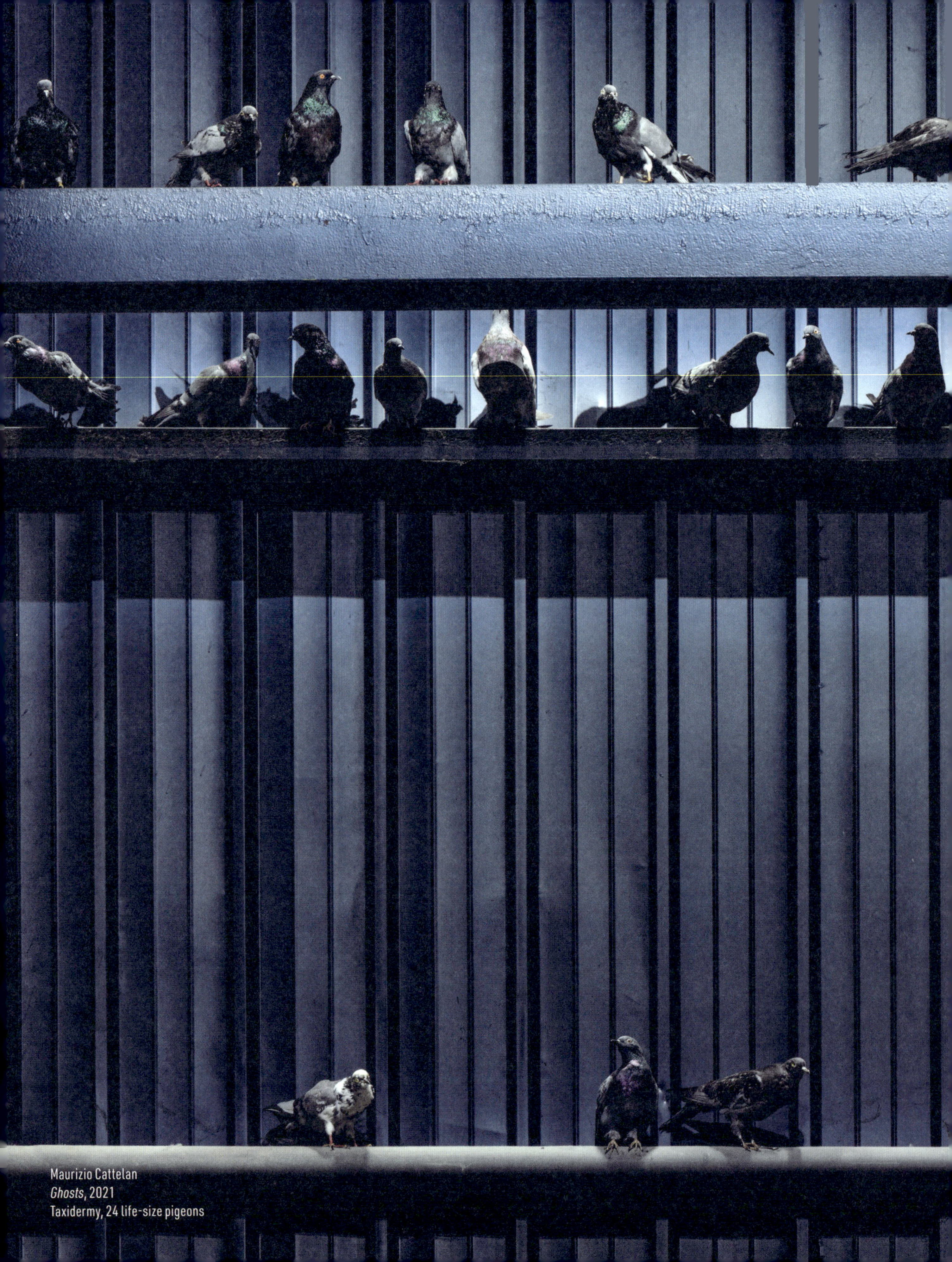

Maurizio Cattelan
Ghosts, 2021
Taxidermy, 24 life-size pigeons

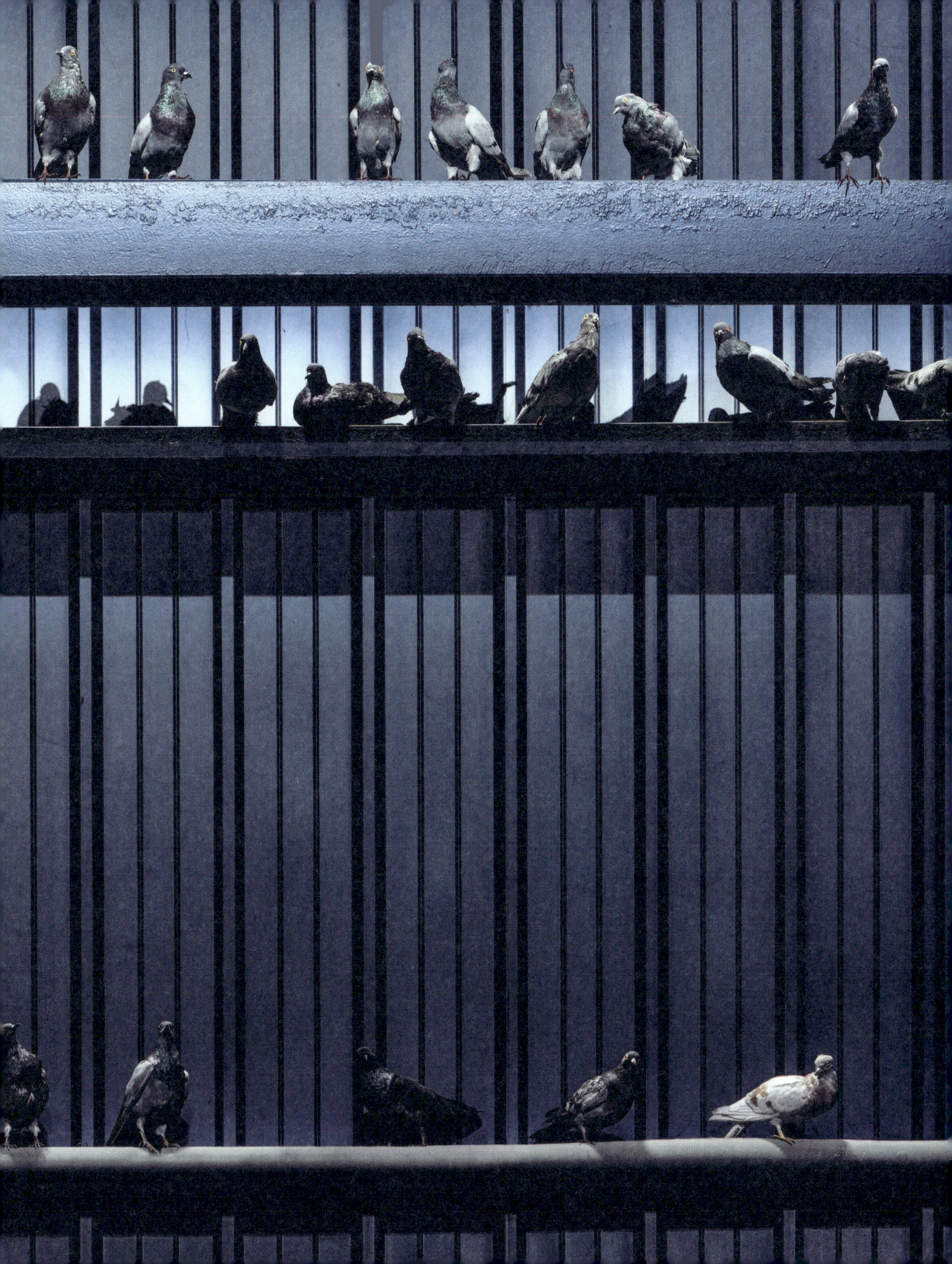

William Kent
Squid, 1965
Black Italian slate, 43 x 32 x 1/4 inches

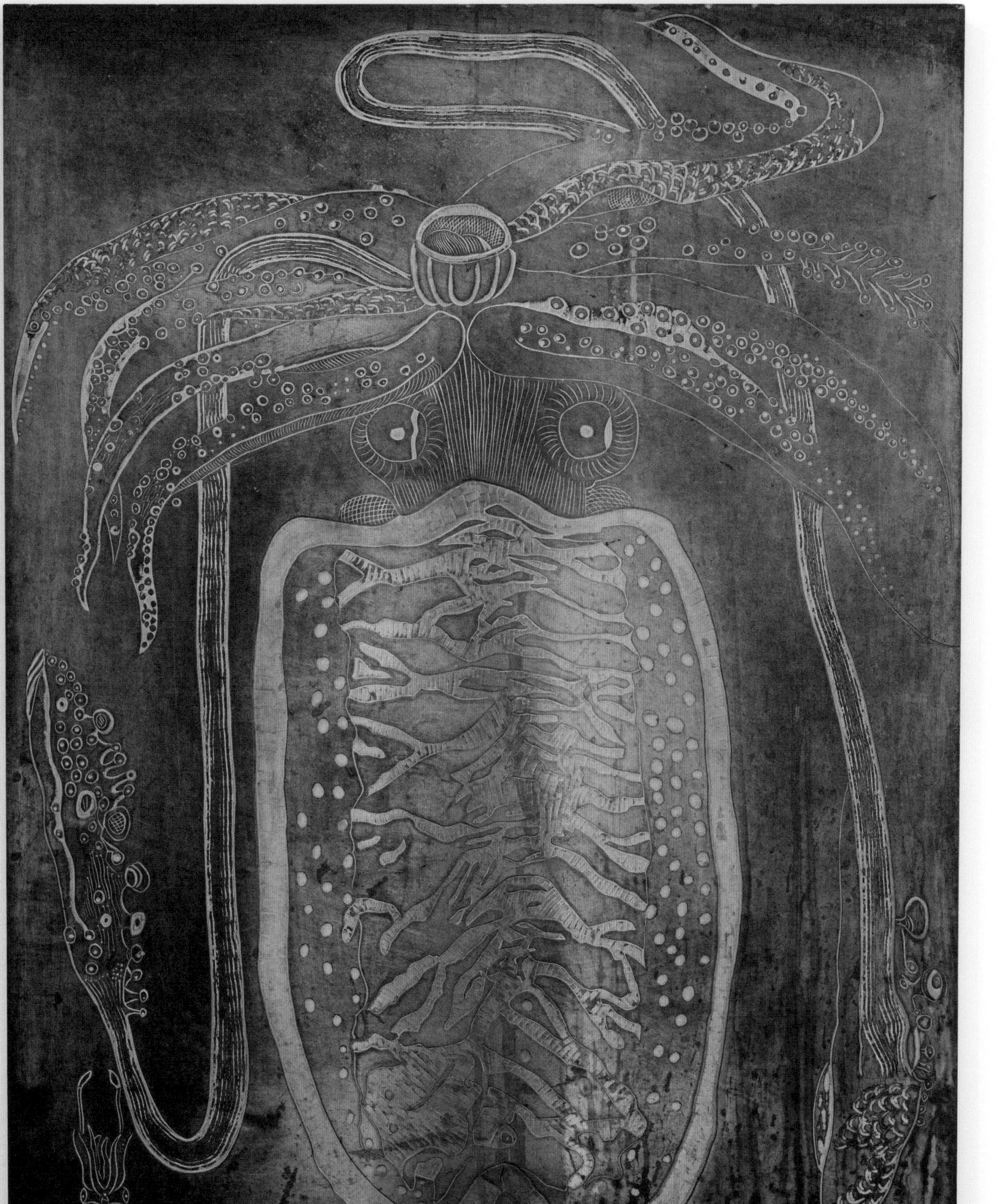

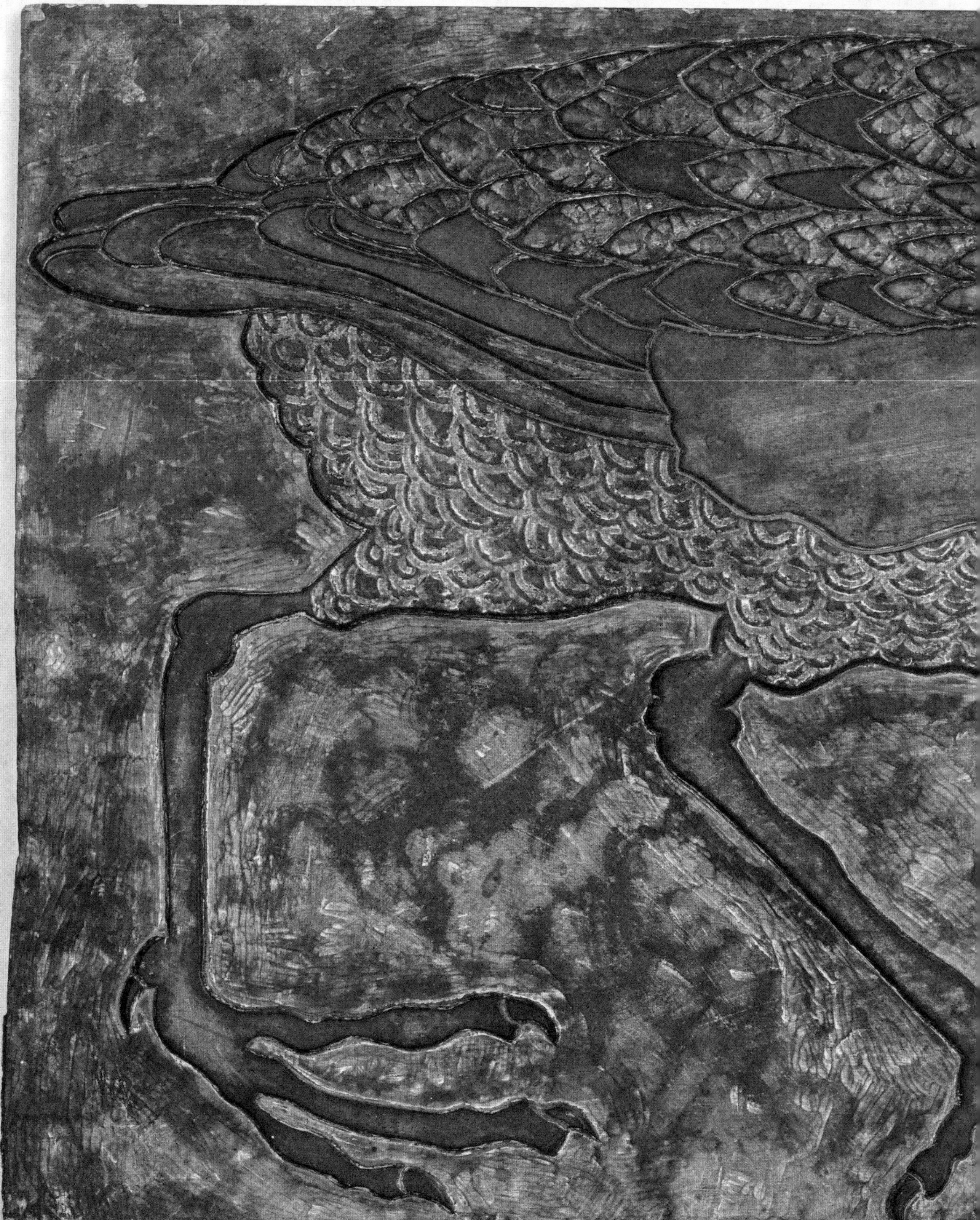

William Kent
Bitten and Beetle, 1968
Black Italian slate, $10^{5}/_{8} \times 17^{1}/_{2} \times {}^{1}/_{4}$ inches

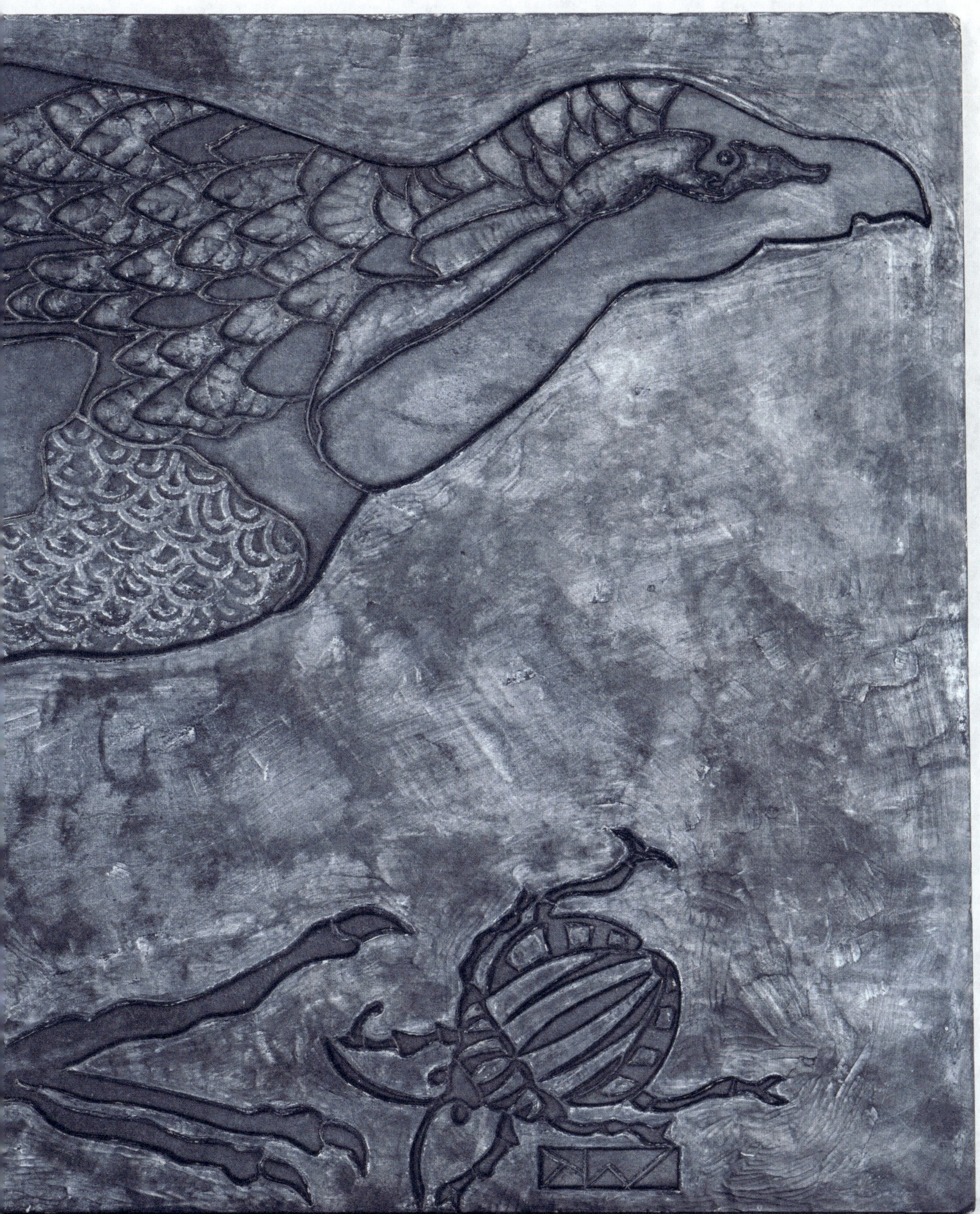

William Kent
Fish and Snake, 1958
Marble, stone, and wood, 33 x 22 x 14 inches

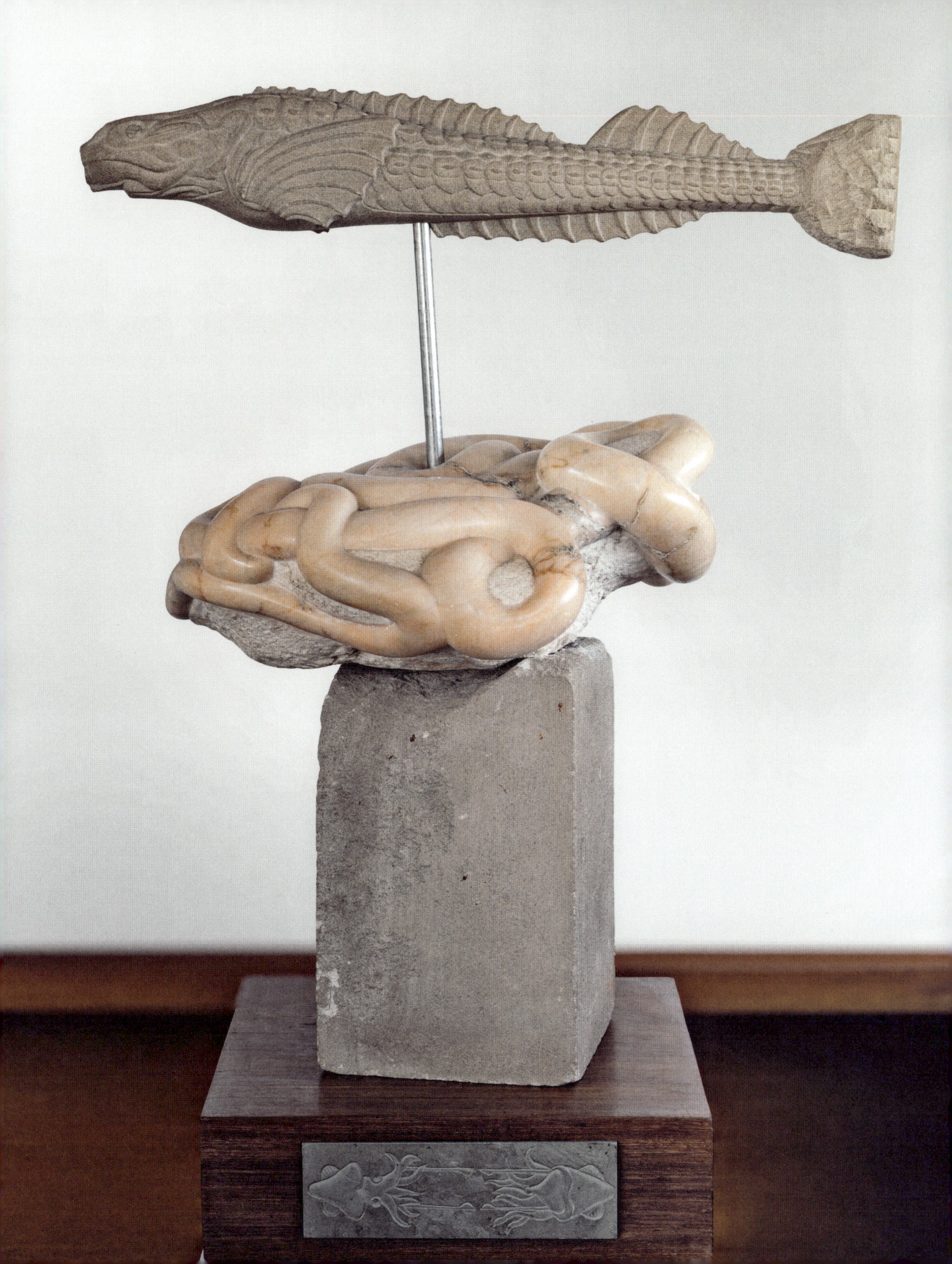

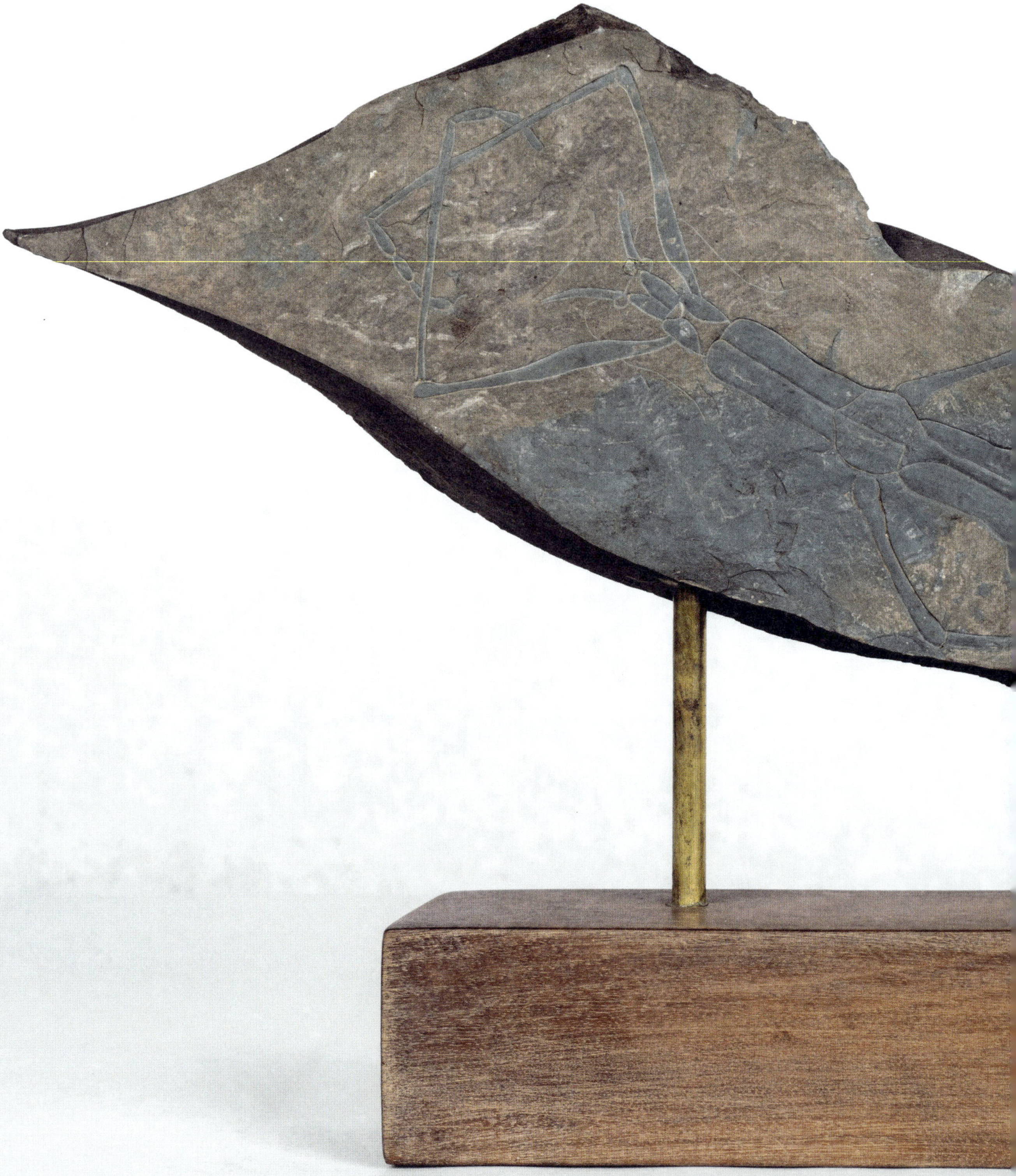

William Kent
Walking Stick, 1958
Black Italian slate, 20 x 8 1/2 x 3/8 inches

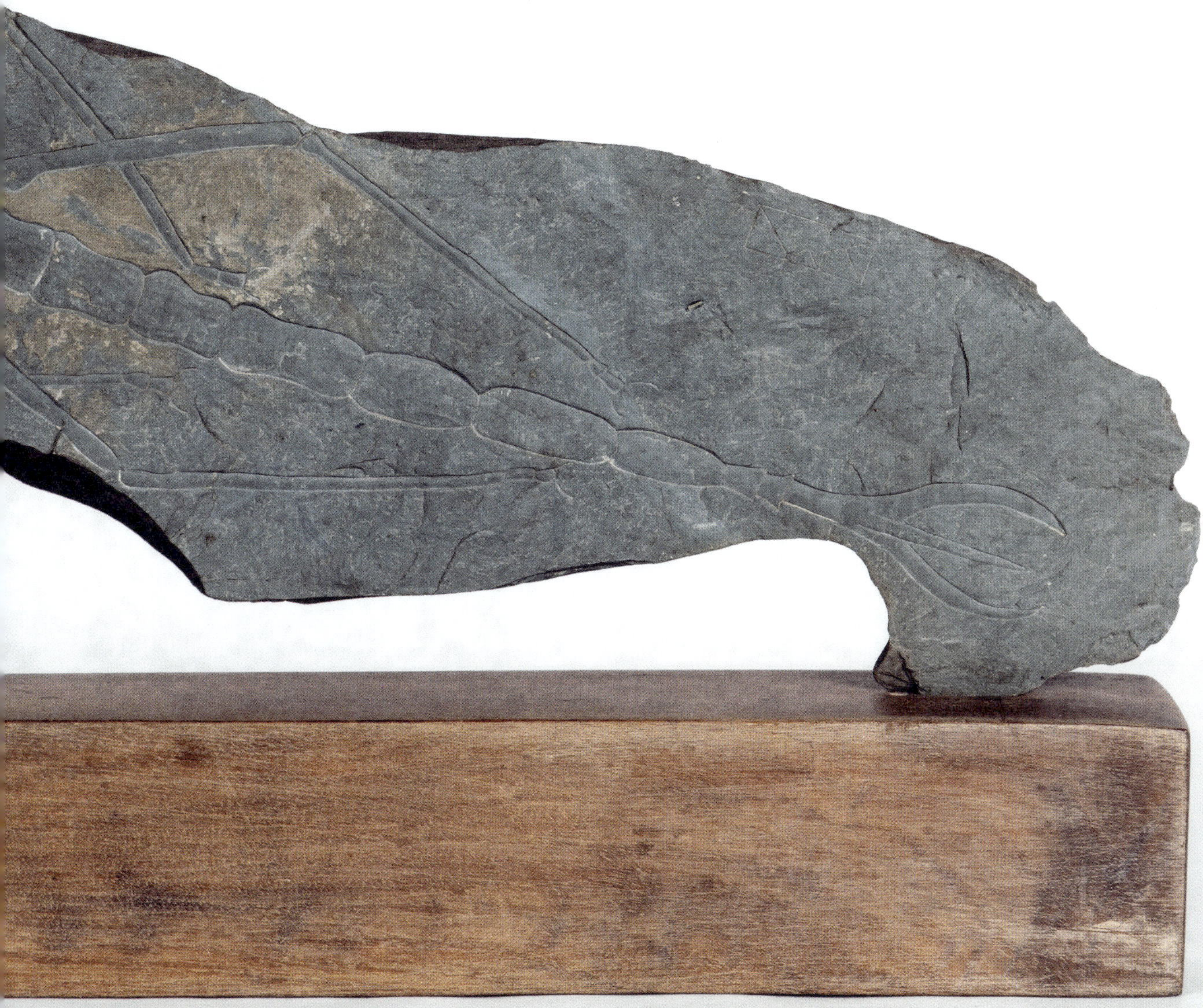

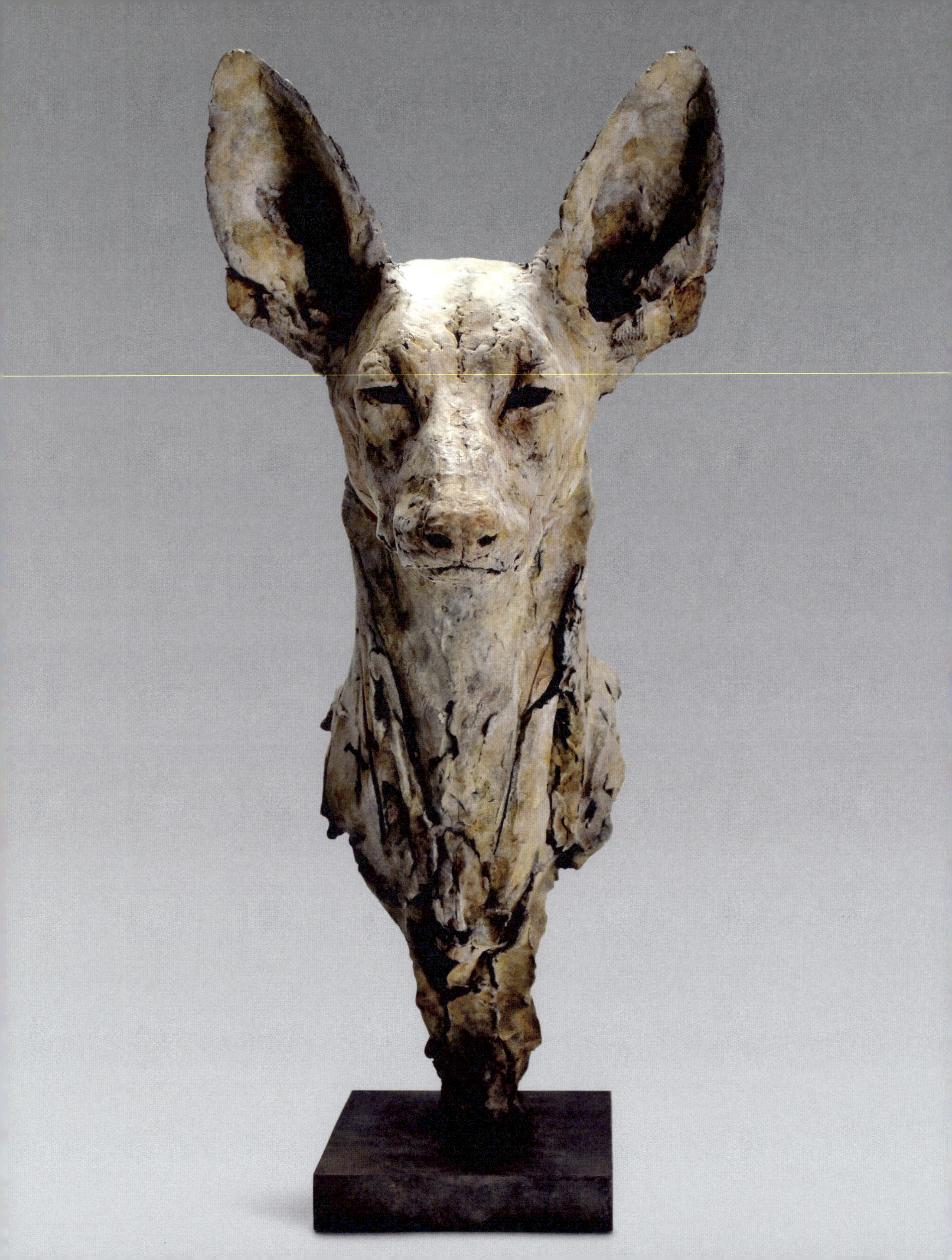

As a sculptor with a background in ceramics, working with a bronze foundry has offered me the opportunity to combine the experimental language of hand-building techniques used for the kiln with more traditional and observational sculpting on an armature. The translation of one medium to another and the way that the fabricated clay voice is evident within the finished bronze sculpture is not only exciting but now forms almost exclusively my current artistic practice. Subjects tend toward animals with which humans have a deep social and historical connection, particularly canine and feline themes. In a world which feels increasingly disconnected from nature, I am interested in attempting to convey our mutualities, empathy, and shared consciousness—exploring notions of a perceived "spirituality" or "otherness," and in elevating the subject beyond its physicality. Referencing representations of Anubis, the ancient Egyptian deity with the head of a jackal, the muse and inspiration for *Pariah* is Nola, our Podenco rescue hound, who at times seems to very much embody her distant ancestry and the sculpture speaks to our interwoven human connection with both.—Nichola Theakston

Nichola Theakston
Pariah, 2025
Bronze, 23 5/8 x 22 x 6 1/4 inches

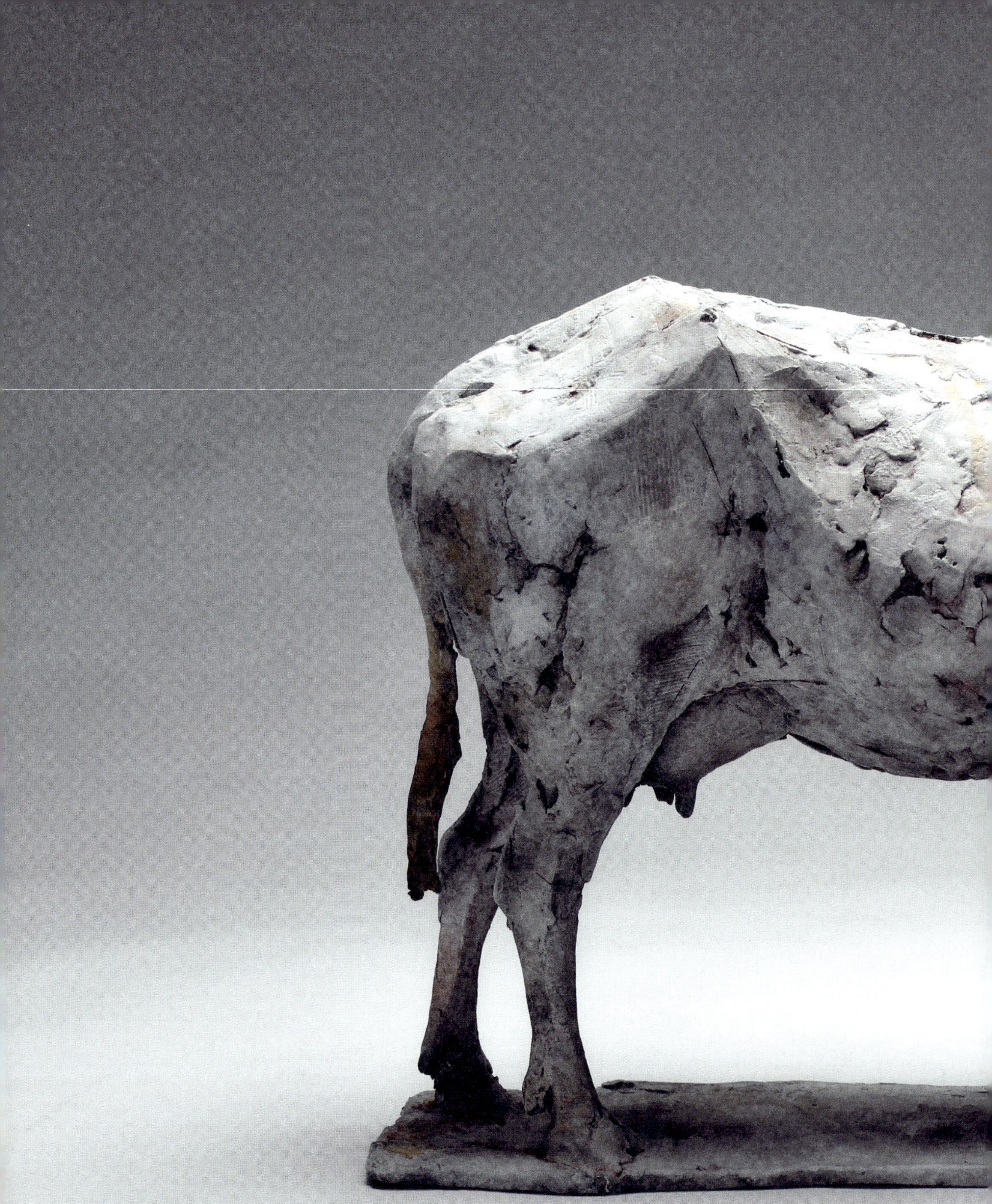

Nichola Theakston
Sacred Cow, 2025
Bronze, $25^{5}/_{8}$ x $16^{1}/_{2}$ x $7^{7}/_{8}$ inches

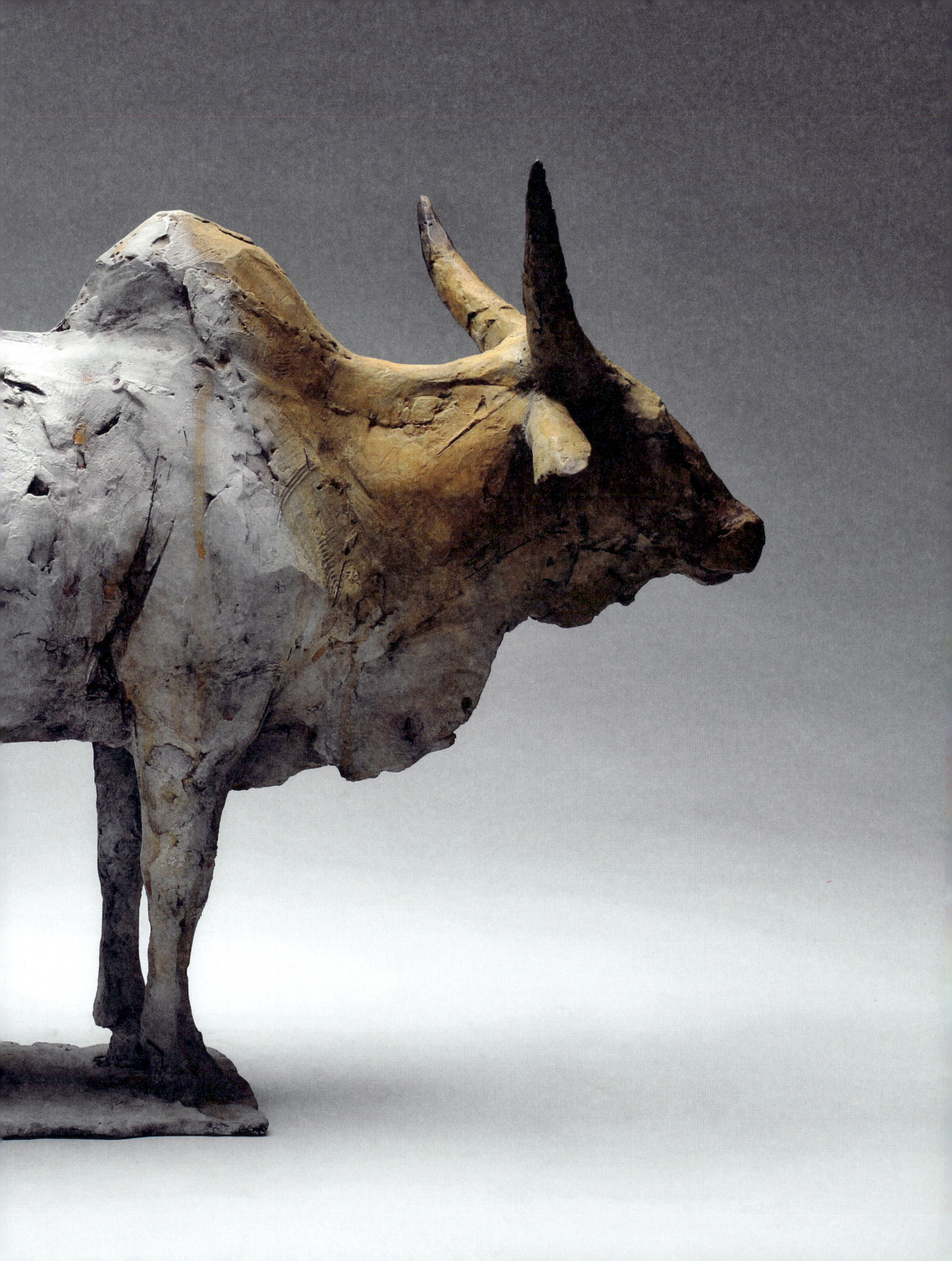

Nichola Theakston
Bastet, 2022
Bronze, $17^3/_8$ x $15^1/_4$ x $10^1/_4$ inches

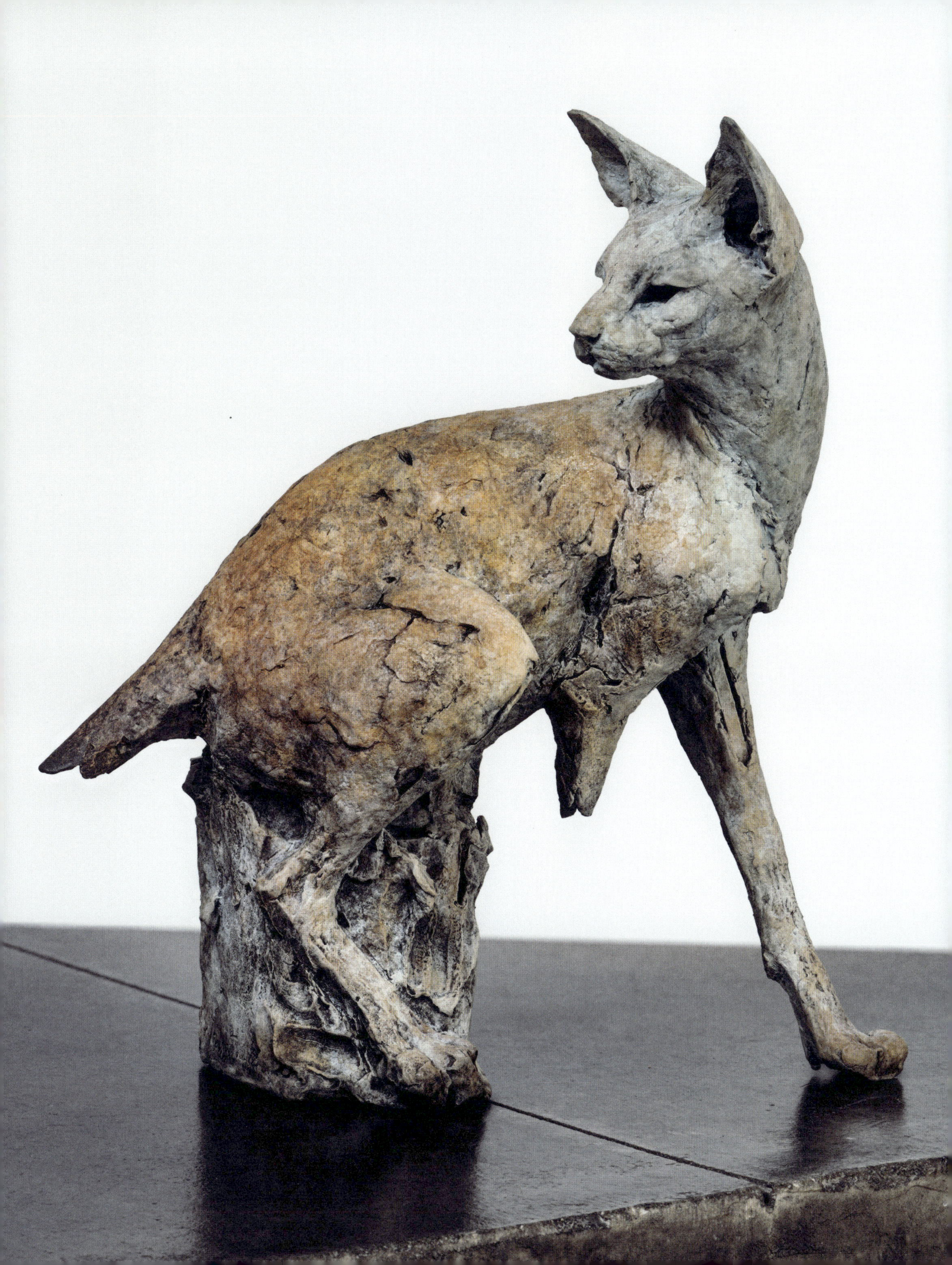

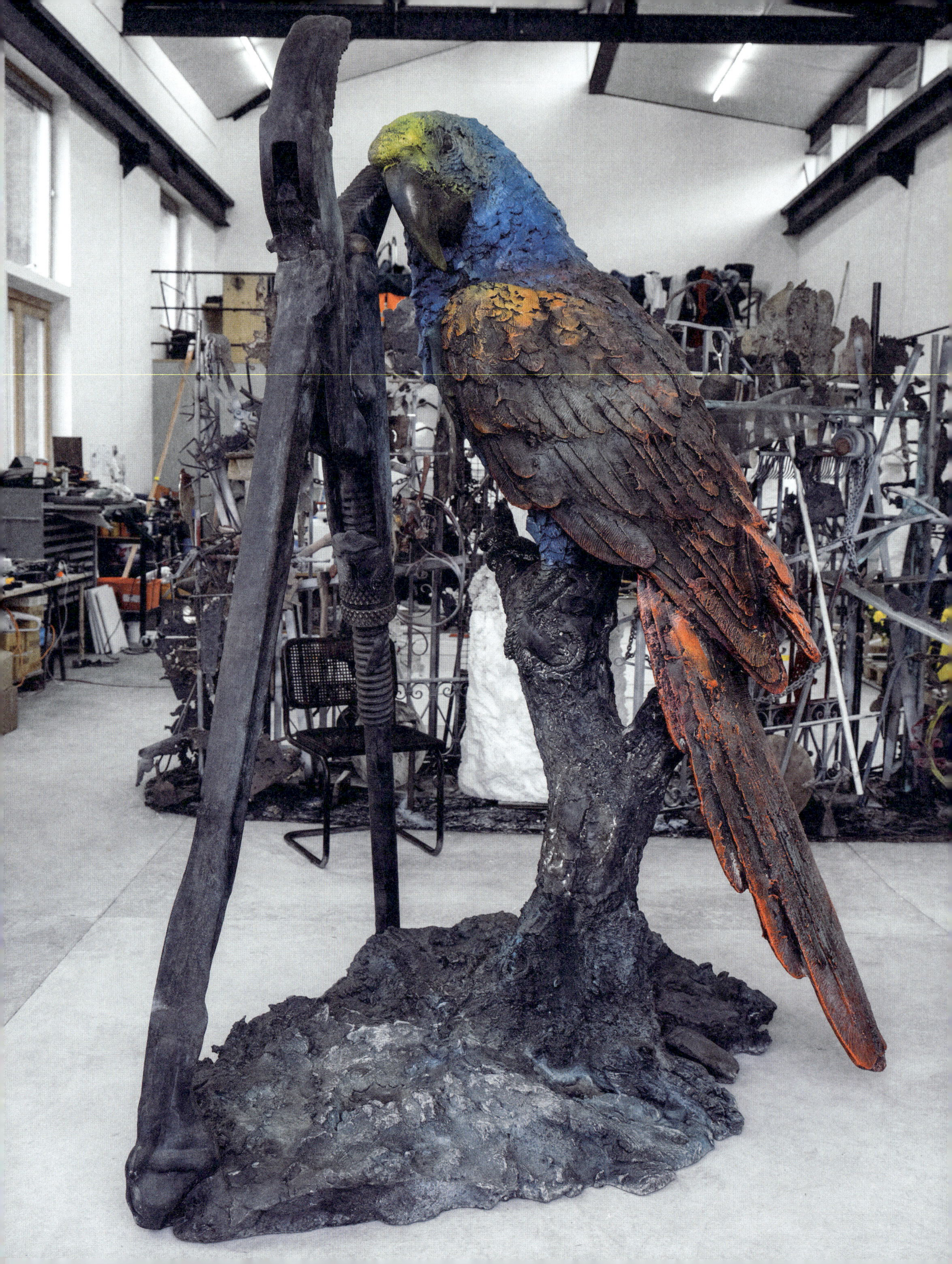

I have been casting bronze sculpture since 1980. The 2024 sculpture, *Bird, Me and Tool*, has been cast and assembled in St. Gallen, Switzerland, at the foundry called Kunstgiesserei St. Gallen. I worked in the studio provided for me by the Sitterwerk Foundation for the past five years, regularly moving back and forth between St. Gallen and Paris. I have built the positives from plaster and wood before they are given to the artisans to mold and cast in bronze. After all these years of making sculpture, I finally have learned to sit with the work and realize it after much looking. The studio and the people at the Kunstgiesserei, with their highly sophisticated sense of collaboration and cooperation, have given me the gift of silence and contemplation so that I can see clearer.–Jim Dine

Jim Dine
Bird, Me and Tool, 2024
Painted bronze, 98 1/2 x 57 x 49 1/4 inches

I spent my childhood in the woods, fields, oceans, and rivers of New England. Outdoors, I was constantly stimulated and felt a deep connection to something much larger. I was fascinated with all the various life forms that inhabited this shared world. One of my first visceral memories of political repulsion was witnessing our society's collective degradation of the environment. None of these feelings have changed. Value and waste are uniquely human elements and social constructions. What we create, celebrate, and/or disregard intrigues me. I use found objects–mostly plastics that I refer to as post-consumer detritus–in an attempt to both celebrate and condemn extraordinary human creativity and the simultaneous shortsightedness of this relentless consumption. Working with "junk" inspires me to look for the potential in what otherwise would be considered mundane. This engages me in a unique perspective shift visually and emotionally. My muses are often the creatures, mostly birds, which I use as a means for this transformation. The practice pushes me to always observe both the natural and the manmade world with a heightened intensity. The subjects often act as Trojan horses for other, more specific social, political, or aesthetic issues I wish the viewer to consider. I've always been intrigued by the work of Alberto Giacometti. A version of one of his *Walking Man* sculptures sold in 2010 for over $104 million. I personally value his work, but this level of market perversion perplexes me when I consider people are starving. Giacometti suffered from anxiety. There's an expression my older brother often says when I discuss his emotional state, as he struggles with depression: "Some days you are the pigeon. Some days you are the statue." Depicting a Giacometti allowed me to obsess on the nuances of his work in a way that only a faithful translation can. The piece is also a statement about how indifferent other species are to human cultural significance, ambitions, and our perceived self-grandiosity. For the pigeon, the Giacometti is not a valuable sculpture. It is just a perch.
–Thomas Deininger

Thomas Deininger
Pigeon on the Giacometti, 2024
Mixed media, 80 x 48 x 48 inches

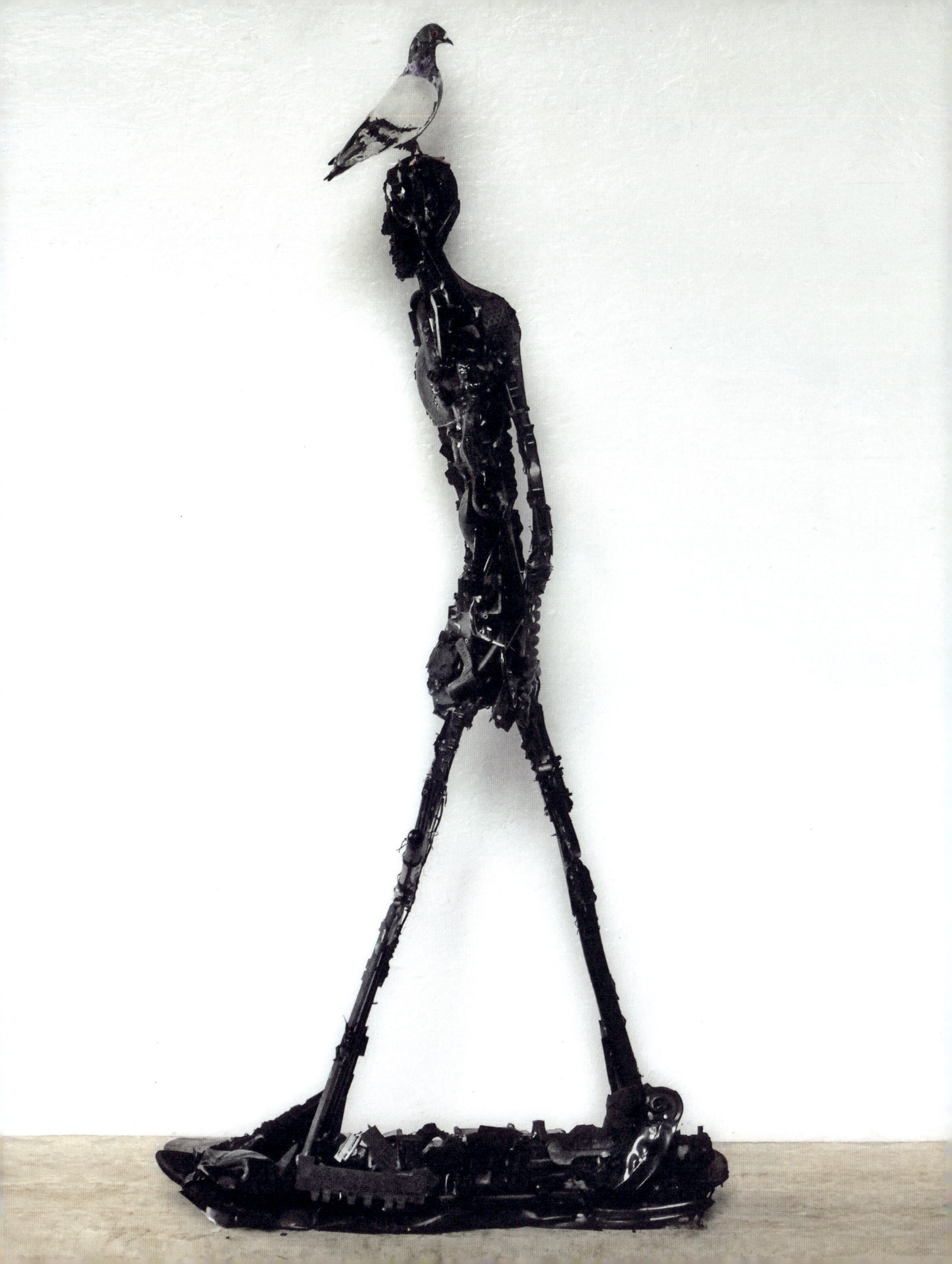

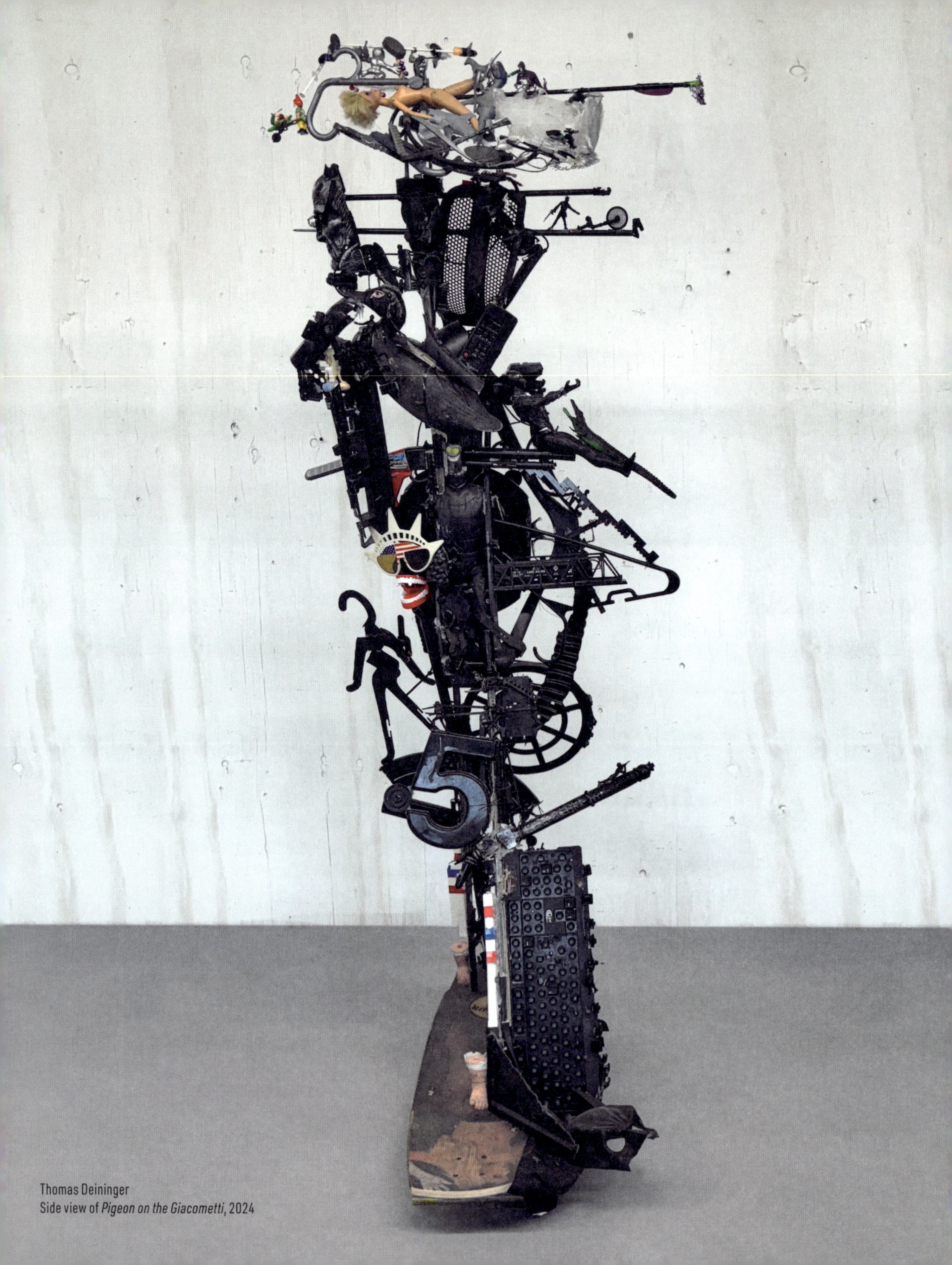

Thomas Deininger
Side view of *Pigeon on the Giacometti*, 2024

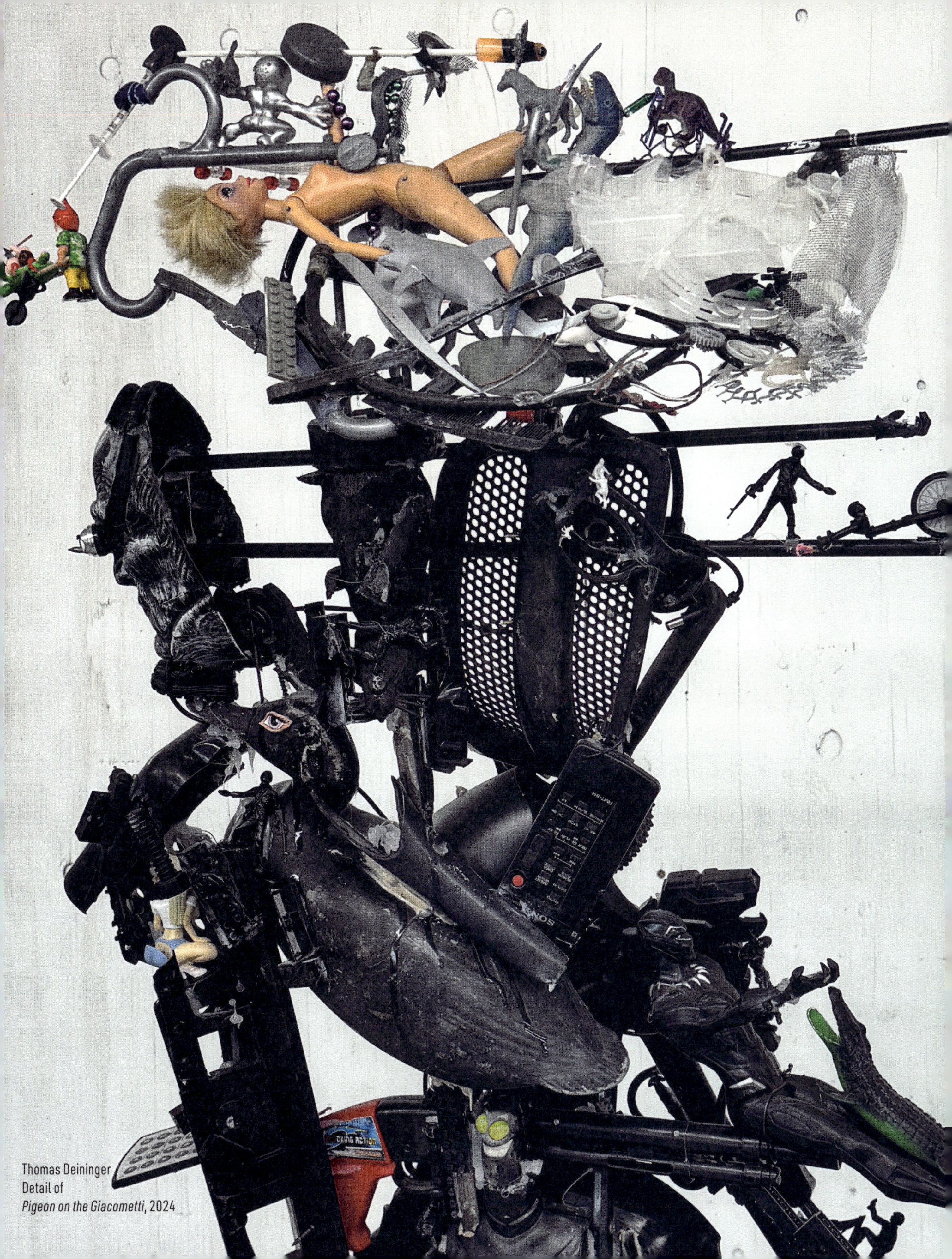

Thomas Deininger
Detail of
Pigeon on the Giacometti, 2024

Back in 1990, I became especially interested in the cultural distinctions we make regarding "Originals," "Copies," and the "Natural." Something that had been in my thoughts for many years was the idea of "fossils," which are generally "nature-made" copies of things from long ago. Fossils can be seen as the representation of things lost, gone, or no longer with us, and can be connected to sadness. In the late 1980s, I had become interested in how we individually define ourselves to ourselves, via symbols. This led me to a project of making over 30,000 "Individual Works," little sculptures, each unique, and a series I called "Drawings," making a few thousand unique "heraldic" shapes, as if each of us could have a symbol that related only to ourselves, not a "group" of people in which we felt we were a member. This led me to also think about how a "community" defines itself, and when I was offered to do a project with Studio Trisorio in Naples, Italy, which is right near the historical Pompeii site, and the present-day town of Pompei. I instantly felt that the history of the lost Pompeii brought a definition to the area. I didn't want to make the project *too* sad, but going through the fossilized artifacts ultimately led me to the human and animal copies, made by casting plaster into the hollow buried areas of the lost remains. The dog fossil became one of the only ones I was able to get permission to copy for the project, so sadness, of course, became a large factor in it. Quantity, copies, things missing from the past, on and on.–Allan McCollum

Allan McCollum
Installation view of *The Dog from Pompei*, 1991

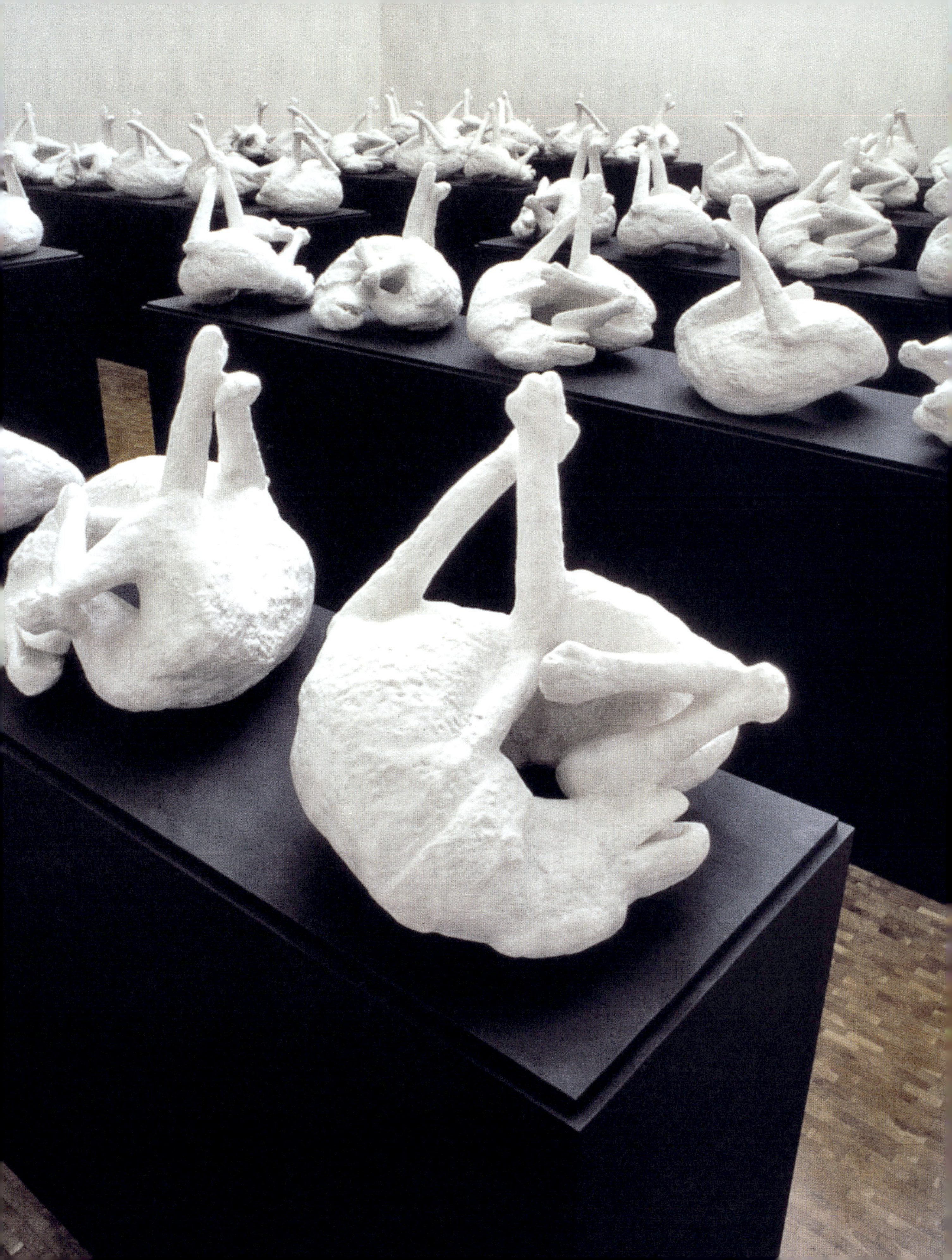

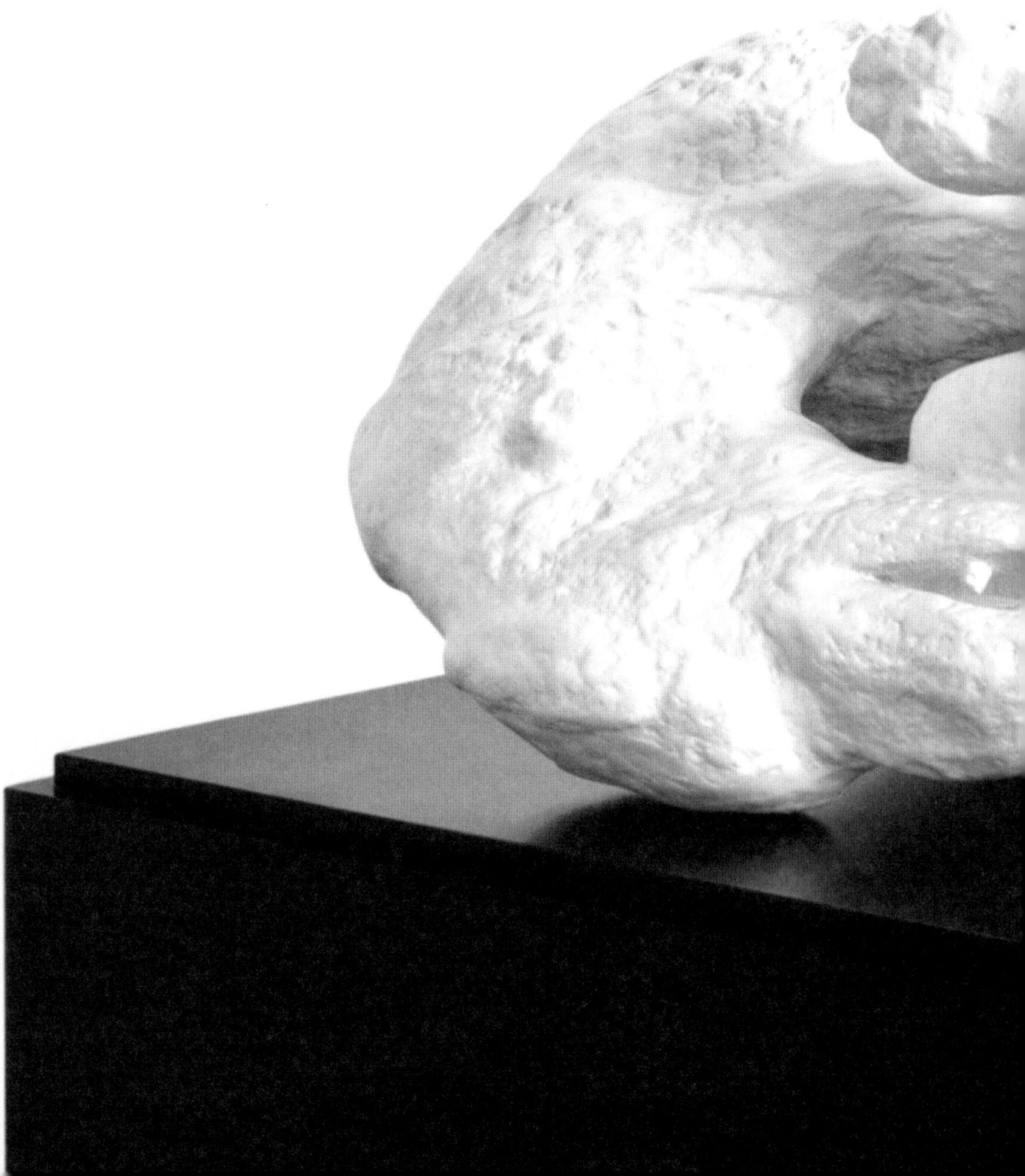

Allan McCollum
The Dog from Pompei, 1991
Cast fiberglass-reinforced hydrocal
20¾ x 20¾ x 20¾ inches

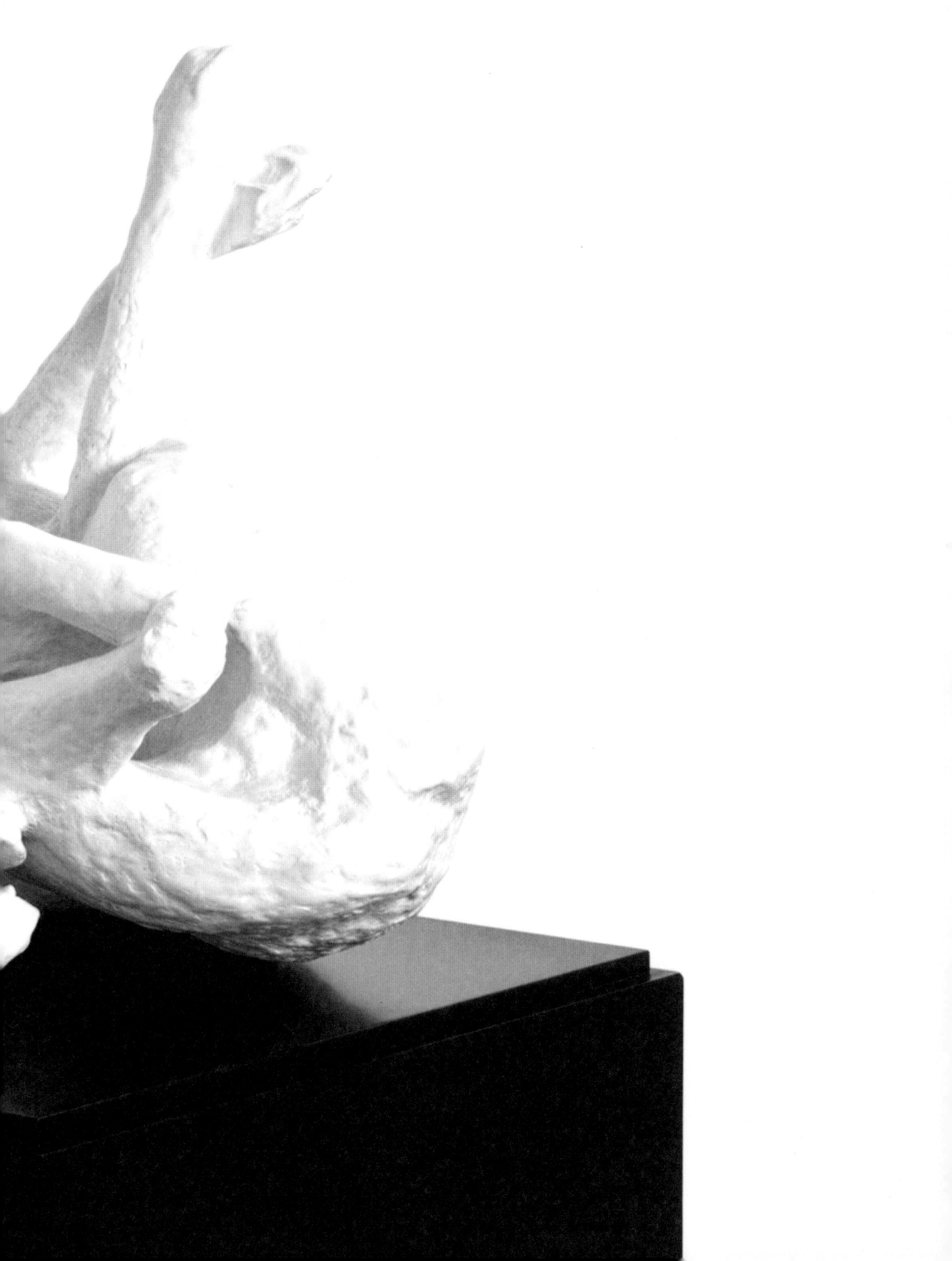

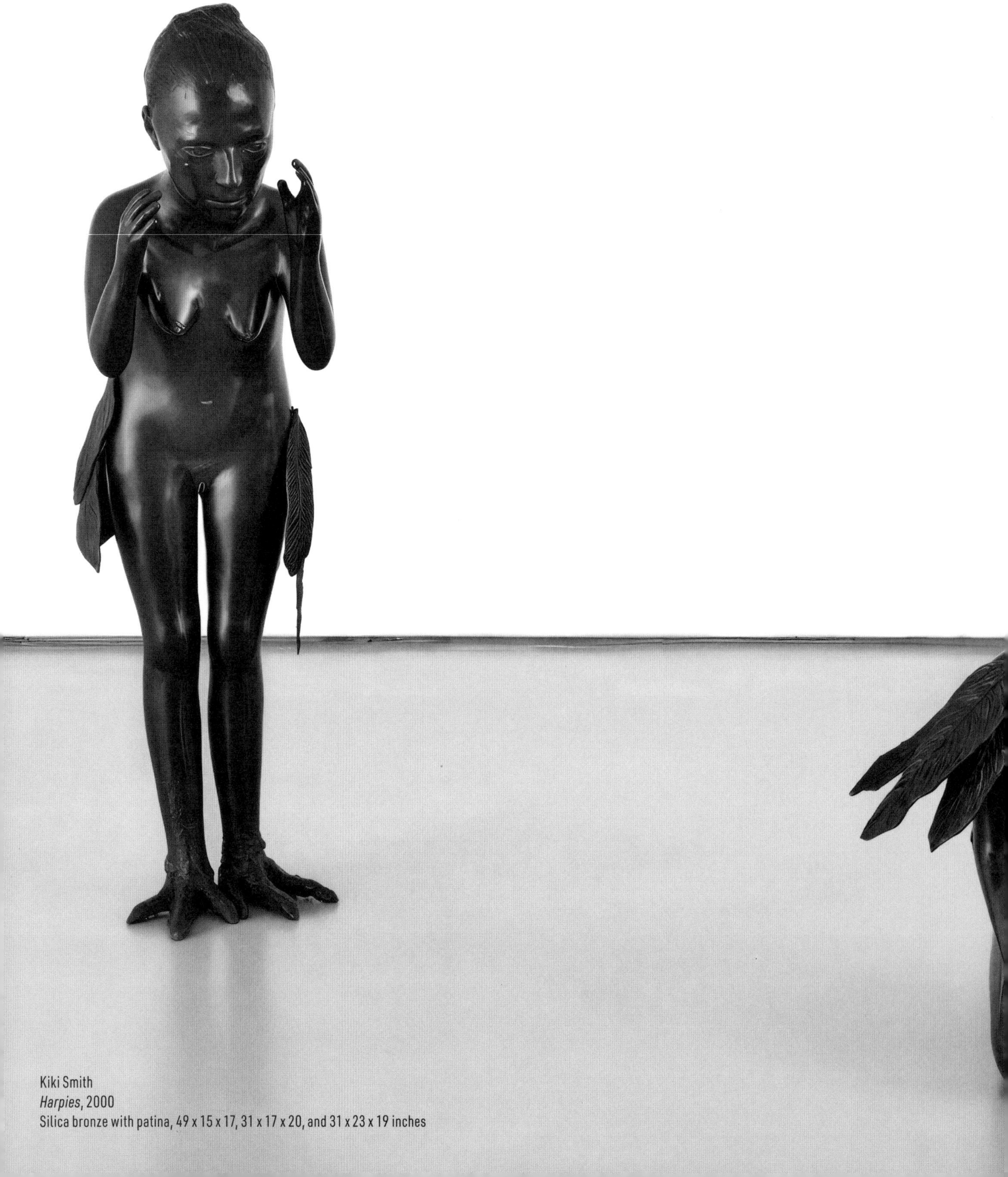

Kiki Smith
Harpies, 2000
Silica bronze with patina, 49 x 15 x 17, 31 x 17 x 20, and 31 x 23 x 19 inches

I was first attracted to the *Harpies* because I liked that they represent strong weather conditions. I liked that they were so ill behaved and had a destructive attitude about them in the environment and to people. They were unruly and somehow were a pleasure to me at the time. That's all I know.—Kiki Smith

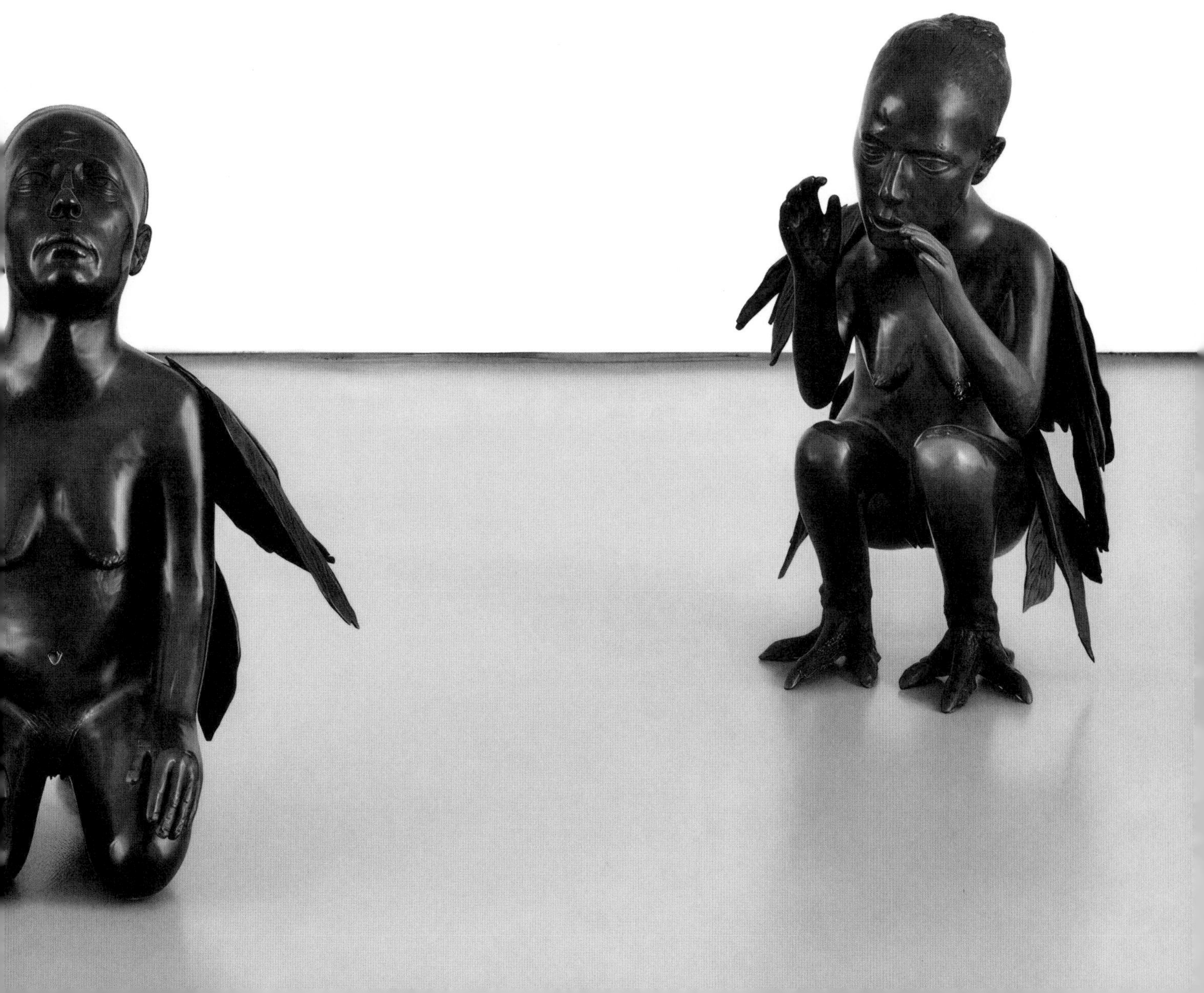

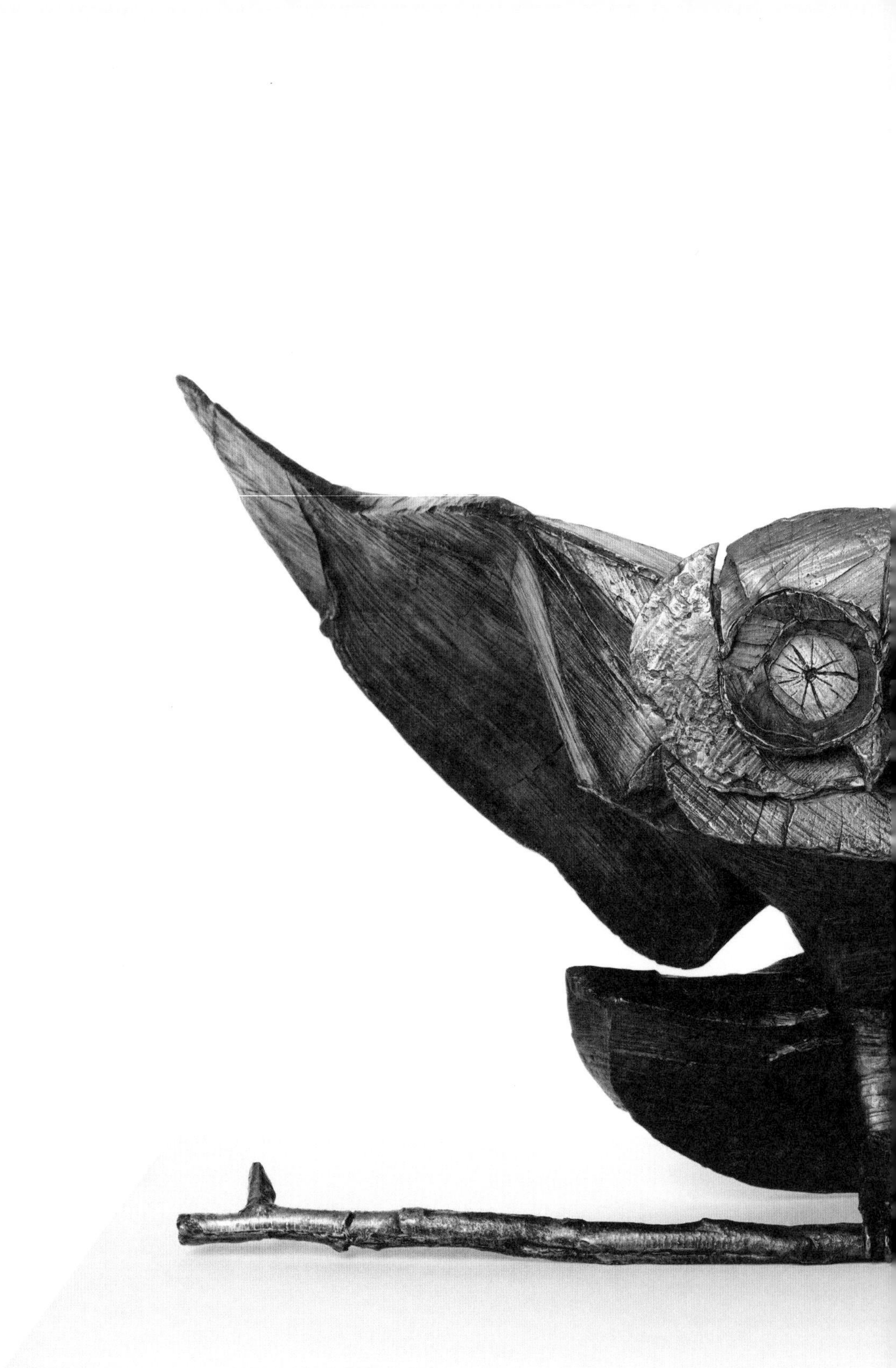

Kiki Smith
Sentry, 2020
Bronze, 18½ x 29 x 17 inches

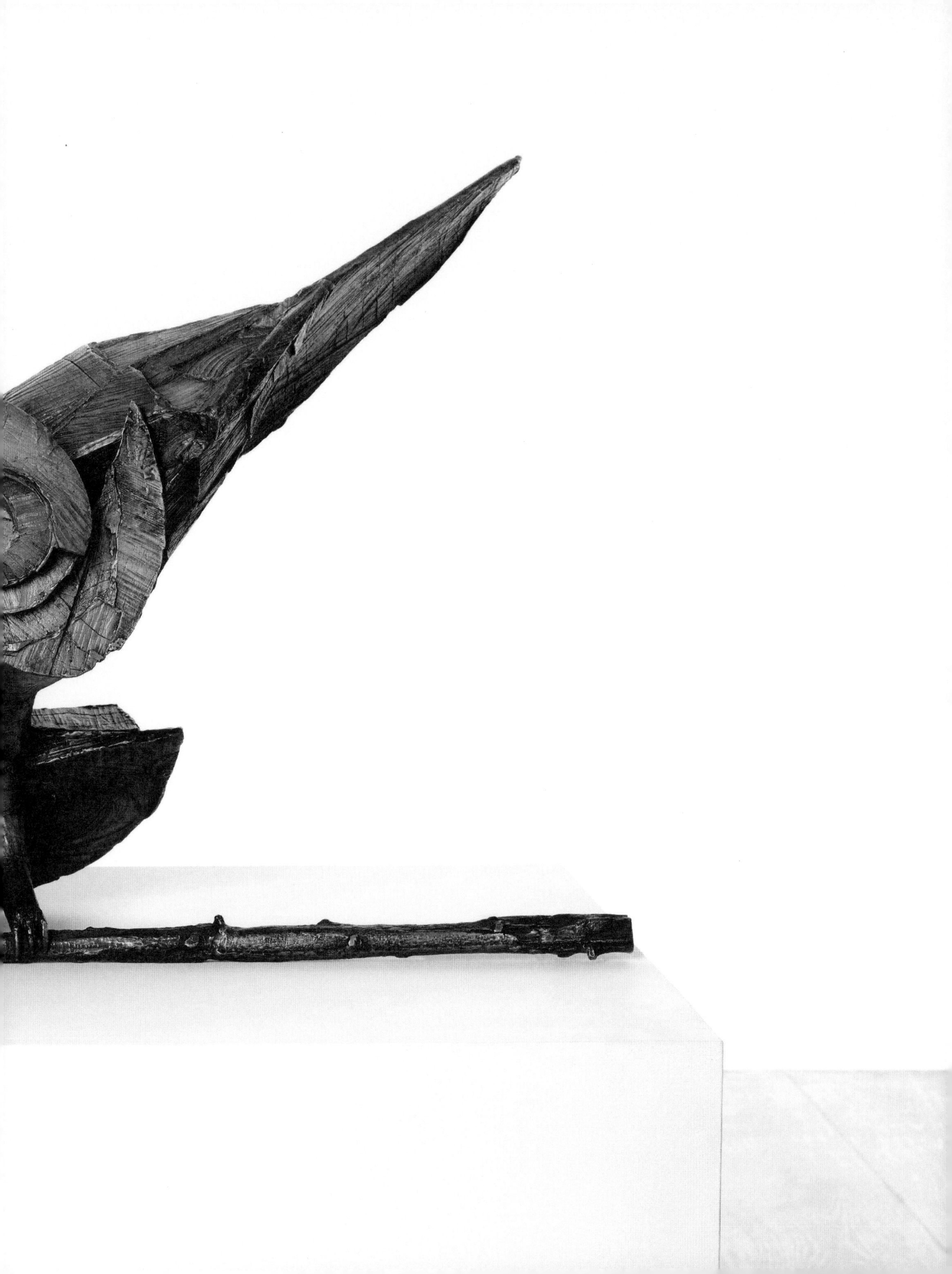

Sherrie Levine
Steer Skull, Horned, 2002
Cast bronze, 18 x 8 x 6 1/4 inches

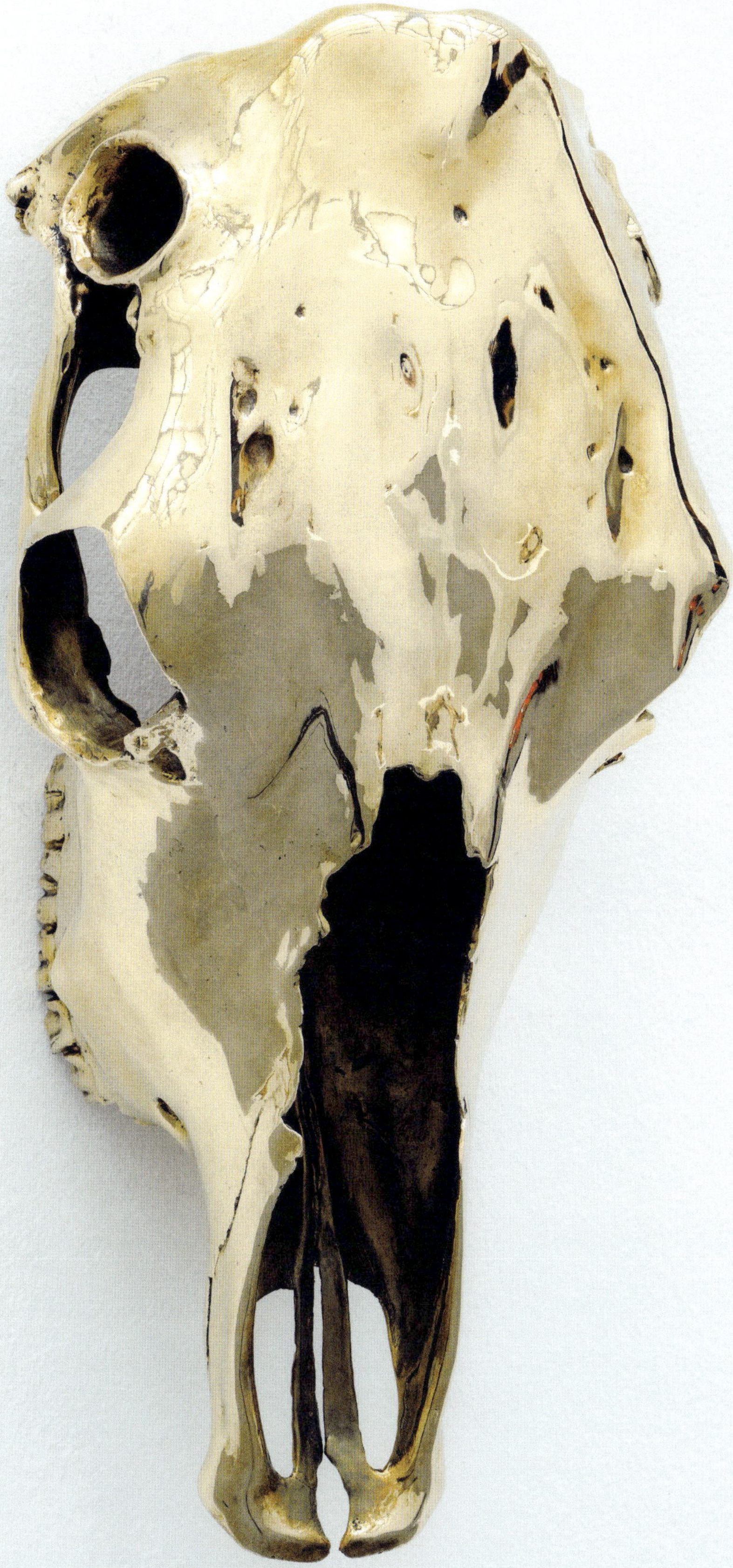

Susan [Rothenberg] always had dogs. She didn't know about horses when she first painted them, but when she came out here she took to my horses. She didn't ride much, she was a walker. We had seven dogs at one time, she attracted them, she painted them, they lived in the studio, and walked and shed on her paintings. She painted my horses with me coming off them. She

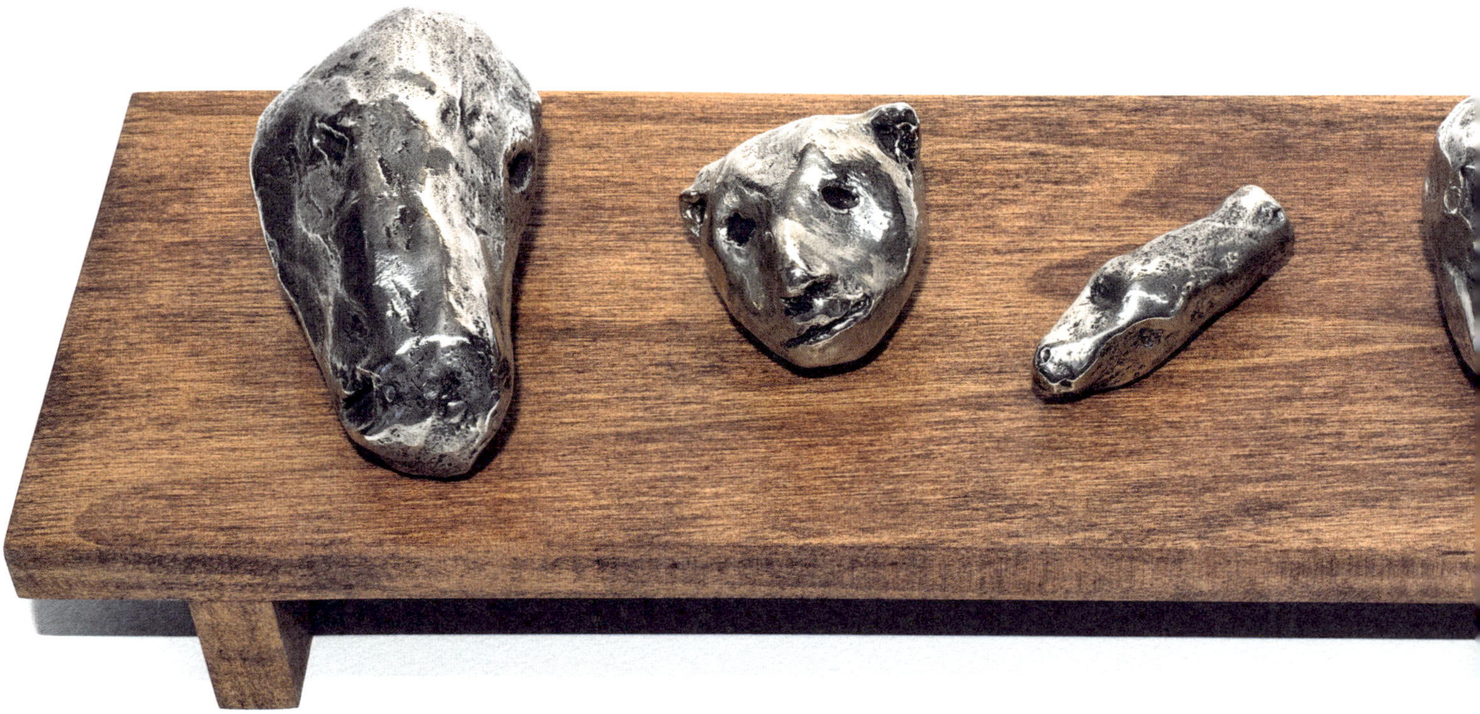

Susan Rothenberg
17 Heads, 2002
Cast, solid sterling silver, 4 x 18 x 4 inches

painted the ravens, she painted a beautiful little blue bird. She made pottery with the clay the Native Americans used on the Pueblo. She tried to use the mud on the paintings. It didn't work so she made sculpture. You know how visceral her paintings are and sometimes it just got off the canvas. She made things to handle. She lived in the land.—Bruce Nauman

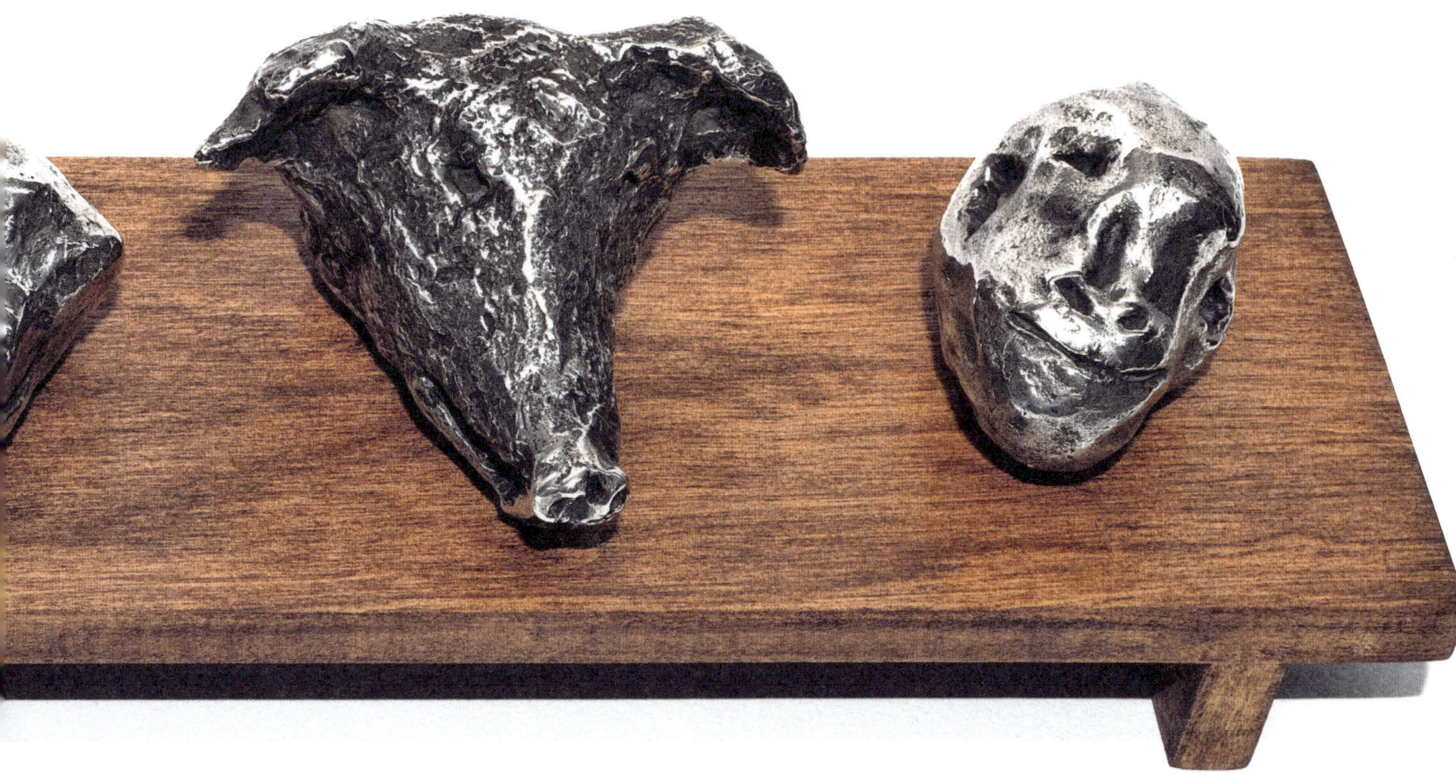

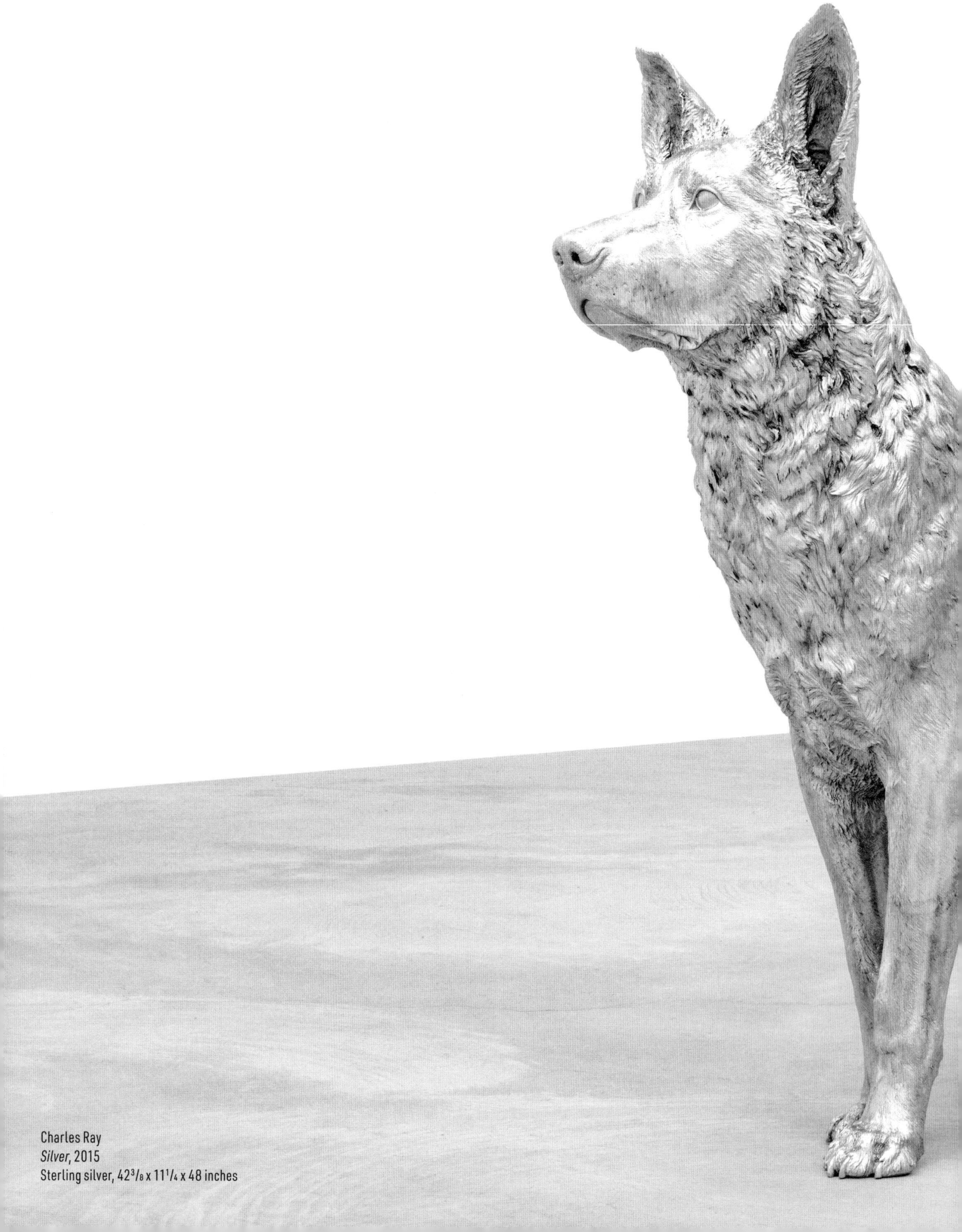

Charles Ray
Silver, 2015
Sterling silver, $42^{3}/_{8}$ x $11^{1}/_{4}$ x 48 inches

Hi, this is Charles Ray, talking about my exhibition at the Art Institute of Chicago. Would you like to know why I made a sculpture of a silver dog now on display in the museum's Modern Wing? The dog's name is Silver, because he's created out of pure silver, and he protects the Museum from the vampires that roam Millennium Park and moonlit evenings. It's common knowledge that after a vampire feeds on human blood, it likes to drink the blood of a dog for dessert. Because vampires are most active on nights of the full moon, the glittering silver of my guard dog sculpture attracts these paranormal beasts. They fall for my trap, and their two sharp teeth bite into the canine's neck of pure silver. They die a chilly but painless death, and their souls return to the grave for eternal rest. If you're interested in learning more, the exhibition is open at the Art Institute through October 4th [2015]. I'm Charles Ray.

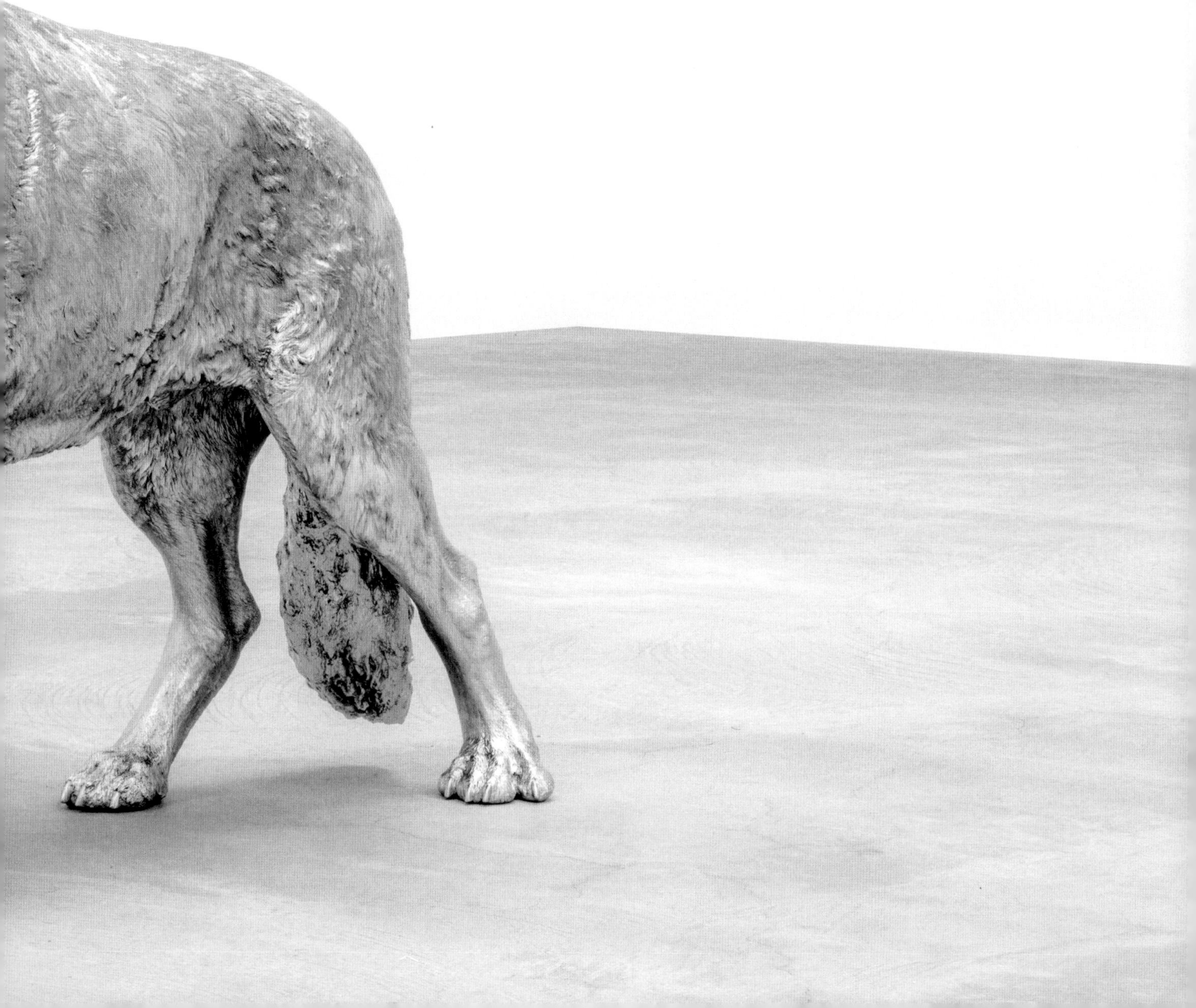

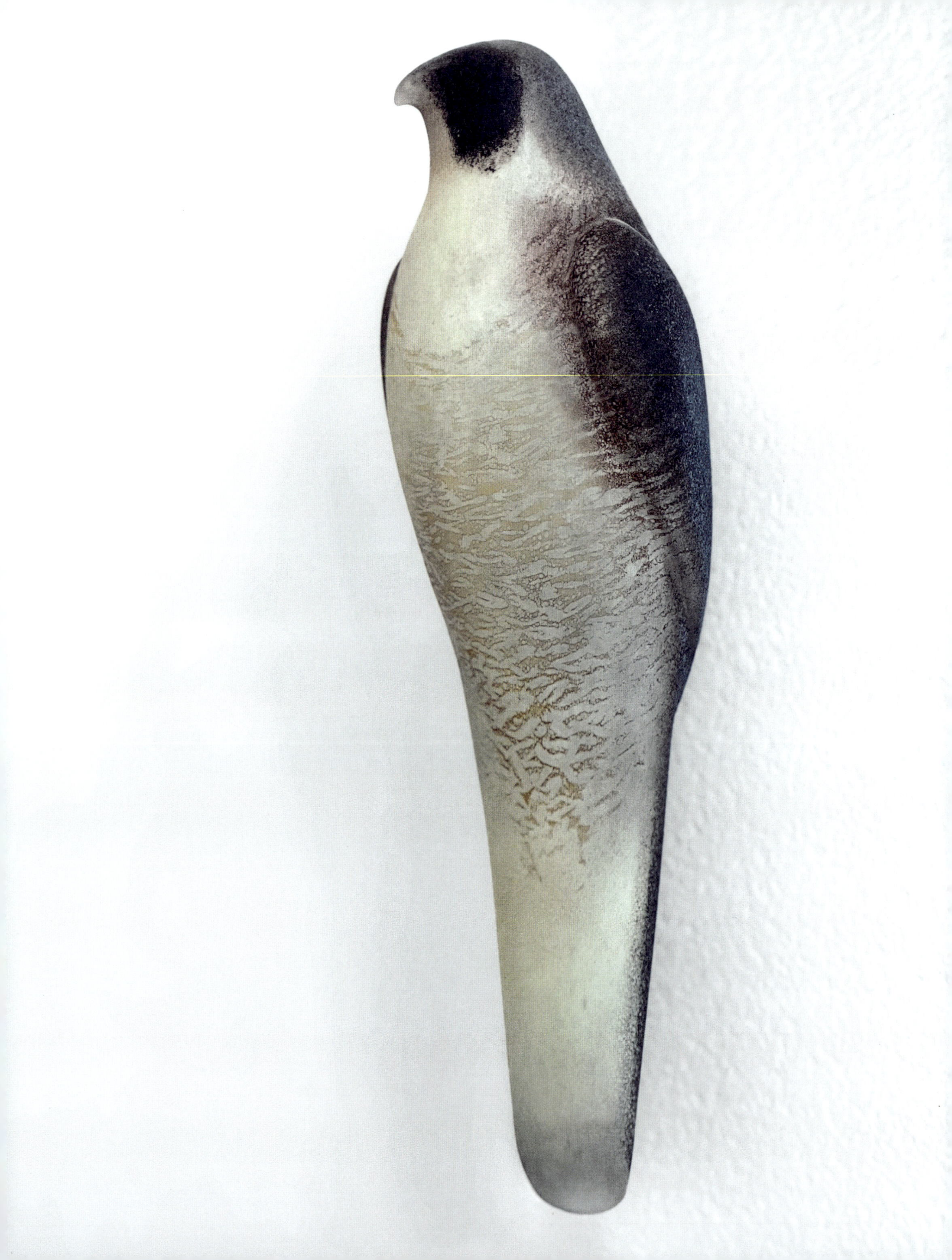

As a youth, sitting in silence in the ancient wings of the Metropolitan Museum in New York, there was and is a love of being fully in the present moment that is given in the face of nature that can lead to one's own better nature. Like Horus, the sun god that gazed both in and out simultaneously, the raptor I see posted in the late-afternoon sun has both a stillness and an awareness, translucent and present. Only the alchemy of glass and the force of stone could represent this presence and stillness. Would it be possible to learn to open our hearts through the sensation of our own inner nature? My art seeks to ask these questions and wishes to study the sense of our own inner life as the fragility of both human and animal nature calls to question an intelligence that we are asked to protect through learning again to listen to our own better nature.
I ask: "Is it possible through art for animal nature to lead to our own better human nature?"–Jane Rosen

Jane Rosen
Hybrid Peregrine, 2024
Hand-blown pigmented glass, 15 x 4 x 4 inches

Jane Rosen
Barred Owl, 2025
Pigmented hand-blown and carved glass and Provençale limestone, 65 x 8 x 10 inches

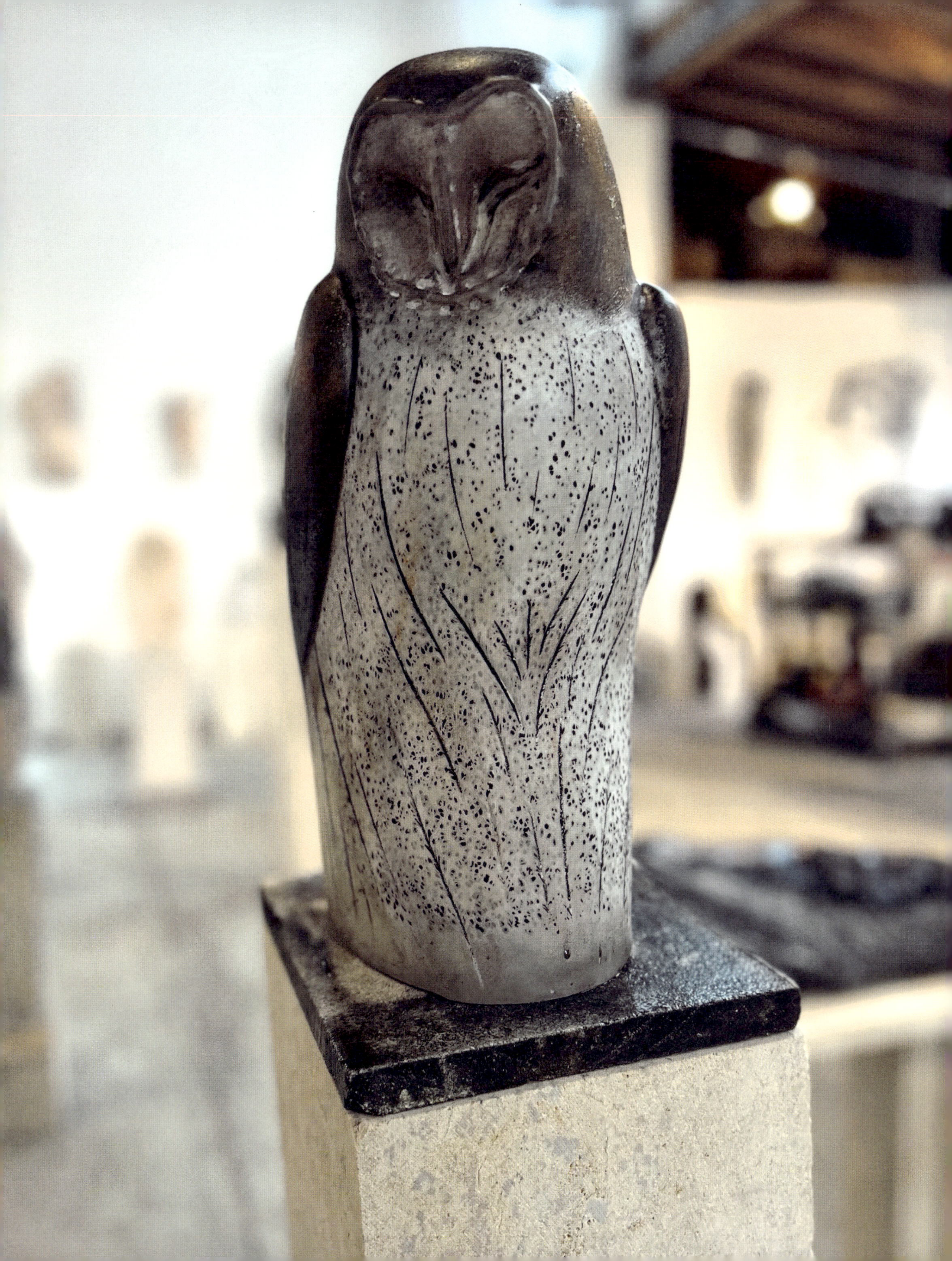

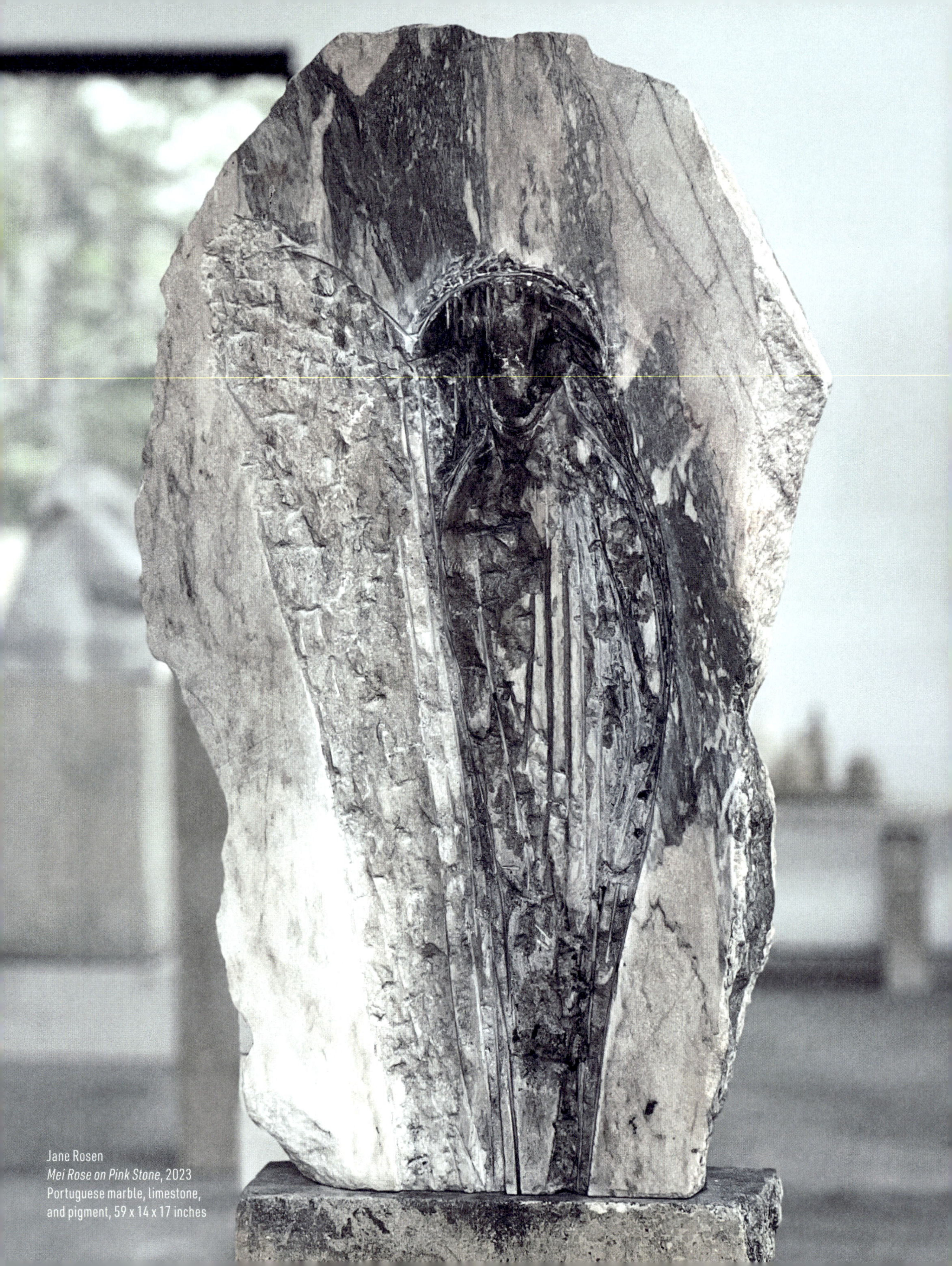

Jane Rosen
Mei Rose on Pink Stone, 2023
Portuguese marble, limestone, and pigment, 59 x 14 x 17 inches

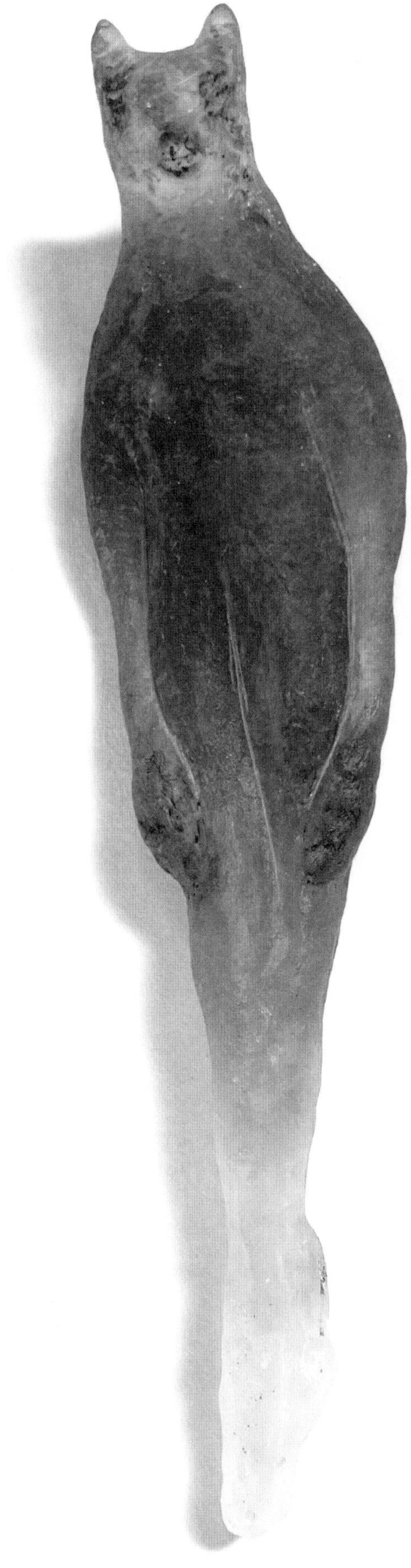

Jane Rosen
Crystal Buddhi, 2017
Kiln-cast crystal, 19 x 5 x 4 inches

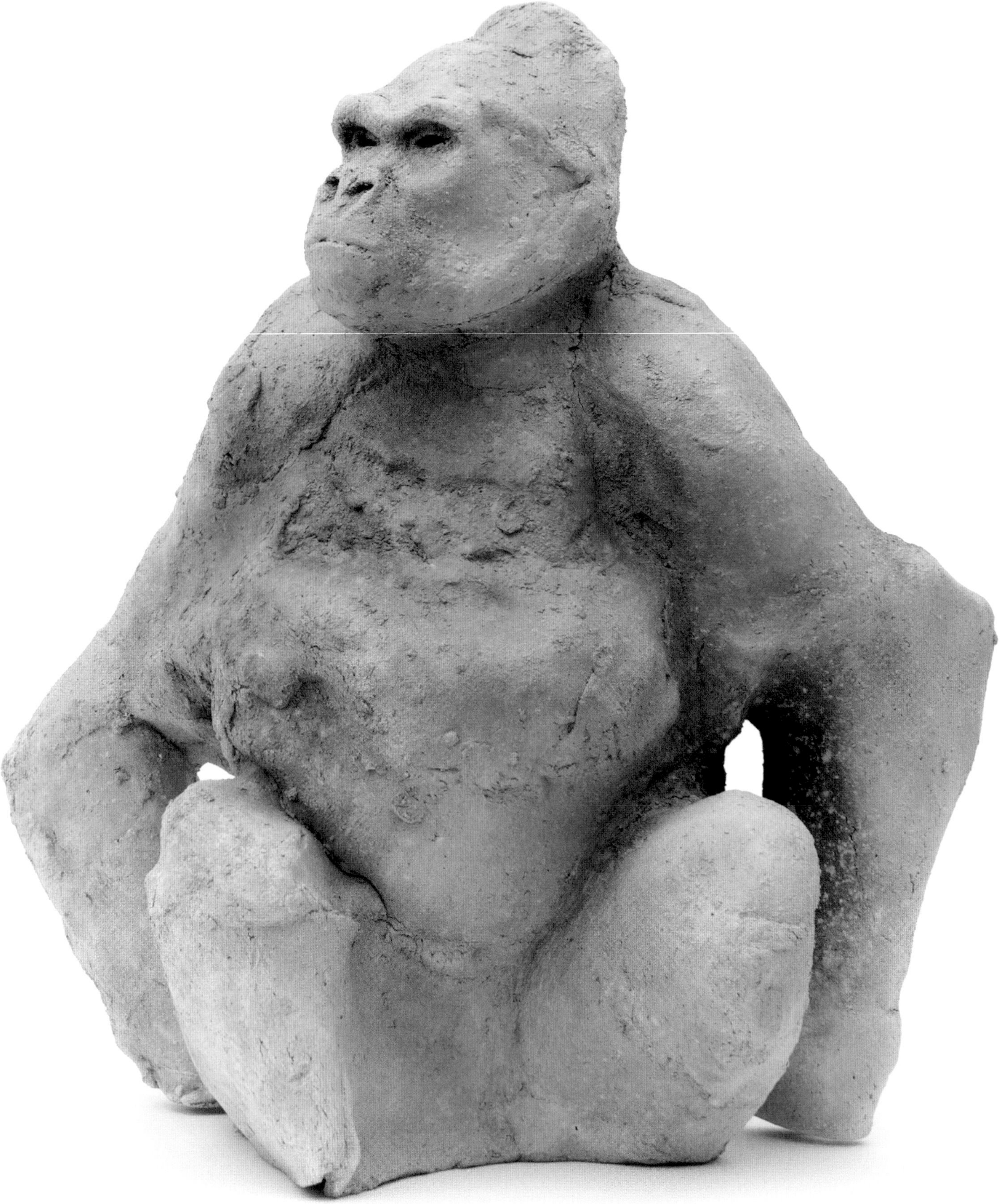

Daisy Youngblood
Little Gorilla, 2020
Low-fire clay, $12^1/_4$ x $11^1/_2$ x $6^3/_4$ inches

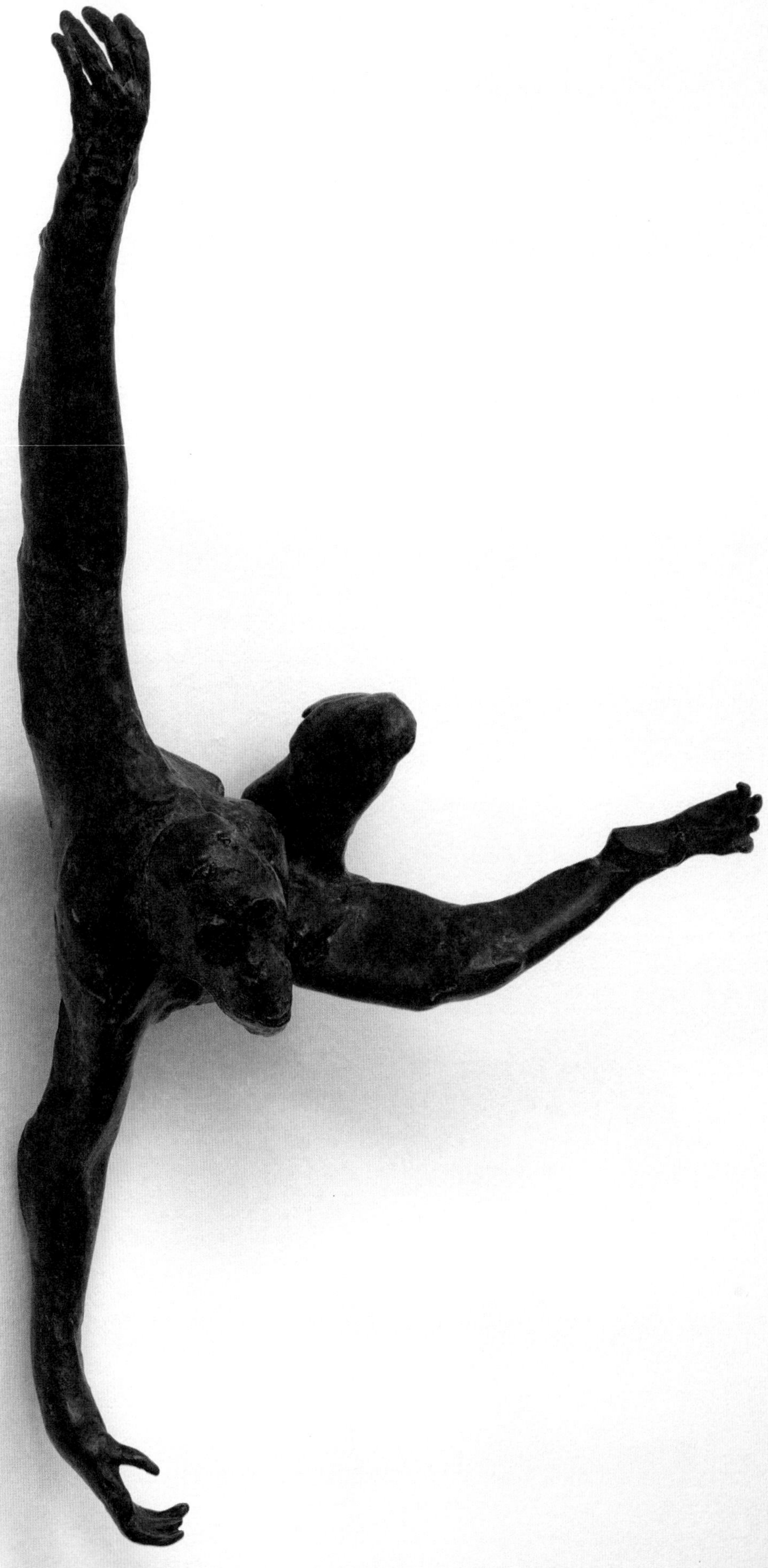

Daisy Youngblood
Leaping 1, 2010
Low-fire clay, 5 x 13 x 4 inches

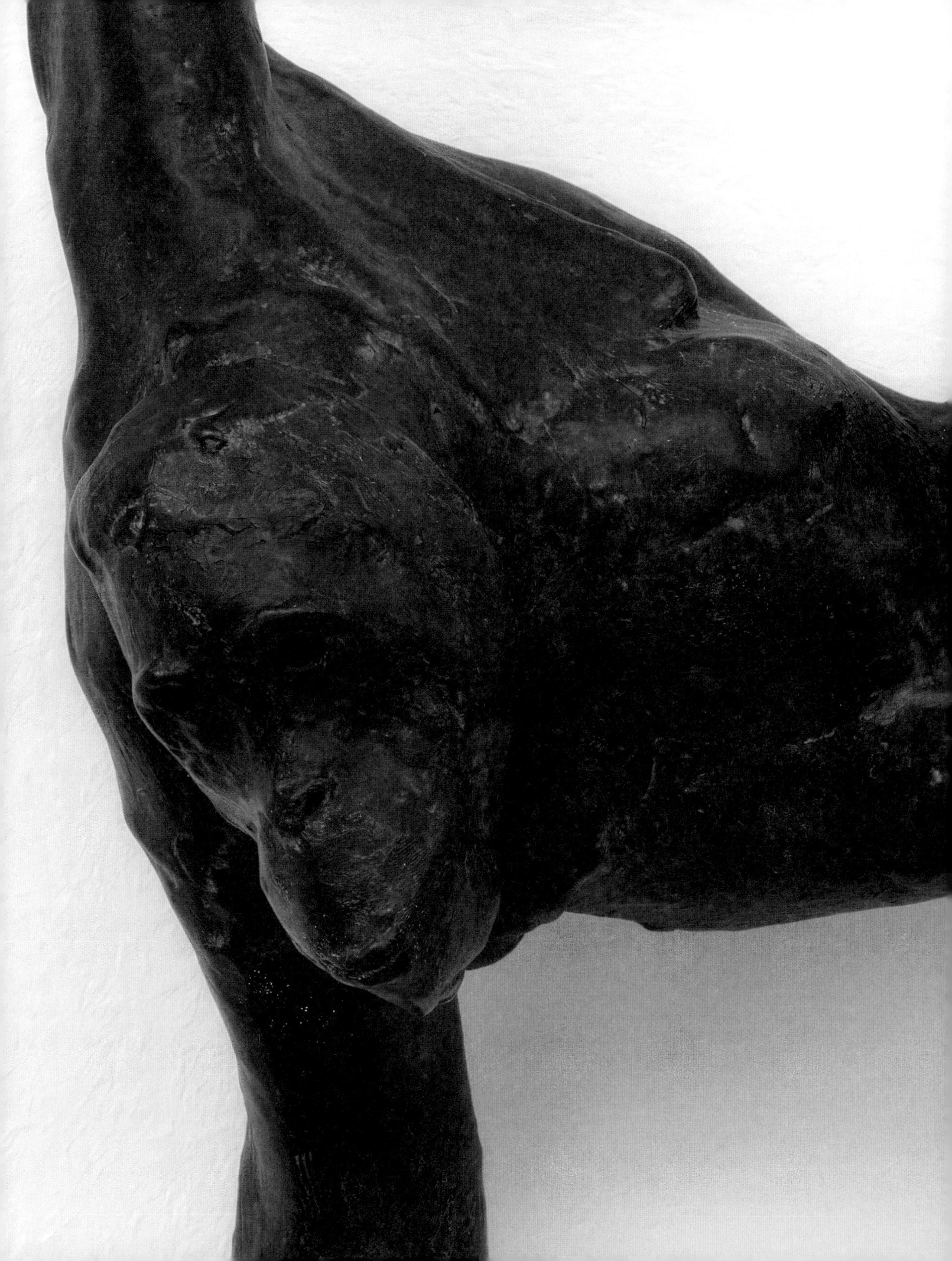

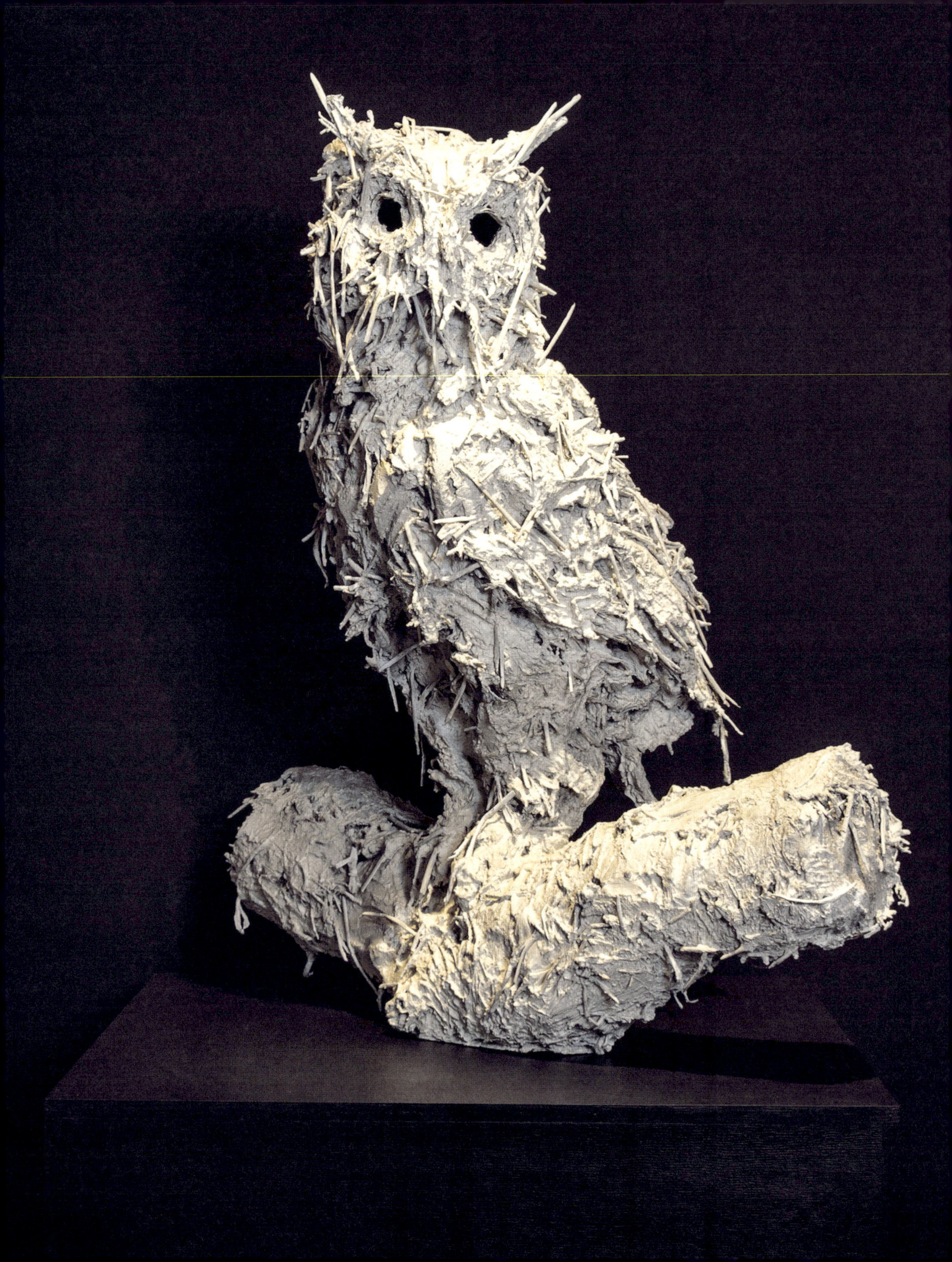

I am an artist because it's the process I have for examining life. I'm a sculptor because I couldn't make my voice work on a flat square. I draw but only on a scale where the edges of the drawing never confront the edges of the paper. I only ever consider the matter I'm investigating, like a poem, choosing a font or a selection of words. To restrict the writing wouldn't be helpful and knowing all the words doesn't make you a poet. It's the feeling and the need to note the feeling. By accident, I communicate. I guess because life experiences are broadly shared, we like to see ourselves as seen. I have arrived at a cast of players who are familiar and emotionally malleable, and within my players I am able to talk my talk. All my work is about me and my small world of mystery. Satisfying and frustrating in equal measures, sometimes I can't quite connect with where I was yesterday and I have no idea where I will be tomorrow. But today, today is a wild blast of play, need, and want. All I need is some stuff, some space, and to be left alone. Some people have a tin of buttons that is their treasure. Some people have libraries or gardens. I have a mind full of sparkling memories, feelings, observations, questions, and notices. I add to it by being awake. I respect my craft, but I am only ever at the beginning, as finishing a work in some ways is a fake event, a necessary interruption. Really I'm just following a thread. In terms of scale, I think all artists have two natural scales, small and large, and finding these is a large part of the success of a work. My small scale is roughly the volume of my hand and my large scale is multiples of my body. Too big and it's flabby, too small and it's fiddly.

–Nicola Hicks

Nicola Hicks
Owl, 2022
Bronze, 20 1/2 x 16 1/2 x 13 inches

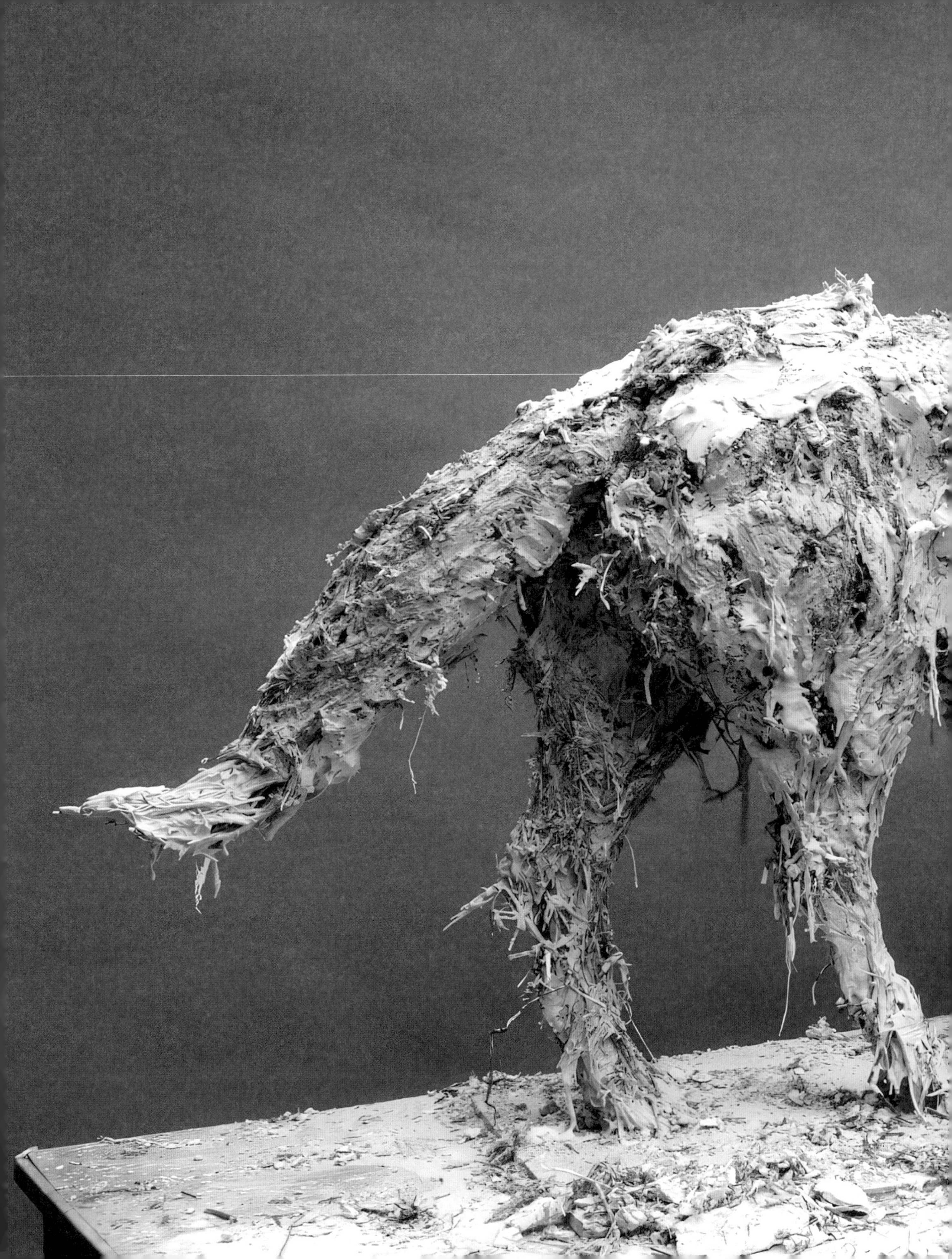

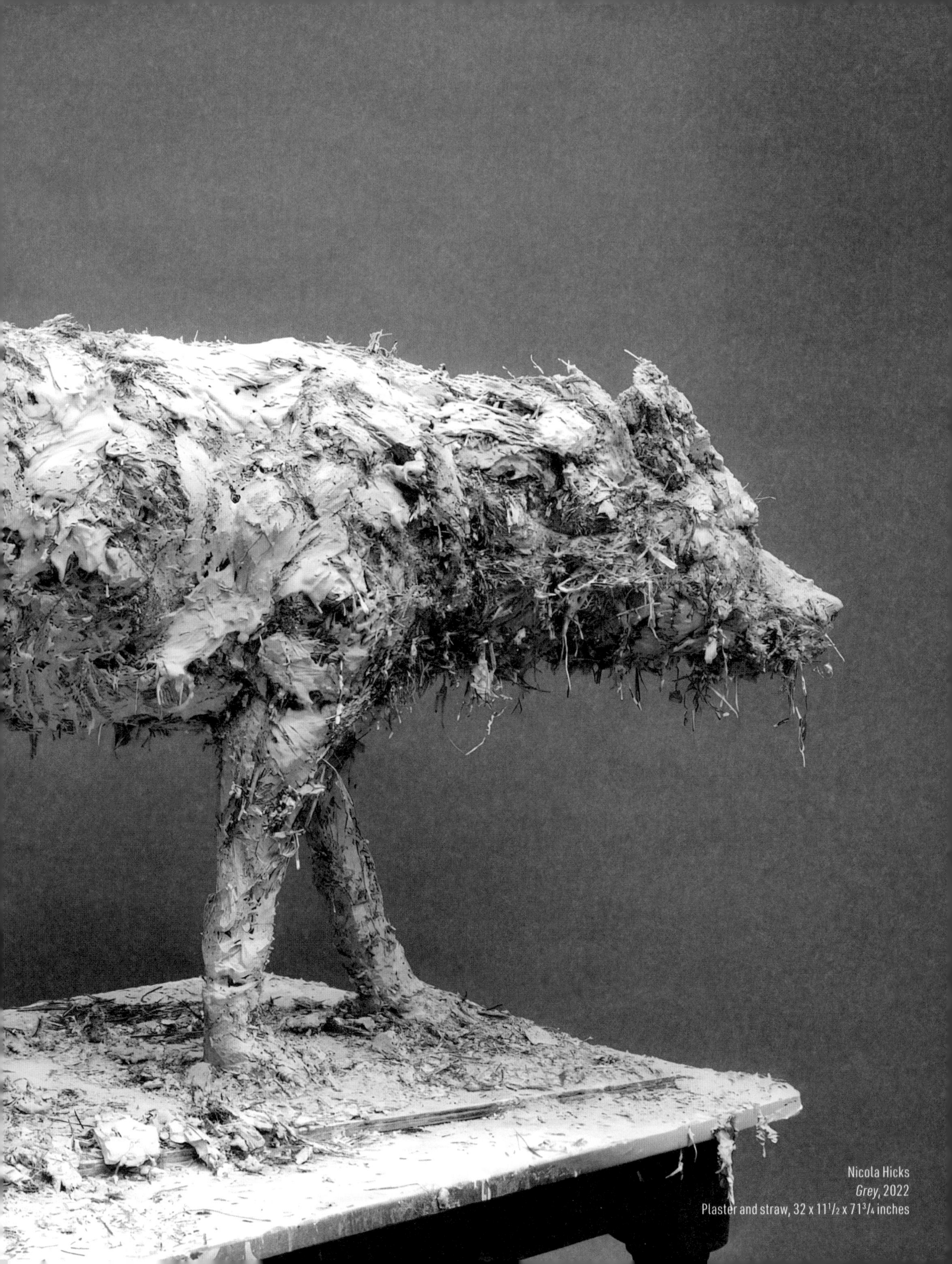

Nicola Hicks
Grey, 2022
Plaster and straw, 32 x $11^1/_2$ x $71^3/_4$ inches

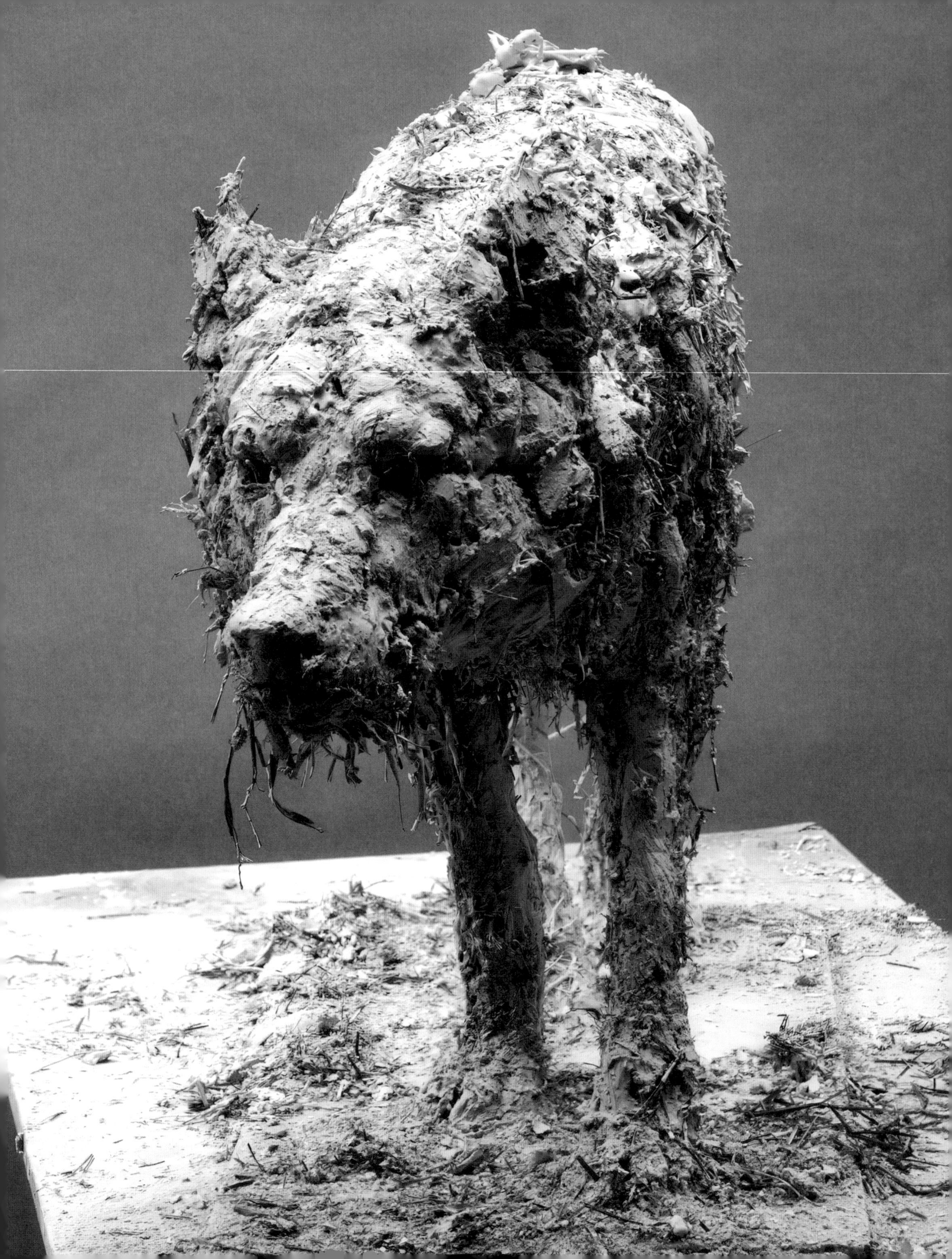

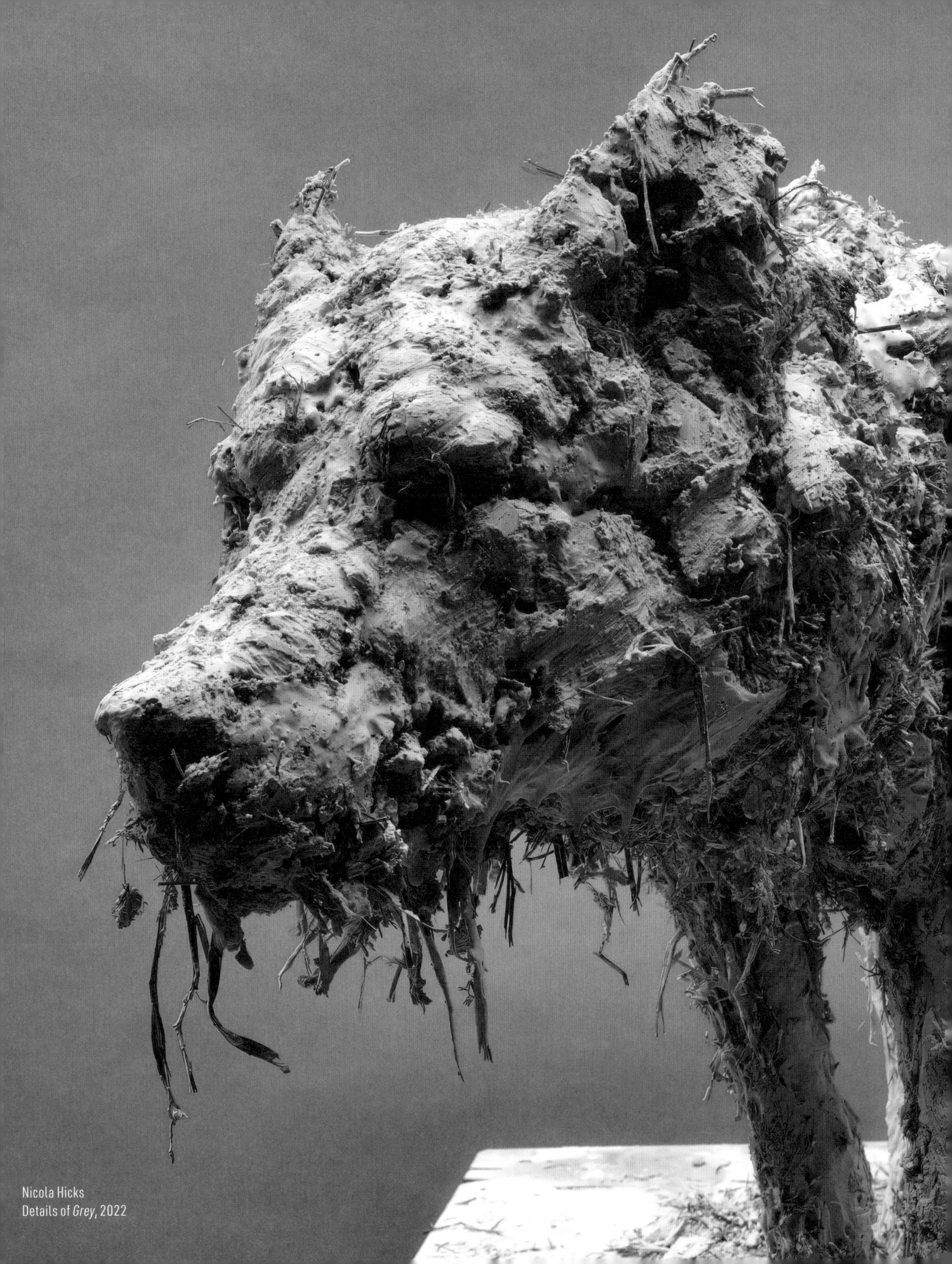

Nicola Hicks
Details of *Grey*, 2022

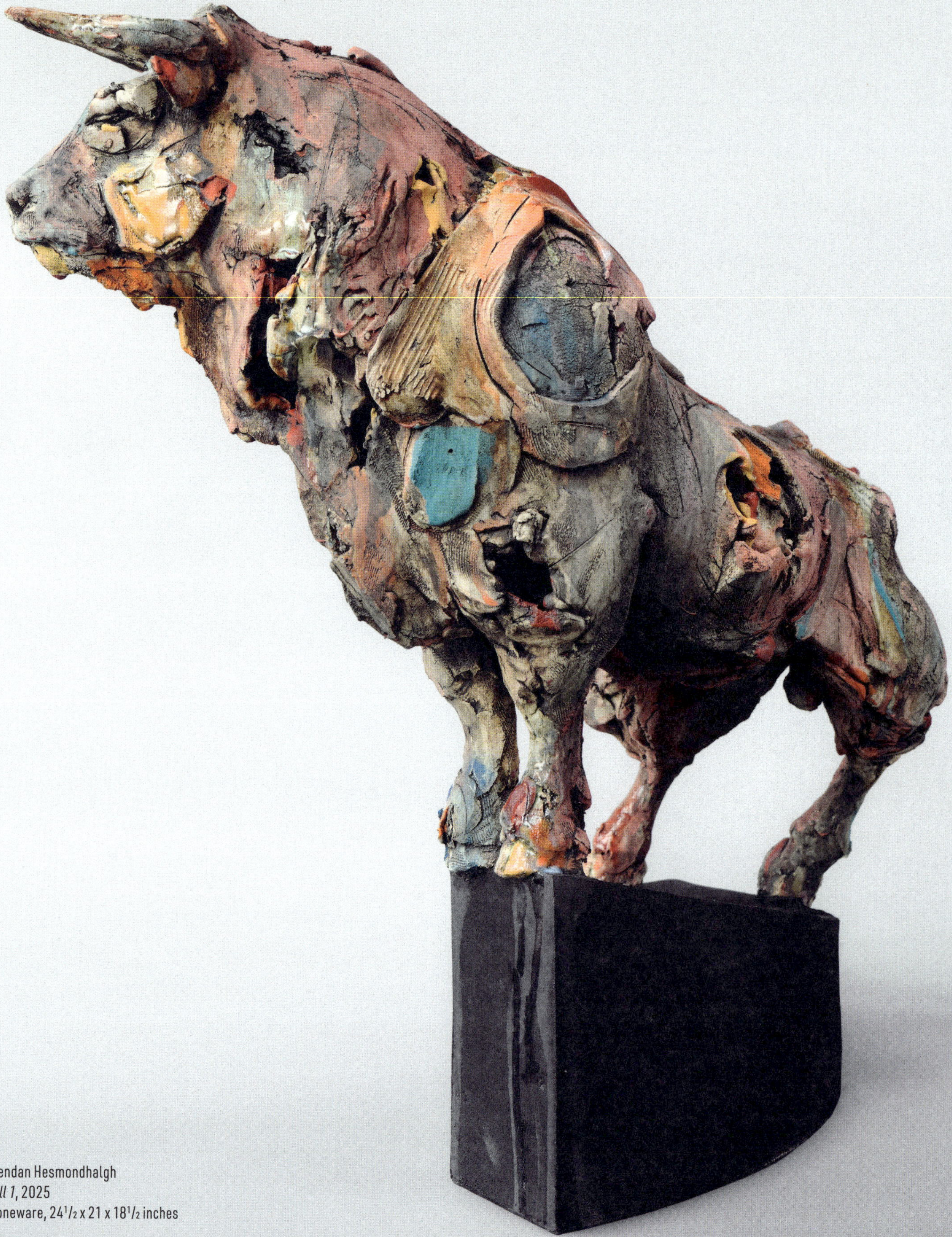

Brendan Hesmondhalgh
Bull 1, 2025
Stoneware, $24^1/_2$ x 21 x $18^1/_2$ inches

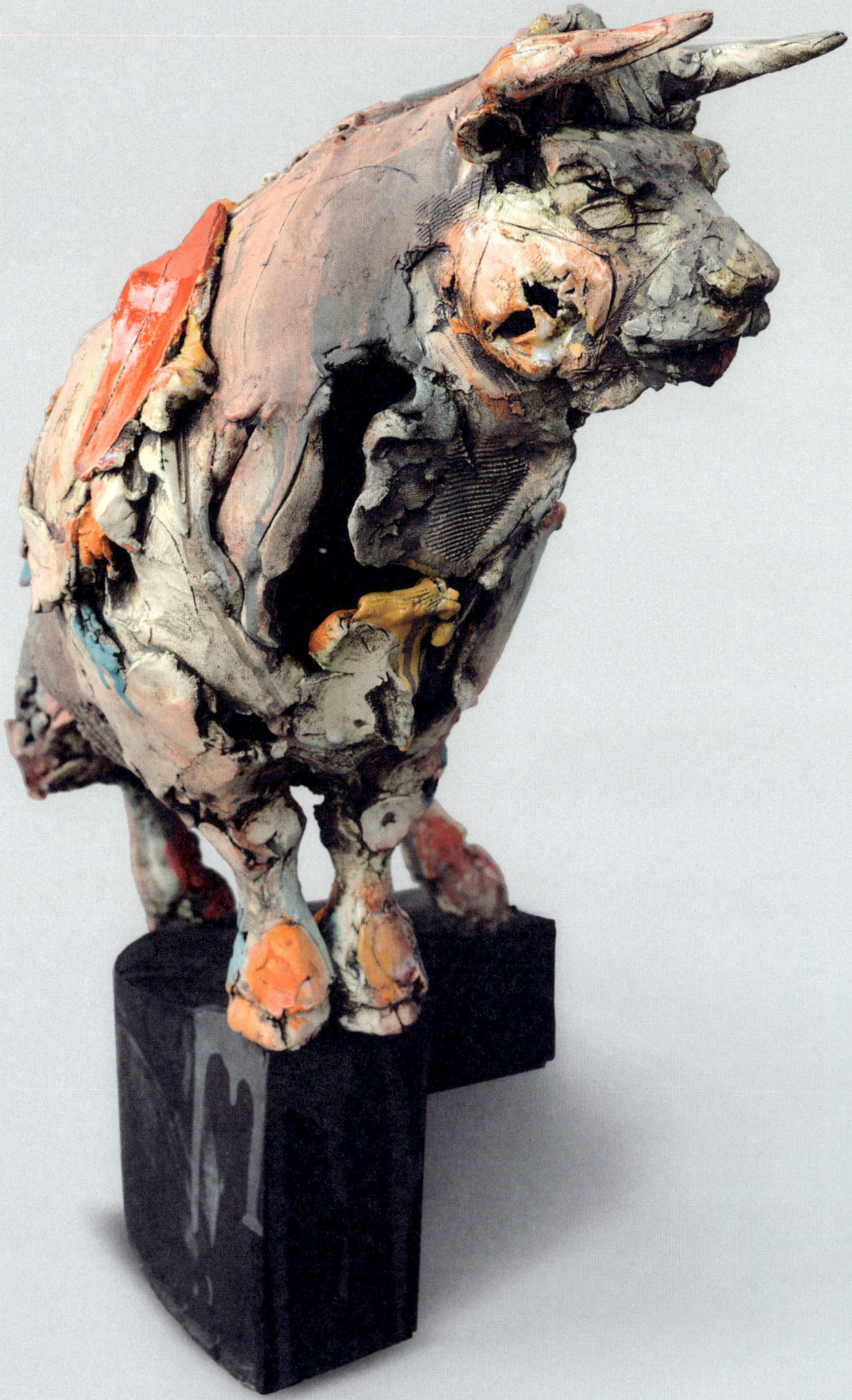

Brendan Hesmondhalgh
Bull 2, 2025
Stoneware, 20½ x 16½ x 13 inches

I began drawing the original foxes posed, and through my friendship with Chelsea [Weathers] and Jenn [Shapland] I was brought back to Susan [Rothenberg] and began to draw her death. When I drew just her hair, I was so deeply moved that I told Chelsea I couldn't draw any more. She pointed out that the fox configuration I had been drawing could be a sculpture, and I said that I used to have that profession, and together we began the whole fox and coyote sculpture series. Ellen [Babcock] joined later and made the molds for the plaster pieces.—Bruce Nauman

Bruce Nauman
2 plaster foxes head to foot with plaster can and hammer, 2024
Plaster, burlap, threaded rods, plastic wrap, mud, tape, wire, ax handles, and hammers, 101 x 32 1/2 x 12 1/2 inches

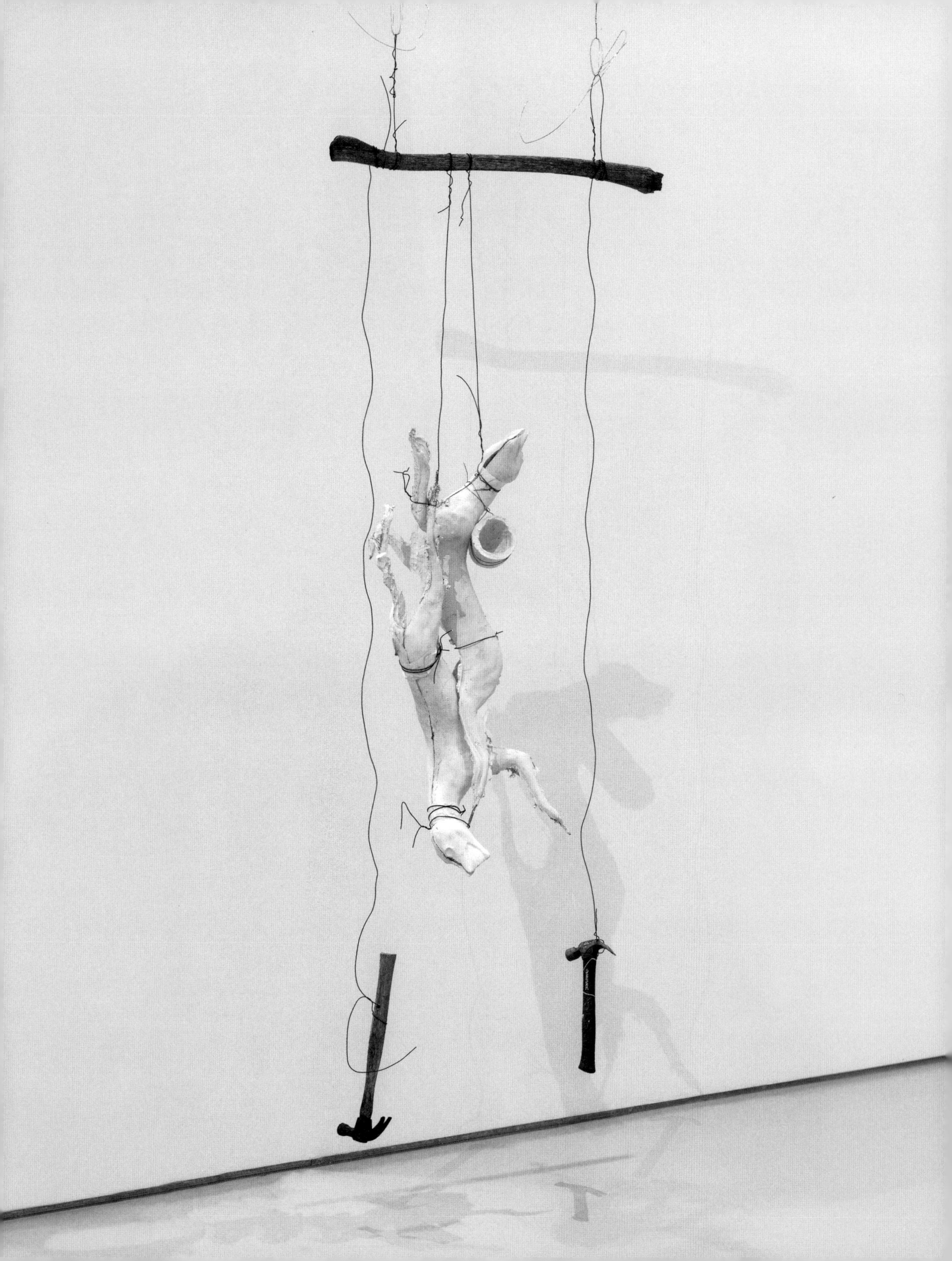

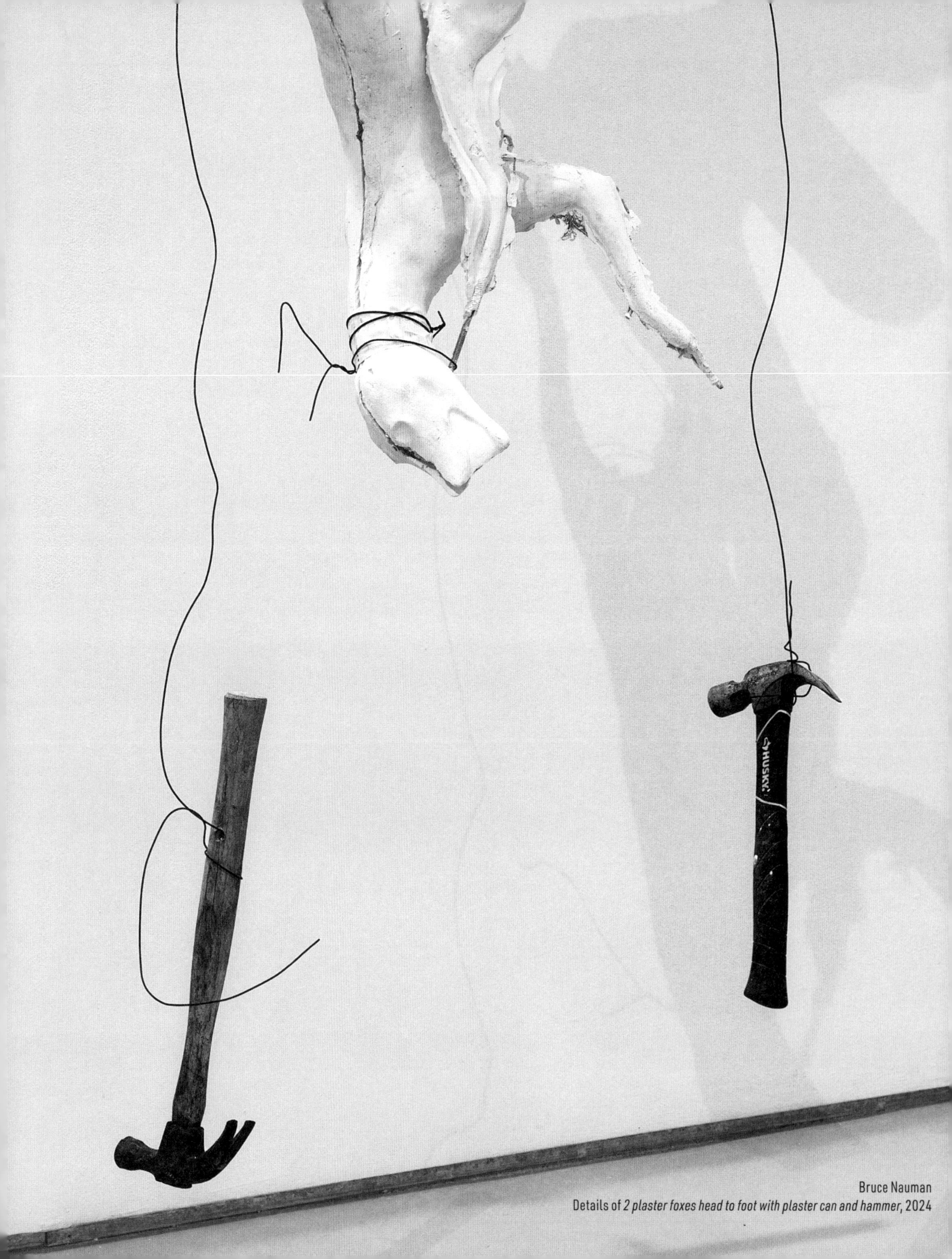

Bruce Nauman
Details of *2 plaster foxes head to foot with plaster can and hammer*, 2024

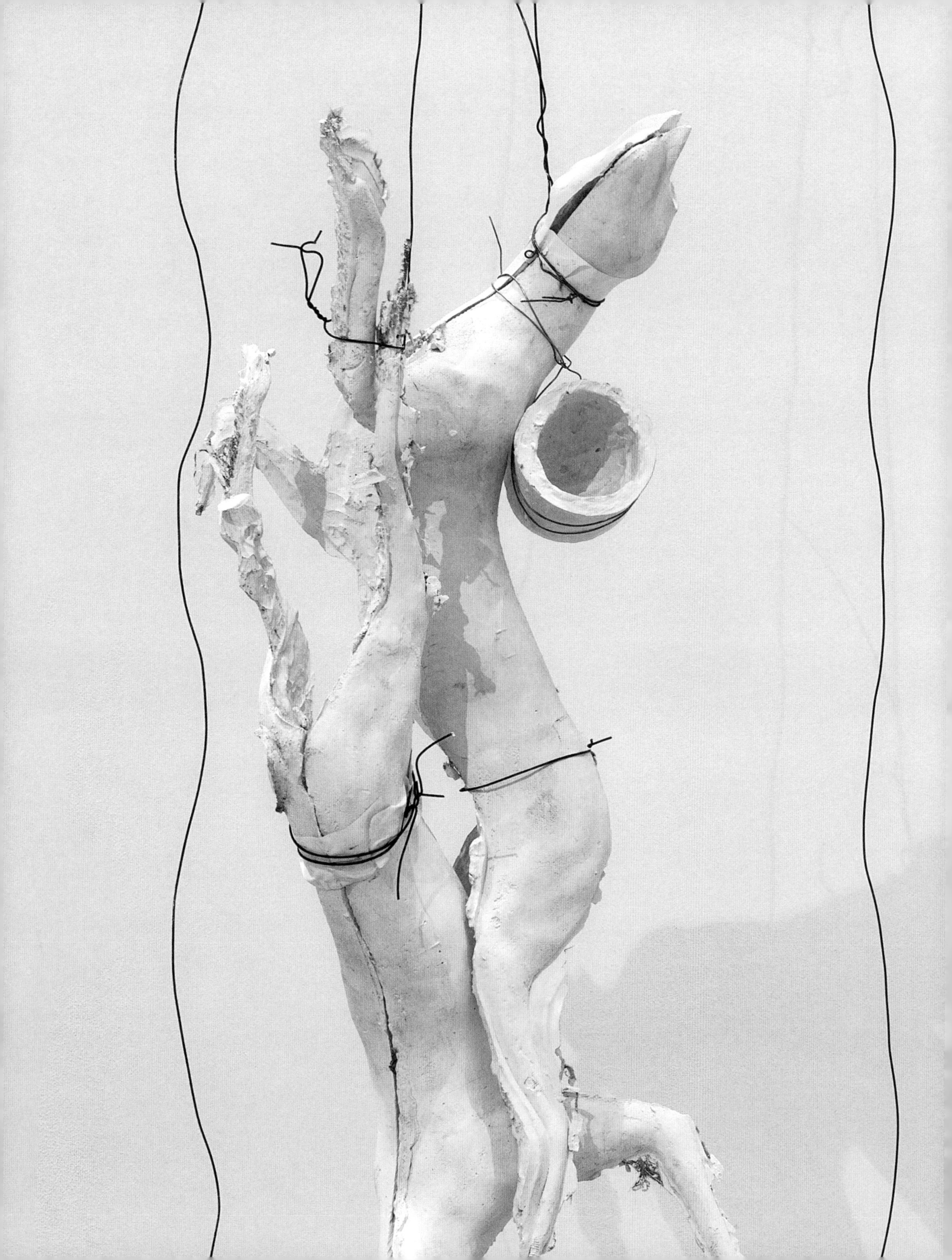

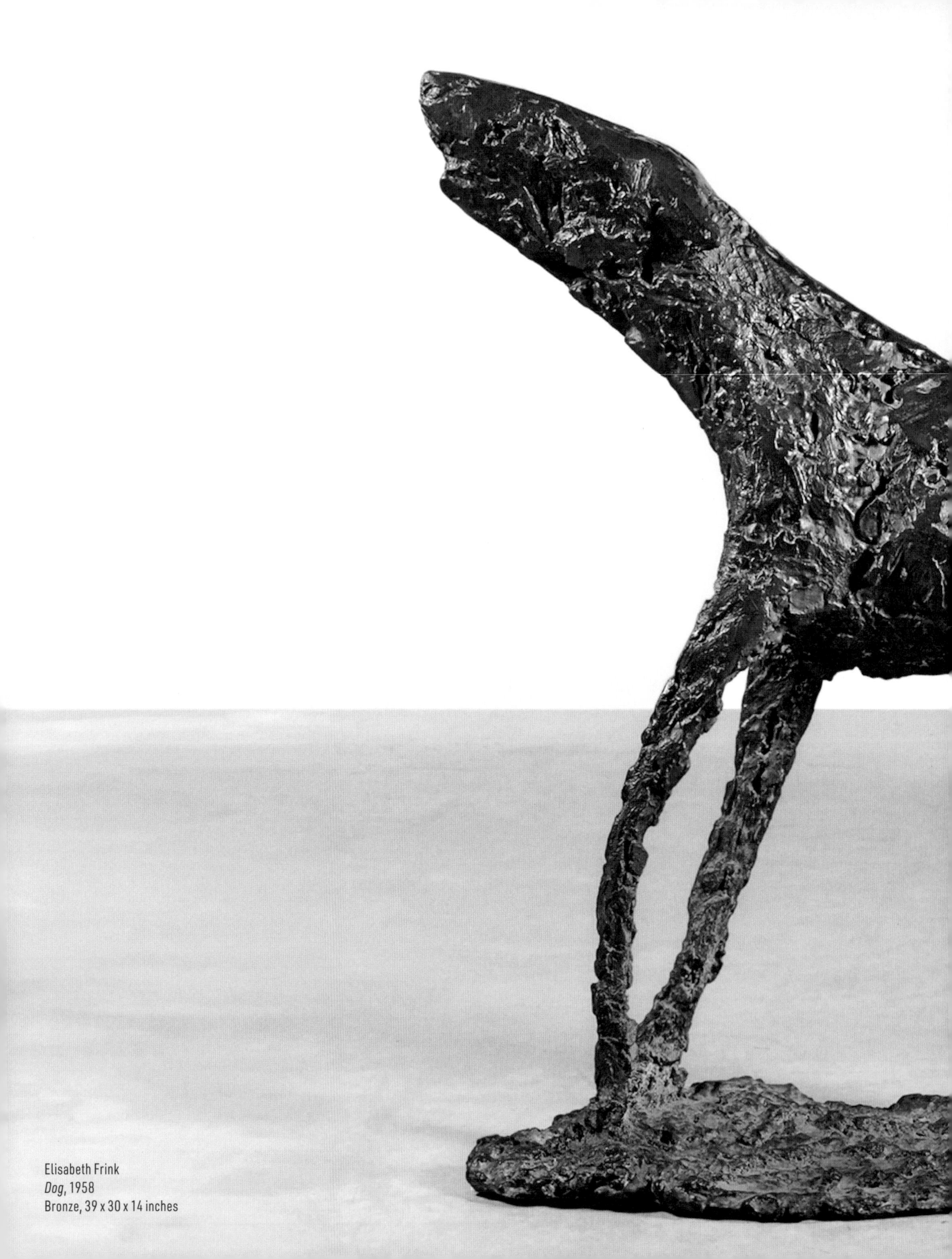

Elisabeth Frink
Dog, 1958
Bronze, 39 x 30 x 14 inches

I am interested that men and animals are confronted with combat in their lives. I try to create the stress and tension this causes. I admire strength under stress.–Elisabeth Frink

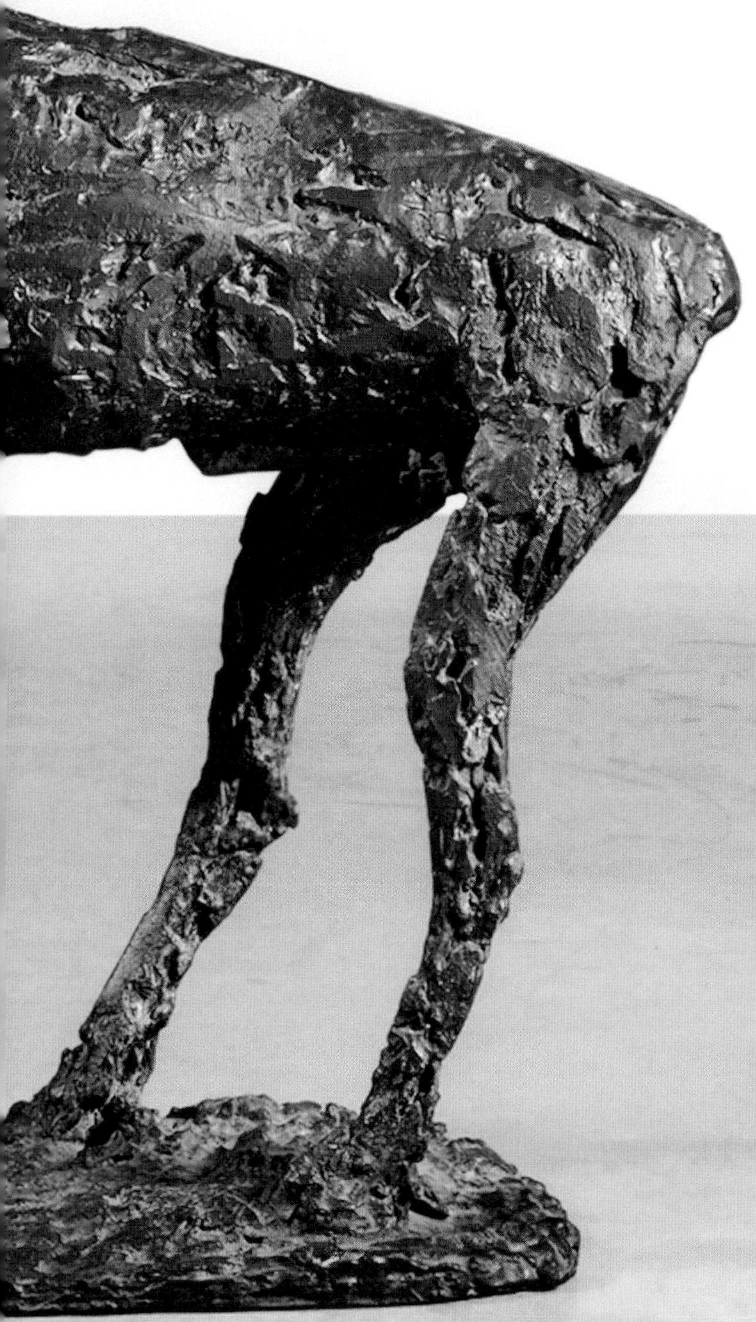

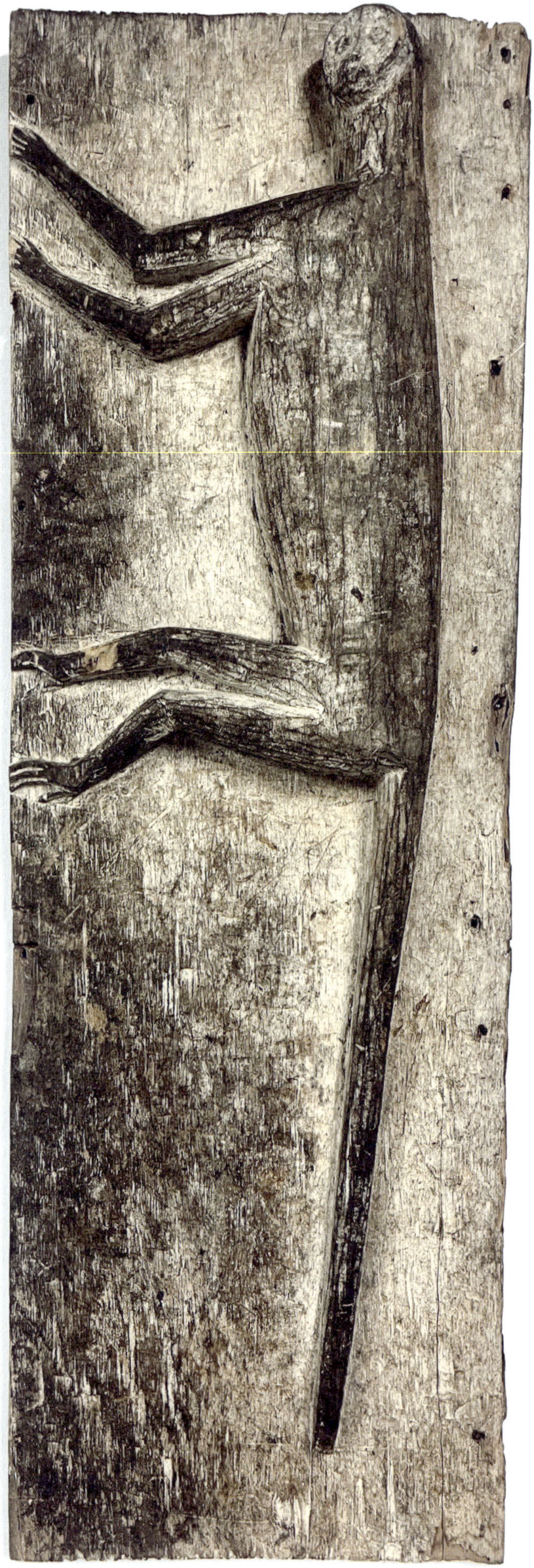

Mentawai people
Monkey Panel, 1930–1939
Carved wood, 37 x 12 x 1 inches

Mentawai people
Monkey Panel, circa 1900
Carved wood, 67 x 15 x 5 inches

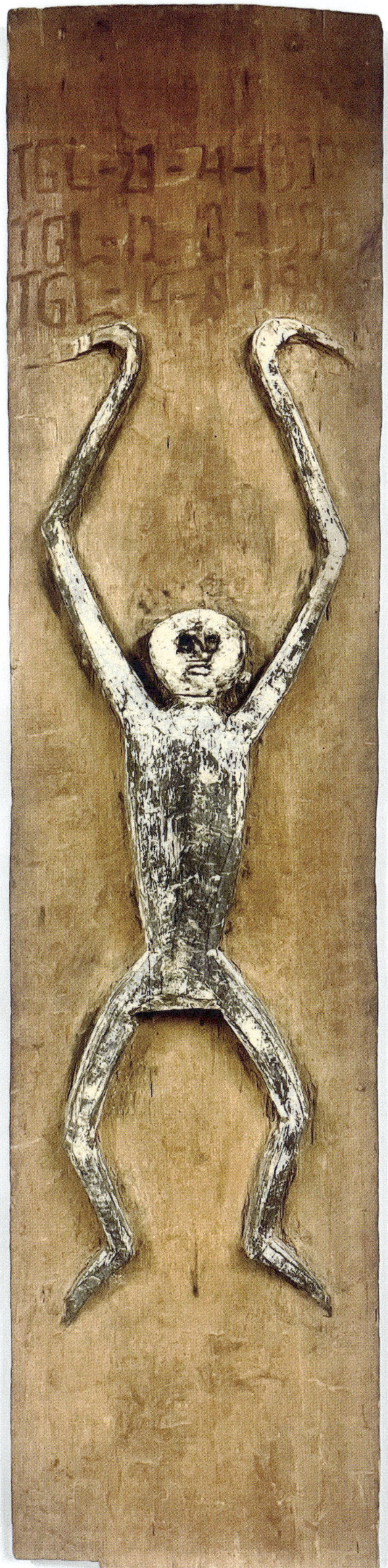

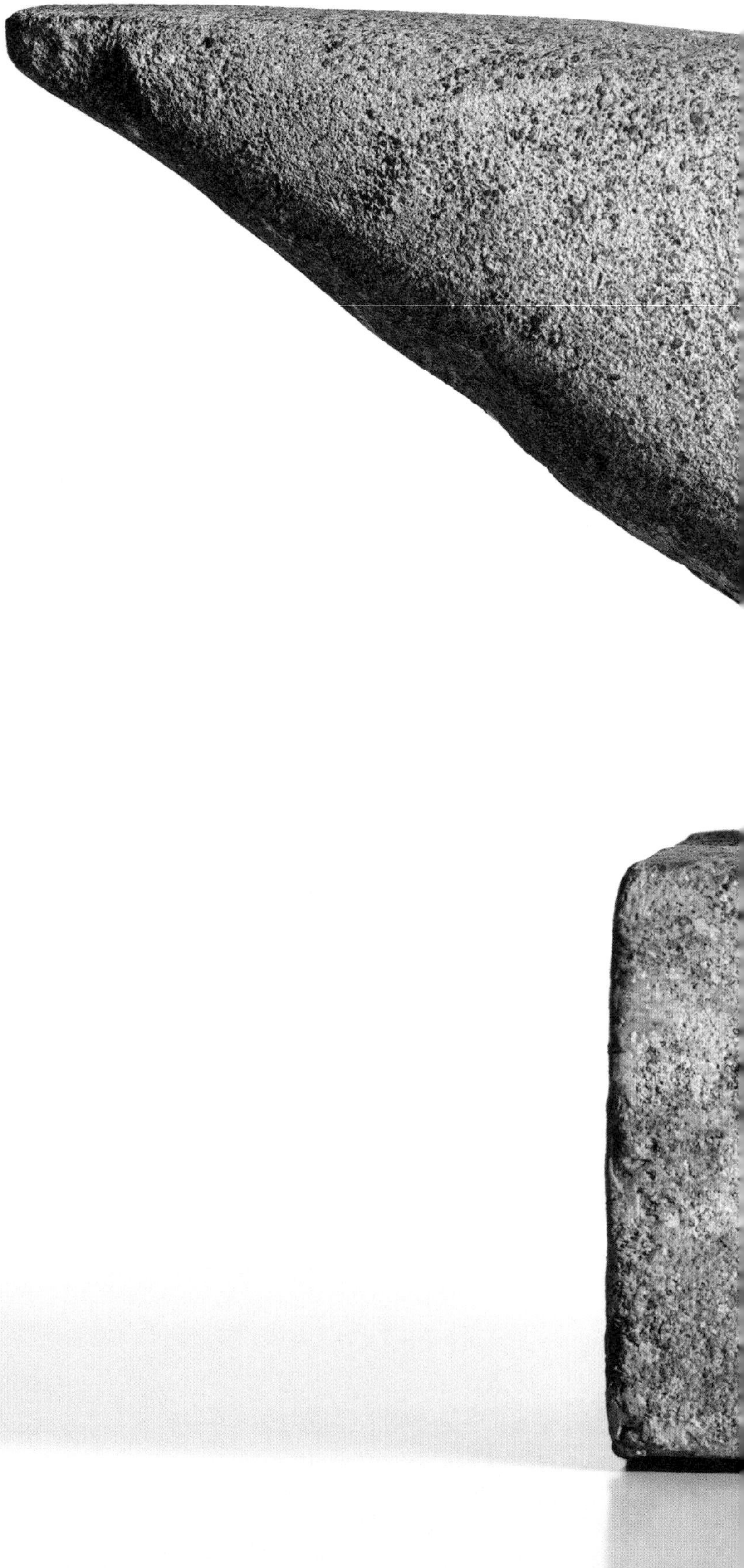

William Edmondson
Bird, circa 1930
Carved stone, $9^1/_2$ x $12^1/_4$ x 5 inches

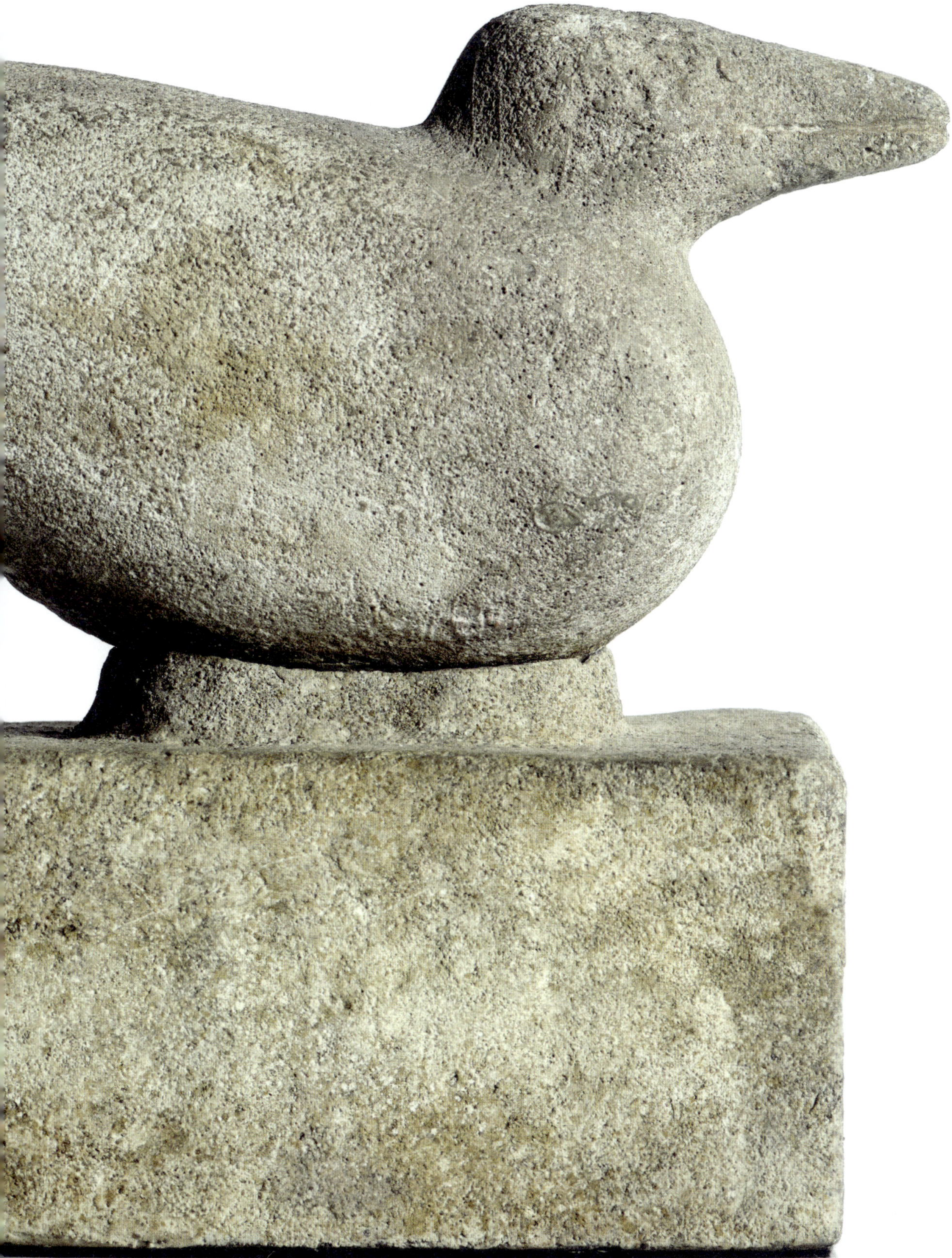

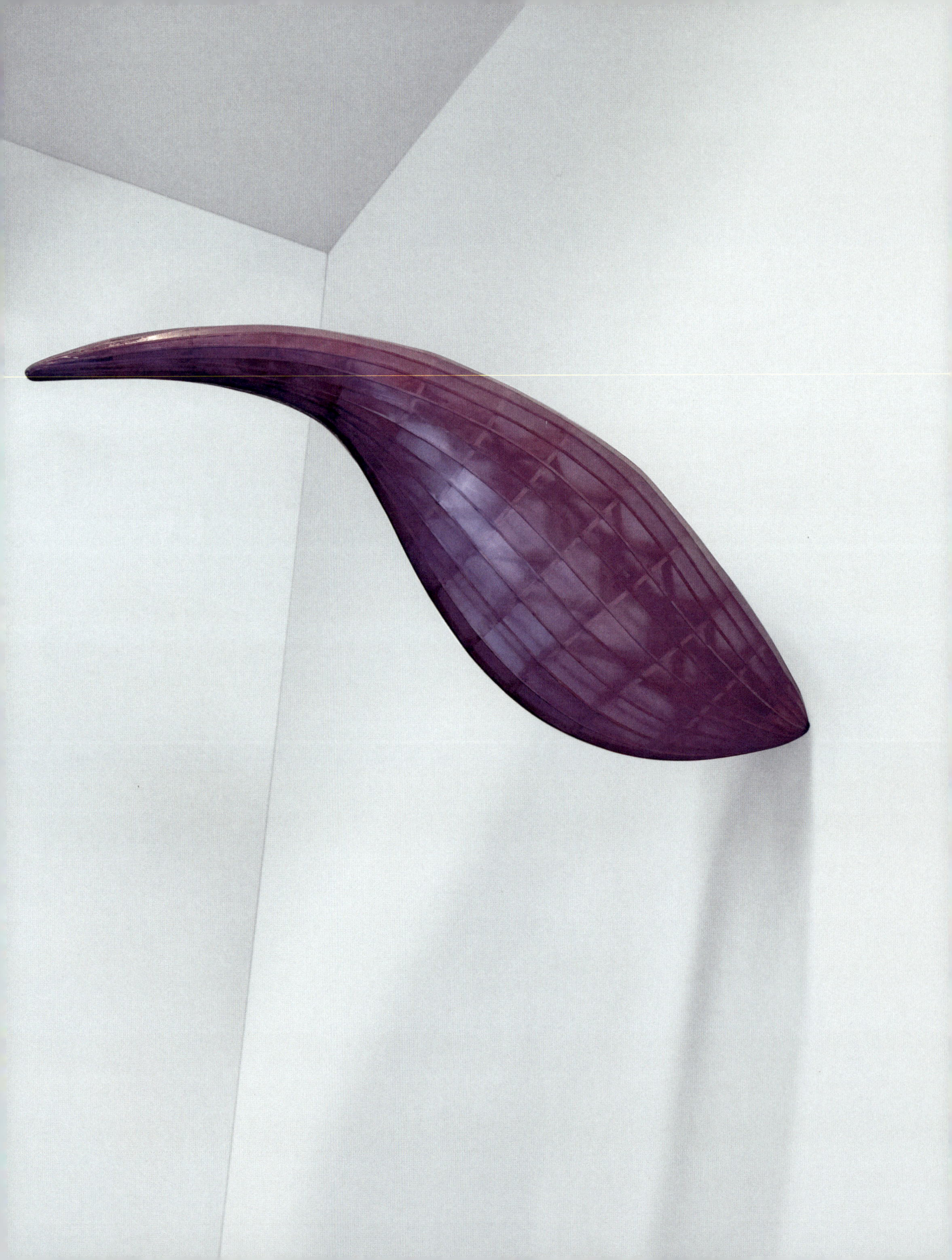

Ceta-II is the shape of a sea creature as it rises from the watery depths into the air above to draw an enormous breath–mysterious, exhilarating, beautiful–then, gliding down weightlessly to rejoin the unseen and unknown. For me it is the shape of cetaceans in motion, flourishing in a most magnificent way.

–Bryan Hunt

Bryan Hunt
Ceta-II, 2018
Wood, synthetic fabric, and steel, 43 x 20 x18 inches

The first sculptures I made in plaster in the early 1980s were large simple forms—a closed fist, a foot. They could have been the solid cores of the huge open frame-like constructions in wood or steel that I had made the previous decade. But now I decided to come down in scale and work more spontaneously. I made some tubes of chicken wire, bent them in the middle, and covered them with burlap soaked in plaster. Then I added handfuls of Structolite, a kind of slow-setting plaster with a lightweight aggregate. The image I first had in mind of this articulated form was that of an arm bent at the elbow, or a leg at the knee. But as the group of sculptures proceeded, the image of a horse's head emerged. There are ten sculptures in the series. It is only with the last four—VII, VIII, IX, and X—that I seem to have decided that the horse's head was definitely the subject. A decade later I made two more horse heads on a larger scale—a Greek horse inspired by the "horse of the dawn" from the Parthenon and a Chinese horse inspired by the marvelous ceramic horses at the Museum of Fine Arts, Boston.—William Tucker

William Tucker
Horse IX, 1986
Bronze, 30 x 35 x 18 inches

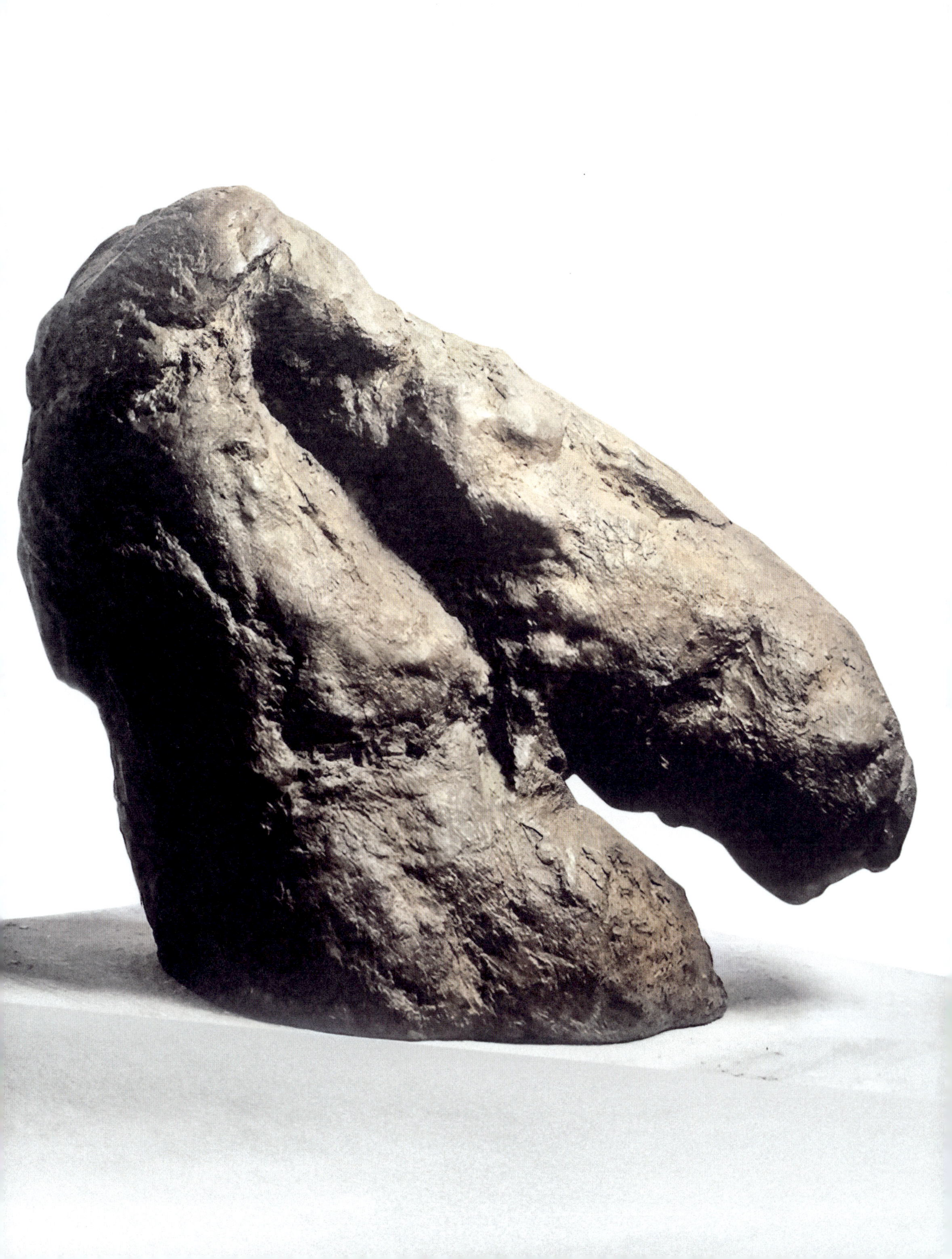

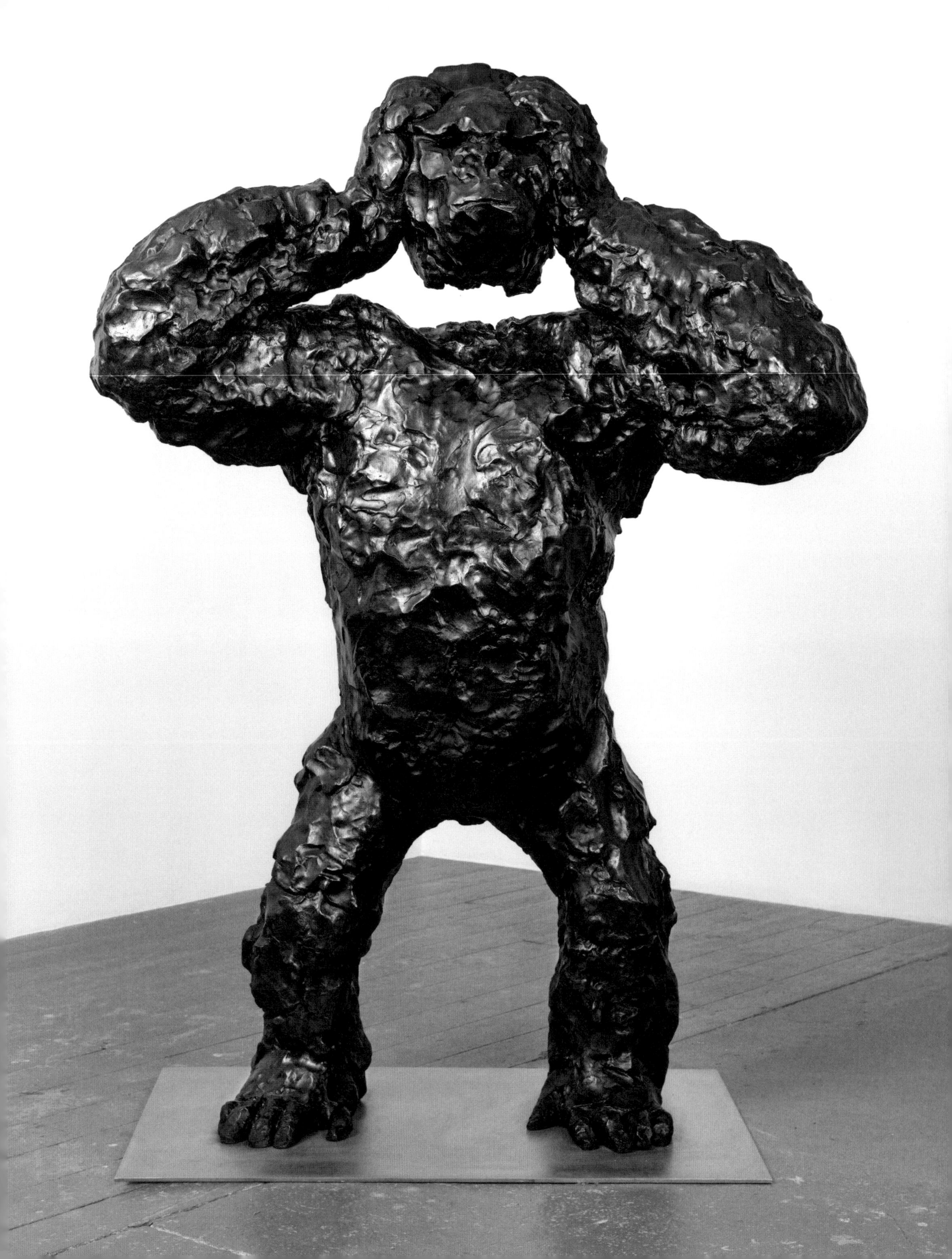

Angus Fairhurst
I'm sorry, and I won't do it again, 2004
Bronze, 86½ x 51¼ x 39¼ inches

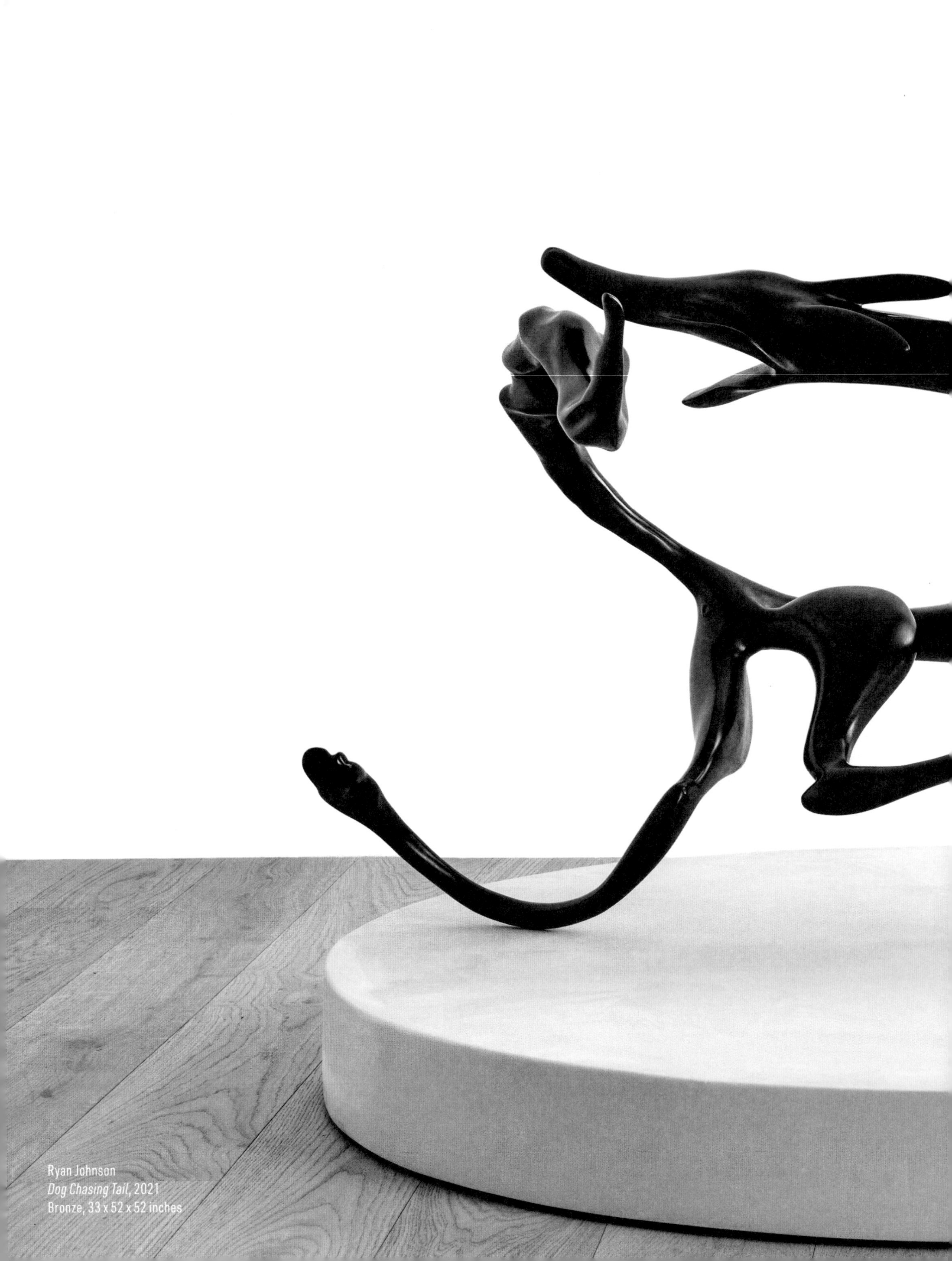

Ryan Johnson
Dog Chasing Tail, 2021
Bronze, 33 x 52 x 52 inches

A dog chasing after its own tail is a common thing to see, absurd in its futility, but also sympathetic–the dog totally absorbed by a hopeless objective. The comedy of the scene gives way to a deeper meaning. Something like the cyclical nature of being. Or the thin line between the pointless and the profound. Making the dog was especially fun and surprising. The idea proposed certain formal problems: How to capture the dog's frenzied motion in static sculpture? This led to all sorts of distortions and elongations, the limbs and tail as a sequence of swirling lines. But the more exciting prospect was for the sculpture to somehow capture a state of being, a feeling more than a description.–Ryan Johnson

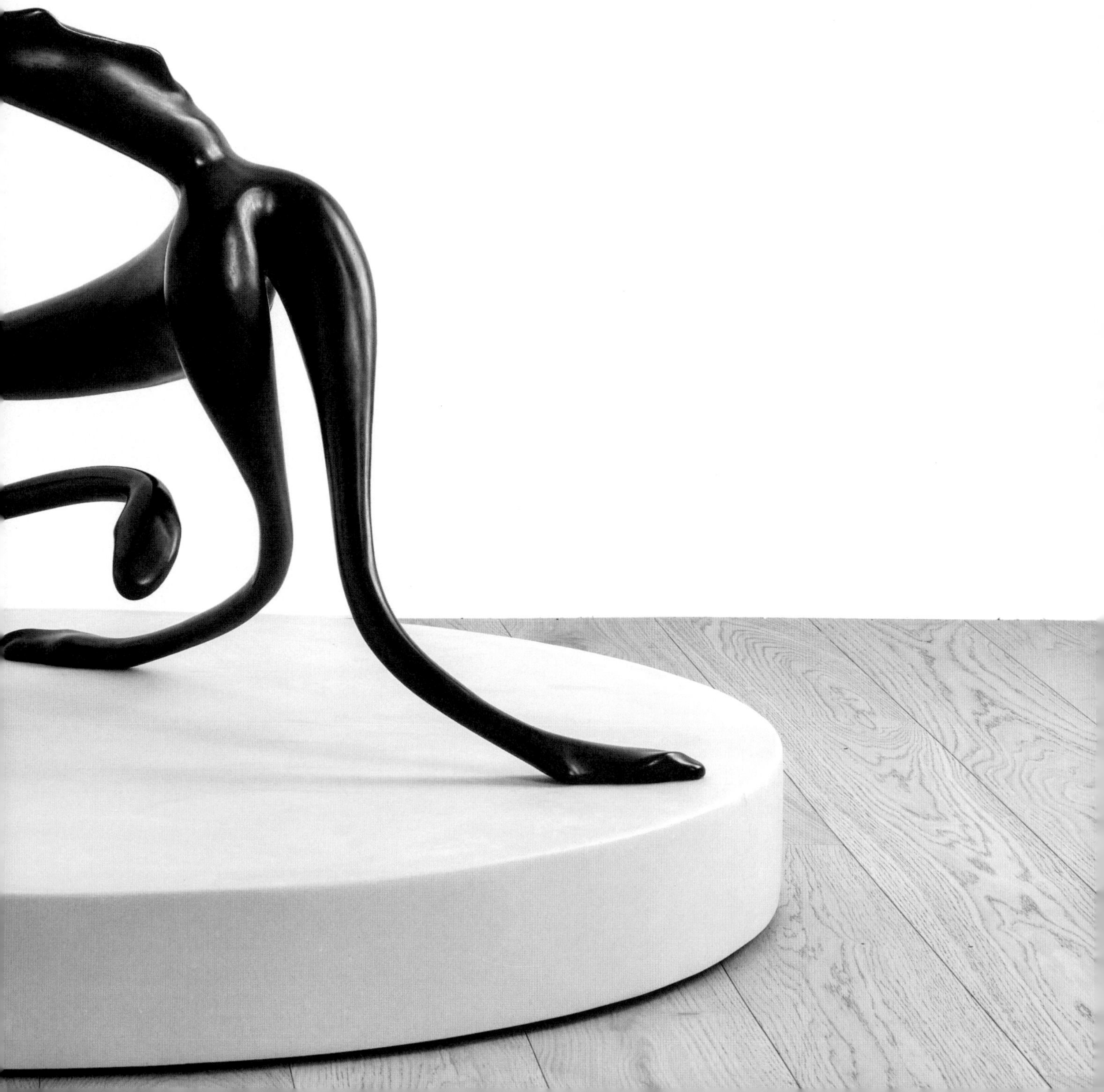

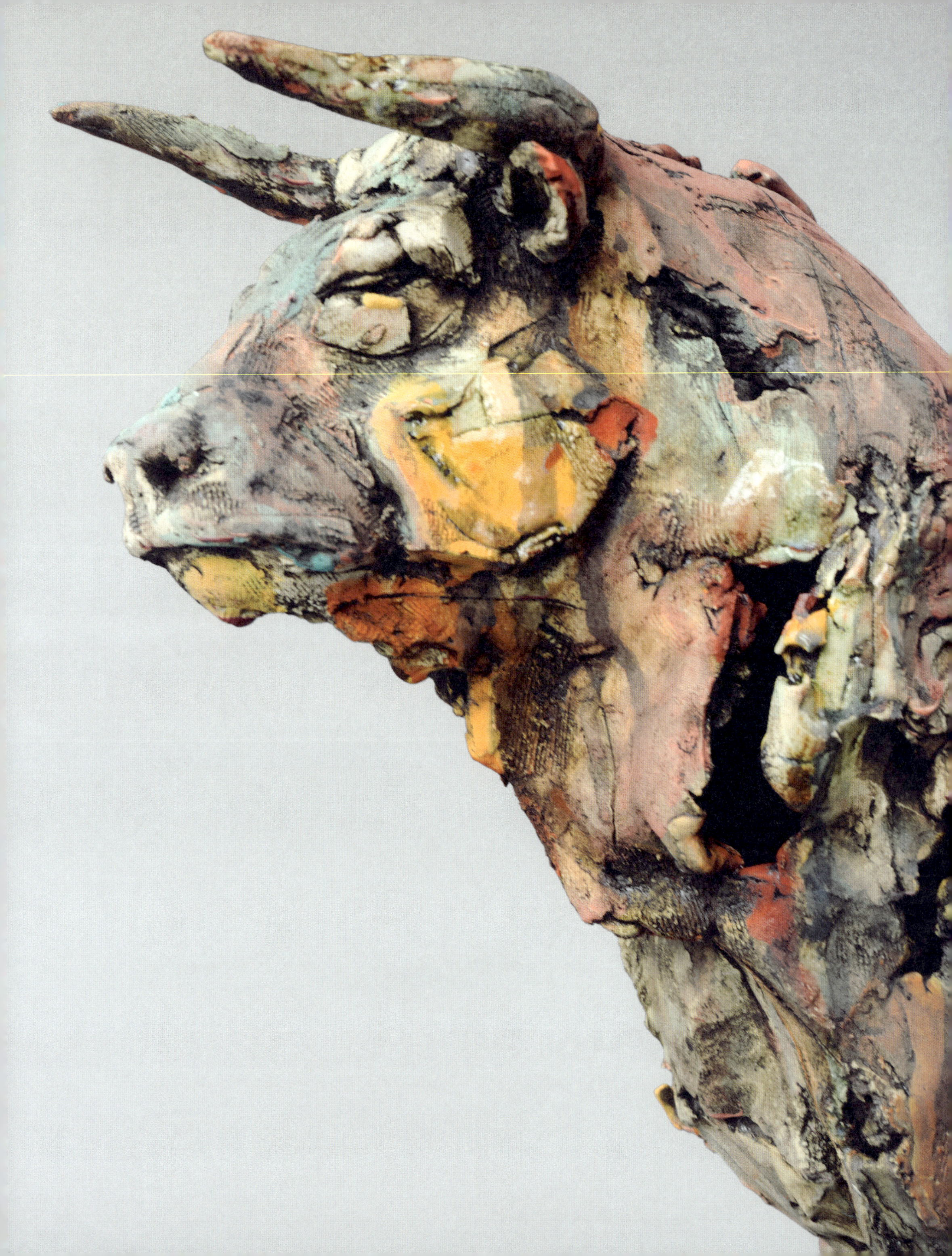

ACKNOWLEDGMENTS

Firstly, I would like to give a heartfelt thank you to all the artists in *The Ark* for their generosity of time and enthusiastic support helping us secure works for this show that have given us such a broad range of power and poignancy through their empathetic and compassionate use of the animal as subject, second self, and muse.

I want to underscore how deeply grateful we are to all those working for and with the artists in the show—their assistants, galleries, collectors, and also the museums who have helped with the loans of works.

Lastly, my most sincere shout out to our team at The Church, especially Joe Jagos and Liam Huberty under the superb stewardship of Sheri Pasquarella, our Executive Director, for making this actually happen. Their professionalism, diligence, attention to detail, and clarity of process has been not only an honor to watch but also an education on how things actually get done and done right.

I also would be remiss if I did not tip my hat to Joe Jagos who suggested *The Ark* as a suitable title for this show.
—**Eric Fischl**, Co-founder of The Church

The Church would like to thank the exhibition's curator (and The Church's co-founder), Eric Fischl, for his ambition and vision. We are further indebted to each of the artists in the show.

We extend further thanks to the many lenders, gallerists, and professionals who have made both the exhibition and the catalogue possible. In particular, we acknowledge the tremendous contributions of Joe Jagos, Exhibition Coordinator; Liam Huberty, Project Manager for the catalogue; April Gornik, co-founder of The Church; Suzanne Slesin (Publisher), Frederico Farina (Creative Director), and Julian Cosma (Editorial Assistant) of Pointed Leaf Press; and our full board and team at The Church.

We are grateful for the support of the following who have made this book possible: Per Skarstedt; the Forman Family Foundation; the Fuhrman Family Foundation, New York; the Fund for Visual Arts at The Church; and

Blue Rider Group
MORGAN STANLEY PRIVATE WEALTH MANAGEMENT

Brendan Hesmondhalgh
Detail of *Bull 1*, 2025

INDEX

Monica Banks, 32-35
Louise Bourgeois, 40-43
Rembrandt Bugatti, 10-11
Deborah Butterfield, 36-39
Maurizio Cattelan, 56-59
Thomas Deininger, 76-79
Jim Dine, 74-75
William Edmondson, 122-123
Angus Fairhurst, 128-129
Daniel Firman, 52-53
Elisabeth Frink, 116-117
Jean-François Gambino, 54-55
Brendan Hesmondhalgh, 110-111, 132
Nicola Hicks, 104-109
Bryan Hunt, 124-125
Jörg Immendorff, 48-49
Ryan Johnson, 130-131
William Kent, 60-67
William Kentridge, 24-27
Sherrie Levine, 88-89
Sarah Lucas, 50-51
Kate MccGwire, 44-45
Allan McCollum, 80-83
Mentawai people, 118-121
Bruce Nauman, 112-115
John O'Reilly, 30-31
Charles Ray, 92-93
Germaine Richier, 16-17
Jane Rosen, 94-99
Susan Rothenberg, 90-91
Claudette Schreuders, 22-23
Jaune Quick-to-See Smith, 46-47
Kiki Smith, 84-87
Anthony Theakston, 20-21
Nichola Theakston, Cover, 68-73
Catherine Thiry, 18-19
Rosemarie Trockel, 28-29
William Tucker, 126-127
Patrick Villas, 12-15
Daisy Youngblood, 4, 100-103

CREDITS

Every effort has been made to locate the holders of copyright; any omissions will be corrected in future editions.

Cover: © Nichola Theakston, 2025. Photograph by Nichola Theakston. Lender: collection of the artist.
Front endpapers: *Noah's Ark* by Edward Hicks, 1846. Courtesy of WikiArt.
Page 4: © Daisy Youngblood, 2020. Photograph courtesy of the artist and Salon 94. Lender: collection of Nicolas Rohatyn and Jeanne Greenberg Rohatyn.
Page 7: Photograph of the front entrance of The Church by Michael Heller.
Page 8: Photograph of the interior of The Church by Michael Heller.
Pages 10-11: © Rembrandt Bugatti, 1907. Photograph courtesy of the Sladmore Gallery, London. Lender: Kovner Collection.
Page 12: © Patrick Villas, 2006. Photograph courtesy of the artist. Lender: collection of the artist.
Pages 14-15: © Patrick Villas, 2021. Photograph courtesy of the artist. Lender: collection of the artist.
Page 17: © 2025 Artists Rights Society (ARS), NY / ADAGP, Paris. Photograph by Skyler Smith. Lender: Kovner Collection.
Page 18: © Catherine Thiry, 2017. Photograph by Eric Fischl. Lender: private collection.
Page 21: © Anthony Theakston, 2025. Photograph by and courtesy of the artist. Lender: courtesy of the artist.
Page 22: © Claudette Schreuders, 2019. Photograph courtesy of Jack Shainman Gallery. Lender: courtesy of the artist and the Jack Shainman Gallery.
Page 25: © William Kentridge, 2021. Photograph courtesy of the Forman Family Collection. Lender: Forman Family Collection.
Pages 26-27: © William Kentridge, 2022. Photograph courtesy of the Forman Family Collection. Lender: Forman Family Collection.
Pages 28-29: © 2025 Artists Rights Society (ARS), New York / VG Bild-Kunst, Bonn. Photograph courtesy of the Skarstedt, New York. Lender: Skarstedt Gallery.
Pages 30-31: © John O'Reilly, 2012. Photograph by Gary Mamay. Lender: collection of Eric Fischl and April Gornik.
Pages 33, 34-35: © Monica Banks, 2024. Photograph by Gary Mamay. Lender: courtesy of the artist.
Pages 36, 38-39: © 2025 Deborah Butterfield / Licensed by VAGA at Artists Rights Society (ARS), NY. Photograph courtesy of the Whitney Museum of American Art. Lender: Whitney Museum of American Art, New York, gift of Mrs. Frances Allen.
Page 40: Text: Louise Bourgeois, in conversation with Sarah Donaldson, August 2007. Courtesy the Louise Bourgeois Archive, © The Easton Foundation/VAGA at Artists Rights Society (ARS), NY.
Pages 41, 42-43: © 2025 The Easton Foundation / Licensed by VAGA at Artists Rights Society (ARS), NY. Photograph by Stefan Altenburger. Lender: private collection, New York, NY.
Page 45: © Kate MccGwire, 2023. Image courtesy of the artist. Photograph by John-Paul Bland. Lender: private collection.
Pages 46, 47: © Jaune Quick-to-See Smith, 2021. Image courtesy of the estate of Jaune Quick-to-See Smith and Garth Greenan. Lender: Gochman Family Collection.
Page 49: © The Estate of Jörg Immendorff. Photograph courtesy of the High Museum of Art. Lender: collection of the High Museum of Art, Atlanta, GA, gift of the Alex Katz Foundation.
Page 50: © Sarah Lucas, 2015. Courtesy of Sadie Coles, London. Image courtesy of Salon 94. Lender: collection of Nicolas Rohatyn and Jeanne Greenberg Rohatyn.
Pages 51: © Sarah Lucas, 2015. Courtesy of Sadie Coles, London. Image courtesy of Gladstone Gallery, London. Lender: courtesy of the artist and the Gladstone Gallery.
Page 53: © Daniel Firman, 2025. Photograph courtesy of the artist. Lender: courtesy of the artist and Ceysson & Bénétière.
Pages 54-55: © In Arte Veritas. Photograph by Gary Mamay. Lender: private collection.
Pages 57, 58-59: © Maurizio Cattelan, 2021. Photograph by Zeno Zotti. Lender: courtesy of the artist and Pirelli HangarBicocca, Milan.
Page 61: © William Kent, 1965. Photograph by Cloe Poisson. Lender: courtesy of the William Kent Art Foundation.
Pages 62-63: © William Kent, 1968. Photograph by Cloe Poisson. Lender: courtesy of the William Kent Art Foundation.
Page 65: © William Kent, 1958. Photograph by Gary Mamay. Lender: collection of Eric Fischl and April Gornik.
Pages 66-67: © William Kent, 1958. Photograph by Cloe Poisson. Lender: courtesy of the William Kent Art Foundation.
Page 68: © Nichola Theakston, 2025. Photograph by Nichola Theakston. Lender: private collection.
Pages 70-71: © Nichola Theakston, 2025. Photograph by Nichola Theakston. Lender: private collection.
Page 73: © Nichola Theakston, 2022. Photograph by Gary Mamay. Lender: private collection.
Page 74: © 2025 Jim Dine / Artists Rights Society (ARS), New York. Photograph courtesy of the artist. Lender: courtesy of the artist.
Pages 77, 78, 79: © Thomas Deininger, 2024. Photograph by Russell Owen. Lender: courtesy of the artist.
Pages 81, 82-83: © Allan McCollum, 1991. Image © Galerie Thomas Schulte. Photograph courtesy of Petzel and the artist. Lender: courtesy of the artist and Petzel, New York, NY. Produced in collaboration with the Museo Vesuviano and the Pompei Tourist Board, in Pompei, Italy, and Studio Trisorio, Naples, with the help of New York-based mold maker and caster, Nathaniel Lieb.
Pages 84-85: © Kiki Smith, 2000. Photograph by Lance Brewer, courtesy of the artist and Timothy Taylor. Lender: Forman Family Collection.
Pages 86-87: © Kiki Smith, 2020. Image courtesy of Pace Gallery. Photograph by Richard Gary. Lender: Forman Family Collection.
Page 89: © Sherrie Levine, 2002. Image © Jablonka Collection. Photograph by Nic Tenwiggenhorn. Lender: courtesy of Mark DuBois and Mara Manus.
Pages 90-91: © 2025 The Estate of Susan Rothenberg / Artists Rights Society (ARS), New York. Photograph courtesy of the Sperone Westwater Gallery. Lender: Sperone Westwater Gallery, New York, NY.
Pages 92-93: © Charles Ray, 2015. Photograph courtesy Matthew Marks Gallery. Lender: courtesy of John McEnroe Gallery.
Page 94: © Jane Rosen, 2024. Photograph courtesy of the artist. Lender: courtesy of Bienvenu Steinberg & C. Gallery, New York, NY.
Page 97: © Jane Rosen, 2025. Photograph courtesy of the artist. Lender: courtesy of Bienvenu Steinberg & C. Gallery, New York, NY.
Page 98: © Jane Rosen, 2023. Photograph courtesy of the artist. Lender: courtesy of Bienvenu Steinberg & C. Gallery, New York, NY.
Page 99: © Jane Rosen, 2017. Photograph courtesy of the artist. Lender: courtesy of Bienvenu Steinberg & C Gallery, New York, NY.
Page 100: © Daisy Youngblood, 2020. Photograph courtesy of the artist and Salon 94. Lender: collection of Nicolas Rohatyn and Jeanne Greenberg Rohatyn.
Pages 102, 103: © Daisy Youngblood, 2010. Photograph courtesy of Dorsey Waxter. Lender: courtesy of the artist and Van Doren Waxter, NY.
Page 104: © Nicola Hicks, 2025. Image © Maya Frodeman Gallery. Photograph courtesy of Maya Frodeman Gallery. Lender: Maya Frodeman Gallery.
Pages 106-107, 108, 109: © Nicola Hicks, 2025. Image © Maya Frodeman Gallery. Photograph courtesy of Maya Frodeman Gallery. Lender: Maya Frodeman Gallery.
Page 110: © Brendan Hesmondhalgh, 2025. Photograph by David Fulford. Lender: courtesy of the artist.
Page 111: © Brendan Hesmondhalgh, 2025. Photograph by David Fulford. Lender: courtesy of the artist.
Pages 113, 114, 115: © 2025 Bruce Nauman / Artists Rights Society (ARS), New York. Photograph courtesy of the Sperone Westwater Gallery. Lender: courtesy of the artist and the Sperone Westwater Gallery, New York, NY.
Pages 116-117: © 2025 Artists Rights Society (ARS), NY / DACS, London. Photograph courtesy of Sotheby's, London. Lender: Kovner Collection.
Page 118: Mentawai People, 1930-1939. Photograph by Noah Khoshbin. Lender: Watermill Center Collection and the Robert Wilson Arts Collection.
Page 121: Mentawai People, 1900. Photograph by Noah Khoshbin. Lender: Watermill Center Collection and the Robert Wilson Arts Collection.
Pages 122-123: © William Edmondson. Photograph by Skyler Smith. Lender: Kovner Collection.
Page 124: © Bryan Hunt, 2018. Photograph © 2025 Bryan Hunt / Artists Rights Society (ARS), NY. Photograph by the artist. Lender: collection of the artist.
Page 127: © William Tucker, 1986. Photograph by William Tucker. Lender: collection of the artist.
Page 128: © The Estate of Angus Fairhurst, courtesy Sadie Coles HQ, London. Photograph courtesy of Sadie Coles HQ, London. Lender: collection of Sean and Tamara McCarthy.
Pages 130-131: © Ryan Johnson, 2021. Photograph by Daniel Levin. Lender: courtesy of the artist and Marinaro Gallery.
Page 132: © Brendan Hesmondhalgh, 2025. Photograph by David Fulford. Lender: courtesy of the artist.
Back endpapers: Simon de Myle, *Noah's Ark on Mount Ararat*, 1570. Private Collection.
Back cover: © Ryan Johnson, 2021. Photograph by Daniel Levin. Lender: courtesy of the artist and Marinaro Gallery.
Not reproduced: Joan Brown, *Donald*, 1966. Copper over wood, 31½ x 12¼ x 35 inches. Forman Family Collection.

The Church
48 Madison Street
Sag Harbor, NY 11963
631 919 5342
www.thechurchsagharbor.org

PUBLISHER Suzanne Slesin
CREATIVE DIRECTOR Frederico Farina
EDITORIAL ASSISTANT Julian Cosma
COPY EDITOR Amelia Kutschbach
ISBN 978-1-938461-73-6
LIBRARY OF CONGRESS NUMBER 2025905832
FIRST EDITION
PRINTED IN SPAIN

 Pointed Leaf Press, LLC., 136 Baxter Street, Suite 1C, New York, NY 10013 www.pointedleafpress.com

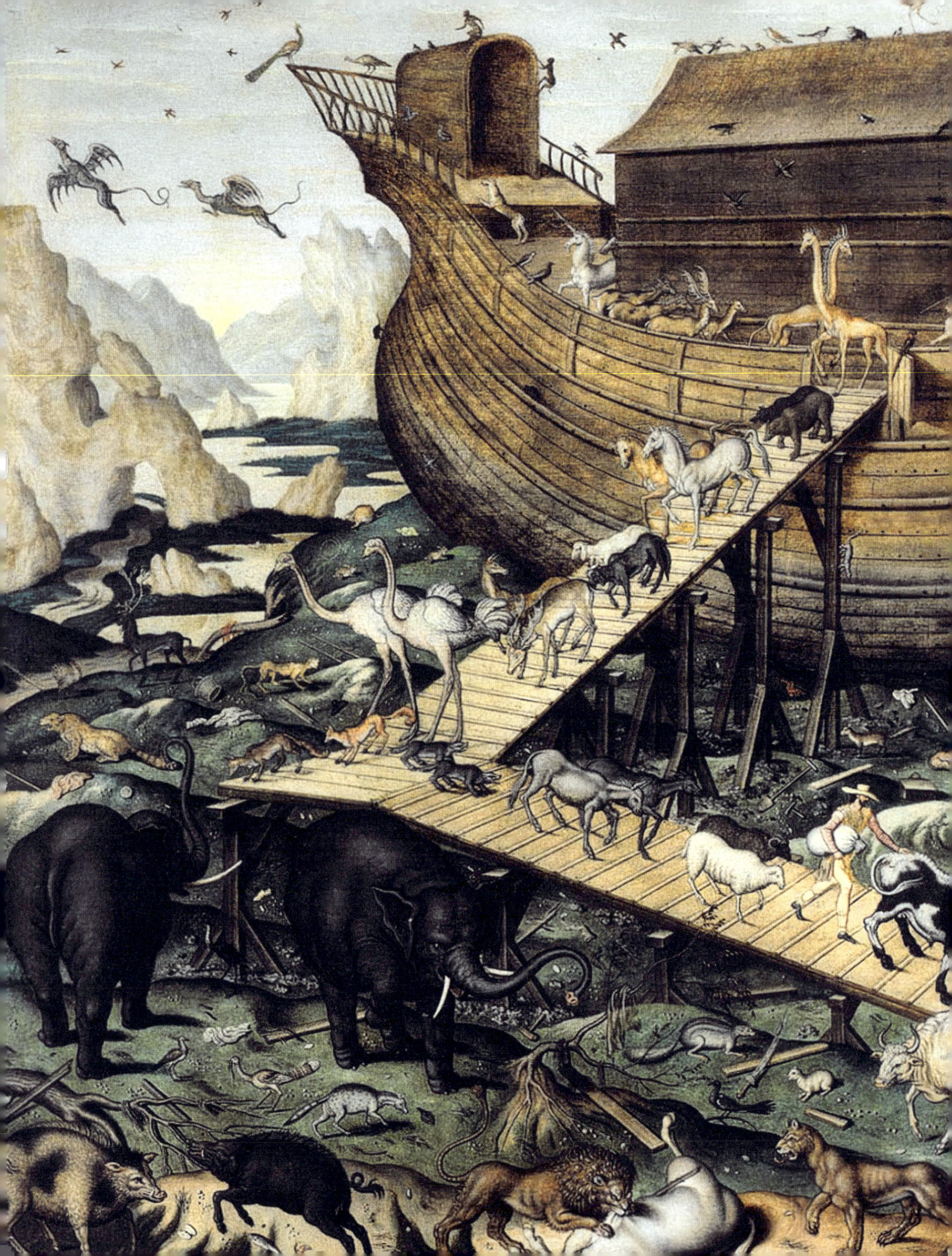